Merry Laughter and Angry Curses

Contemporary Chinese Studies

This series provides new scholarship and perspectives on modern and contemporary China, including China's contested borderlands and minority peoples; ongoing social, cultural, and political changes; and the varied histories that animate China today.

A list of titles in this series appears at the end of this book.

Merry Laughter and Angry Curses
The Shanghai Tabloid Press, 1897-1911

Juan Wang

UBCPress · Vancouver · Toronto

© UBC Press 2012

All rights reserved. No part of this publication may be reproduced, stored in a retrieval system, or transmitted, in any form or by any means, without prior written permission of the publisher, or, in Canada, in the case of photocopying or other reprographic copying, a licence from Access Copyright, www.accesscopyright.ca.

21 20 19 18 17 16 15 14 13 12   5 4 3 2 1

Printed in Canada on FSC-certified ancient-forest-free paper
(100% post-consumer recycled) that is processed chlorine- and acid-free.

Library and Archives Canada Cataloguing in Publication

Wang, Juan, 1960-
  Merry laughter and angry curses : the Shanghai tabloid press, 1897-1911 / Juan Wang.

(Contemporary Chinese studies, 1206-9523)
Includes bibliographical references and index.
Also issued in electronic format.
ISBN 978-0-7748-2338-8 (bound); ISBN 978-0-7748-2339-5 (pbk.)

  1. Tabloid newspapers – China – Shanghai – History. 2. Tabloid newspapers – Social aspects – China – Shanghai – History. I. Title. II. Series: Contemporary Chinese studies.

PN5364.W35 2012   079'.5113209041   C2012-903633-1

Canadä

UBC Press gratefully acknowledges the financial support for our publishing program of the Government of Canada (through the Canada Book Fund), the Canada Council for the Arts, and the British Columbia Arts Council.

Financial support from the Association for Asian Studies is also greatly appreciated.

UBC Press
The University of British Columbia
2029 West Mall
Vancouver, BC V6T 1Z2
www.ubcpress.ca

Contents

List of Illustrations / vii

Acknowledgments / ix

Introduction / 1

1 Community of Fun / 24

2 Officialdom Unmasked / 54

3 Imagining the Nation / 85

4 Confronting the "New" / 112

5 Questioning the Appropriators / 136

6 The Market, Populism, and Aesthetics / 156

Conclusion / 178

Notes / 186

Glossary of Chinese Terms and Names / 209

Bibliography / 218

Index / 226

Illustrations

1 Sample issue of *Fun (Youxibao)* / 3

2 Sample issue of *Splendid World (Shijie fanhuabao)* / 7

3 Sample issue of *Grove of Laughter (Xiaolinbao)* / 8

4 Sample cover pages of *Illustrated Fiction (Xiuxiang xiaoshuo)* / 9

5 Photograph portrait of Li Boyuan / 10

6 Photograph portrait of Wu Jianren / 11

7 Bribing an official / 65

8 Frightened official meets with Westerner / 66

9 Officials smoking opium / 67

10 Official bedridden with venereal disease / 68

11 Opening a new-style school / 147

12 Smoking opium while talking excitedly about reform / 152

Acknowledgments

Numerous individuals and institutions have helped me, over many long years, to complete the research and writing that went into this book. I am deeply indebted to all of them.

Professors Harold Kahn of Stanford University and Timothy Brook of the University of British Columbia played key roles in this project. Professor Kahn arranged for the East Asian Library of the Hoover Institution at Stanford University to acquire microfilms of Shanghai tabloid newspapers, which greatly facilitated my research. His patience, encouragement, and sharp criticism sustained me throughout my graduate work, and he continued to give me generous support whenever I sought it, even after he had retired and I had moved on to a teaching career.

Despite his busy academic life, Professor Brook always found time to provide advice and assistance. He has been an invaluable critic of my work, as well as a source of understanding and encouragement during difficult moments.

Many other scholars have made this book possible. In particular, several people from the Shanghai Academy of Social Sciences facilitated my research in that city during the 1999-2000 academic year. Chen Meng Xiong, from the Academy's Institute of Literature, arranged, and accompanied me to, interviews with several tabloid writers of the Republican era and informed me about relevant source materials. Cheng Zai and Li Tiangang, from the Institute of History, also provided assistance, the former by giving me access to a tabloid newspaper in the institute's archive and the latter by providing me with materials about Shanghai.

The Institute of Modern History at Academia Sinica provided an inspiring scholarly environment as I revised my manuscript in Taipei in 2008 and 2009. Huang Ko-wu, Chen Yung-fa, Chang Ning, Peter Zarrow, Wu Jen-shu, and Han Seunghyun helped in numerous ways, some answering queries when I needed their expertise, others providing relevant materials. Wang Fan-sen, from the Institute of History and Philology at the Academia, brought an important source to my attention.

My gratitude extends to Emily Andrew, senior editor at UBC Press, for guiding this book to publication. Without her faith in this work and her critical eye, it would have been much more difficult to see the light at the end of the tunnel. In addition, I thank Megan Brand at UBC Press for guiding the manuscript through to final production. I am also grateful to three anonymous reviewers and a board member at the Press whose criticisms and suggestions helped make this a much better book.

I am indebted to my partner, Peter Lichtenstein, for his generous editing, enduring support, and encouragement.

My growth as a historian and author would have been impossible without assistance from various institutions. Stanford University provided funding for my doctoral research and dissertation. The Shanghai Academy of Social Science hosted my research. The Institute of Modern History at Academia Sinica granted me a postdoctoral research fellowship. Purdue University provided generous leave time and grant support for completion of this book.

I also wish to thank the journals *Late Imperial China* (The Johns Hopkins University Press) and *Twentieth-Century China* (Maney Publishing) for allowing me to use previously published material in this book.

I gratefully acknowledge the libraries that I utilized extensively, including the Shanghai Municipal Library, the Nanjing Municipal Library, the East Asian Collection of the Hoover Institution, the University of Chicago Library, and the Guo Tingyi Library of the Institute of Modern History at Academia Sinica.

Finally, I thank the Association for Asian Studies for assistance in the production of this book with a First Book Subvention.

Merry Laughter and Angry Curses

Introduction

Late Qing China witnessed a revolution in print journalism. Modern newspapers and magazines written for Chinese audiences first appeared in the 1850s and 1860s in Hong Kong and in treaty port cities such as Guangzhou and Shanghai. Foreign missionaries and entrepreneurs owned and published most of these publications, but the so-called Hundred Days' Reform movement between 1895 and 1898 saw a sudden surge in the publication of Chinese-owned reform newspapers and magazines throughout the country. Emperor Guangxu initiated this development when he encouraged Chinese to publish their own periodicals in order to better communicate with and educate the public. The new reform publications were a crucial part of the Hundred Days' Reform and helped change the public's perception of and relationship to the new, modern media.

Prior to the mid-1890s, the urban literate public saw newspapers as alien and unimportant. When *Shenbao,* a foreign-owned newspaper catering to Chinese readers, appeared in Shanghai in the early 1870s, few knew what it was. Many thought it had no educational value, while others feared that it would distract young students from their studies.[1] Even in 1893, when *Xinwenbao,* a foreign-owned Shanghai daily, began publication, many considered it an insignificant "sideline" business.[2] The Sino-Japanese War of 1894-95 changed people's attitudes, however: eagerly awaiting news from the front every day, they began to take newspapers seriously. The Hundred Days' Reform movement that created the publishing frenzy further stimulated popular enthusiasm for newspapers.

During the last fifteen years of the Qing Dynasty (1644-1911), periodical publications – newspapers and magazines – became the preeminent medium of public communication. Reading affordably priced newspapers became a daily practice for the ever-growing reading public, a public that consisted mainly of urban readers as well as some wealthier, well-connected rural readers. Joan Judge shows how Shanghai newspapers expanded from a few hundred copies per issue in the mid-1890s to production runs that served hundreds of thousands of readers.[3] Leo Ou-fan Lee and Andrew J. Nathan estimate that about a hundred notable periodicals were published at any one time in the last decade of the Qing, with a national circulation of 300,000 copies.[4] Peter G. Zarrow puts regular readership of the Chinese press in the last years of the Qing at two to four million.[5]

Large increases in both the number of periodicals and their circulation made up only one side of this late Qing revolution in print journalism. The fluid political, social, and intellectual environment also shaped how late Qing readers related to periodicals. Readers used newspapers not only to get the daily news but also as a gateway to the larger world of knowledge that would help them gain advantage in those rapidly changing times. In the summer of 1898, government examinations began requiring essays on government policy (celun). Examiners prepared questions about current affairs as reported in newspapers, and examinees wrote their essays based on these same sources.[6] Officials, literati, and aspiring students all relied on newspapers for timely information and new knowledge.

More significantly, as newspapers and magazines became increasingly bold, the reading public became much more knowledgeable about national political and intellectual debates previously hidden from them. They could now, more or less openly, express their opinions and sentiments through the media. Periodicals thus became a major instrument of change, ushering late Qing China into an age in which previously unspeakable and unprintable ideas could be expressed and circulated.

In the last two decades of the Qing, Shanghai became the publishing centre of China, with significantly more periodicals than anywhere else in the country. Although mainstream "serious" periodicals such as the Shanghai papers *Shibao* and *Shenbao* stood at the forefront of late Qing political, social, and cultural changes,[7] the city's tabloid press was also a vital part of the revolution in print journalism and played a unique role in shaping late Qing public opinion and sentiments.

The Tabloid Press

The Shanghai tabloid press included both newspapers and magazines. They were tabloid in nature because they aimed primarily to entertain. The Chinese refer to tabloid newspapers as *xiaobao*, meaning "little" or "minor" papers, to distinguish them from *dabao*, meaning "big" or "important" papers.[8] The former had a reputation for frivolity, whereas the latter were considered serious and weighty. China's first modern tabloid newspaper appeared in Shanghai on 24 June 1897. It had a fitting name: *Fun (Youxibao)* (Figure 1). Its publisher, editor, and writer was Li Boyuan (1867-1906), a talented thirty-year-old literatus.

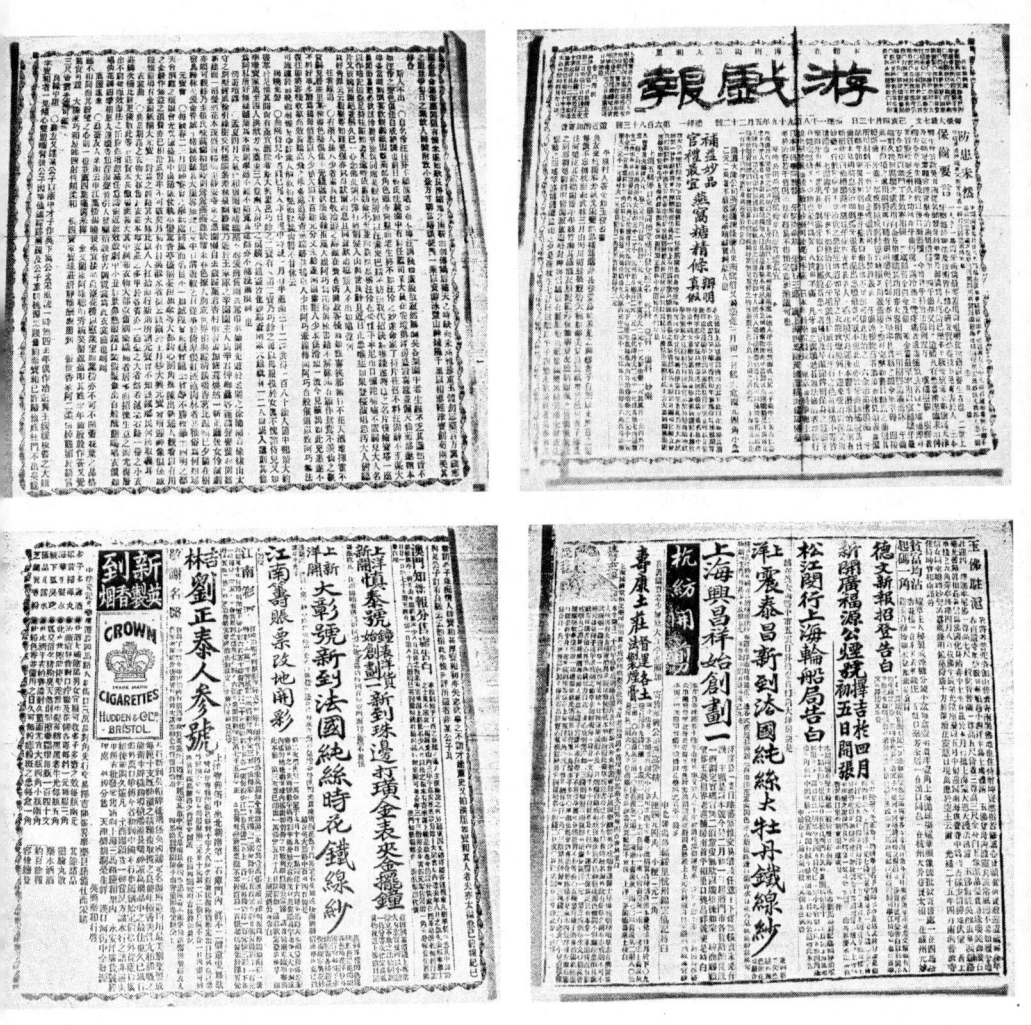

Figure 1   Sample issue of *Fun* (*Youxibao*), 22 May 1899.

Fun was an instant success. Based on Li Boyuan's own estimates, its circulation in its first three months equalled, if not surpassed, those of the major Shanghai papers.[9] *Fun*'s success opened the floodgates: four more tabloids appeared within six months and five in 1898 and 1899. *Fun* and *Anecdotes (Caifengbao)*, which began publication in 1898, attracted the most readers.

The early tabloids, published between 1897 and 1900, focused almost entirely on pleasure and amusement. They contained no important national or international news or much information about the modern world. Li Boyuan structured the content of each issue of *Fun* according to a fixed formula: one headline piece followed by eight short pieces. The headline piece, usually shorter than two or three hundred words, could be an essay, a rhapsody, a poem, or a letter from a reader or contributor. The short pieces were usually anecdotes, mostly about Shanghai's pleasure and entertainment society. A poetry section featuring the work of readers and tabloid writers often followed the eight short pieces. *Fun* sponsored both popularity contests for courtesans and erudite literary games, held poetry competitions, and reported on the best pleasure venues in the city. The headline pieces and the poetry were typically well written and sophisticated. The content and format of other tabloids resembled those of *Fun*.

It was no accident that the late Qing tabloid industry flourished first in Shanghai and then became a predominantly Shanghai phenomenon. By the 1890s, Shanghai had become the most important commercial, financial, industrial, and cultural metropolis in China, as well as its largest international port city. Its population grew from between 800,000 and 900,000 in 1895 to 1,289,353 by 1910.[10] Foreign concessions proliferated, not only because of international trade but also because of an influx of Chinese migrants, many from nearby Jiangsu and Zhejiang provinces.

Migrants flocked to Shanghai to take advantage of the war-free and cosmopolitan environment and the city's vibrant consumption and entertainment milieu. Most migrants were literati, merchants, and landlords. Some were well-off and could afford a life of leisure; others came to find jobs. Entrepreneurs and investors sought to take advantage of economic opportunities; others were fleeing legal or political problems. All found in Shanghai a source of luxury and entertainment, and many patronized the city's brothels, teahouses, restaurants, and theatres. Courtesan culture thrived and became a mainstay of Shanghai's pleasure industry.

Shanghai also had a robust reading market, given its large, literate population and, by the turn of the century, its preponderance of literati and the well-to-do. In 1903, more than 3,000 literati worked in Shanghai's cultural and educational institutions, including presses and publishing houses, schools, libraries, and museums; by 1909, this number had risen to 4,000.[11] Yuan Jin provides a sense of the 1890s Shanghai reading public: of every hundred residents, sixty had a rudimentary level of literacy and between five and ten were literati of some sort; ten to thirty percent of women could read, and about one to two percent could write poetry.[12] S.A. Smith estimates that 300,000 people in Shanghai were reading newspapers in the early years of the twentieth century.[13]

According to Catherine Yeh, by the mid-1880s, the reading market had grown large enough to support the publication of independent entertainment periodicals, such as *Dianshizhai Pictorial (Dianshizhai huabao)* and guidebooks to the courtesan world.[14] No newspaper then in Shanghai made entertainment its primary focus, however. No paper covered prostitution, although hundreds of brothels were concentrated in the International Settlement alone.[15] No paper provided information about the city's teahouses, although the largest of them served over a thousand guests at one time and held daily performances such as *shuoshu*, which combined storytelling and singing. The tabloids filled this vacuum.

The emergence of the tabloids relied as much on Shanghai's stimulating publishing environment as on the reading market. Li Boyuan came to Shanghai from his hometown in Changzhou in 1896, looking for work. While living in Changzhou, he read Shanghai newspapers regularly and was part of a local social network of literati with connections to literati in the capital Beijing and elsewhere. Fully aware of recent developments in China's newspaper industry, Li decided to enter the business. Possibly helped by an acquaintance, J.D. Clark, publisher of the English newspaper *Shanghai Mercury*, he began publishing a daily, *Guidance (Zhinanbao)*, on 6 June 1896. A Chinese subsidiary of the *Shanghai Mercury*, *Guidance* was similar in format and content to other conventional Shanghai papers such as *Shenbao*. In the first issue, Li echoed the rhetoric of the time: "Western nations have newspapers because they are concerned that people are not informed. Reporting to the ruler and informing the people are essential to the power and prosperity of a nation. Now that we have newspapers in our country, what more can people like us hope to achieve in our careers than repaying the ruler's benevolence and communicating with both the ruler and the people?"[16]

Sales of *Guidance* were disappointing. Although it was one of the earlier papers in what would become a publishing frenzy, it was not distinctive enough to compete with the better-known and more established papers. It lasted just over a year, after which Li embarked on a new publication, *Fun*. There he found his niche, opining that similar Western tabloid newspapers had inspired him both to publish the paper and to name it *Fun*.[17]

Mainstream newspapers served as incubators for tabloid journalists. Many began their careers there, and once they knew the business well, they became entrepreneurial tabloid publishers and writers. This was not a difficult proposition. Compared with Shanghai's mainstream papers, the tabloids required far less start-up and operating capital. They mostly used commercial printing services instead of investing in expensive printing equipment. The tabloid press never made illustrations and pictures a significant feature or selling point, even though stone-based lithography print technology in Shanghai, available since 1876, had lowered the unit production cost of graphic images.[18]

They also saved on newswire services by not reporting any national or international news.

Many tabloid journalists cut costs by renting small rooms from established newspapers or by locating their offices in their homes. Li Boyuan produced *Fun* in his home. His family lived upstairs, while the business was located in a downstairs office with a room for the printing machines. Labour costs were minimal because the production of a daily tabloid required only one or two writers, who also served as editors. In the first eighteen months of *Fun*, Li was the sole writer and editor and managed the business by himself. Later, he hired Ouyang Juyuan to assist him with writing and with managing the business. It was not until the fourth year of operation that Li finally hired a manager to handle such jobs as proofreading, printing, distribution, and advertising. Indeed, a tabloid could be started with only two or three hundred *yuan*.[19]

Although production costs were minimal, revenues were potentially huge, which explains why so many tabloids entered the market. Profits came from both sales and advertising. The price of an issue was the same for all the tabloids, five *wen* in the beginning, rising to seven wen and eventually reaching eleven wen in subsequent years. If a paper sold four thousand copies, a day's revenue would have been twenty-eight yuan, a significant amount.[20] Advertising income provided a hefty addition to sales revenue. In the first three months of *Fun*, advertisements increased from one or two per issue to enough to fill two full pages. A year later, *Fun* had four pages of ads each day, and soon thereafter reached six pages. Its actual content occupied around two pages. In his second year of operation, Li Boyuan invested in a new printing machine and began using better-quality imported paper. *Fun* must have been sufficiently profitable by then to enable him to make these investments.

Other tabloids were just as aggressive in expanding their advertising. Most popular papers quickly reached the same ratio of content to ads as *Fun*, between 1:2 and 1:3. We do not know the exact advertising rates or the income derived from advertising, but we can surmise that tabloid rates were comparable to those charged by the mainstream papers because both had similar types of advertisements and comparable circulations. According to Yao Gonghe, four major categories of ads appeared in Shanghai's mainstream papers: theatrical performances, pharmaceutical products, books, and miscellaneous merchandise. Those papers received significant revenues from ads, and it is safe to say that the same was true of the tabloids.[21]

This early phase of tabloid growth was linked directly to political developments. In 1898, Empress Dowager Cixi cracked down on the 1895-98 reform movement and placed the reform-minded Emperor Guangxu under house arrest. On 29 January 1901, however, she reversed her earlier position and issued the *Xinzheng* (New Policy) edict, ushering in a decade of reforms. The deadly anti-foreign Boxer Uprising (1899-1900), which forced her to flee the capital and which cost China an indemnity of 450 million taels of silver (plus thirty-nine years of accumulated interest), had made Cixi realize that China needed reforms after all. In a last attempt to hold on to power, she issued over thirty edicts from 1901 to 1905, which promoted major reforms in government administration, economic development, education, law, and the military. In both depth and breadth, the reforms went well beyond those of the aborted 1898 initiatives of Emperor Guangxu.

Tabloid writers responded immediately to these developments by starting a second wave of tabloids. The first was *Allegories (Yuyanbao)*, which appeared less than two months after Empress Dowager Cixi's 1901 edict. Ten days later came *Grove of Laughter (Xiaolinbao)*, followed a few weeks later by Li Boyuan's *Splendid World (Shijie fanhuabao)* (Figures 2 and 3). In 1901 and 1902, a total of eleven new tabloids entered the market.

Writers shrewdly detected commercial possibilities in the new political environment. The 1901 edict provided them for the first time with free rein to criticize officials, mock the elite, and scandalize readers. Since 1898, writers had already been criticizing Qing officials, albeit carefully, as well as touching on political issues. In 1901 they became audaciously political and overtly anti-establishment, in a style that was both witty and satirical. This was a genuine watershed in tabloid publishing: politics was now of equal or greater importance than news about Shanghai's pleasure quarters, and the two jostled for space. As a result, the distinction between serious reform and entertainment periodicals became blurred, mainly because both types

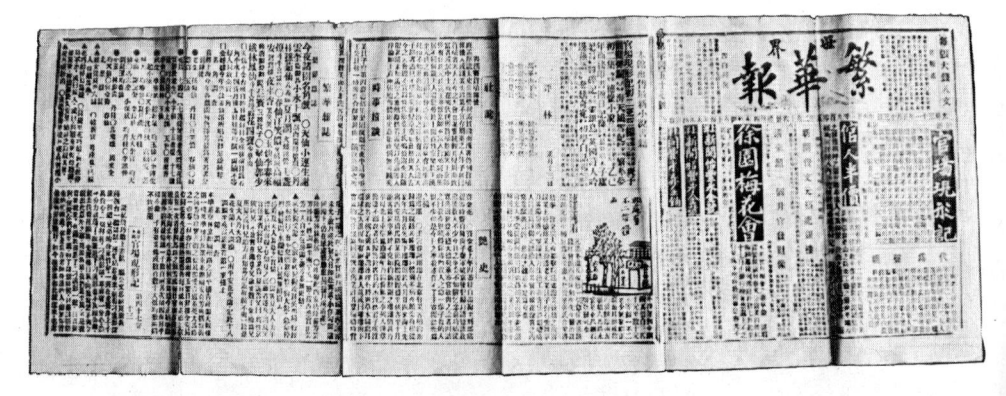

Figure 2 Sample issue of *Splendid World* (*Shijie fanhuabao*), 16 February 1905.

Figure 3 Sample issue of *Grove of Laughter* (*Xiaolinbao*), 2 July 1907.

published entertaining fiction about reform. This distinction sharpened again after 1910.[22]

In 1901, in addition to publishing short pieces about politics, the tabloid newspapers began serializing fiction that dealt with contemporary political, intellectual, and social issues. There was tremendous commercial potential in this kind of literature, but the small format of tabloid newspapers could not accommodate longer literary works. The tabloid magazine was the answer.

Once again, Li Boyuan was the trailblazer, founding the bimonthly literary magazine *Illustrated Fiction (Xiuxiang xiaoshuo)* in May 1903 (Figure 4). Financed by the Shanghai Commercial Press, Li served as editor-in-chief and used the magazine as a venue for publishing many of his own novels. After seventy-two issues, the magazine closed when Li died in April 1906. That November, another tabloid writer, Wu Jianren (1866-1910), began coediting a new fiction magazine, *All-Story Monthly (Yueyue xiaoshuo),* which filled the vacuum left by the demise of *Illustrated Fiction. All-Story Monthly* had twenty-four issues, ending in January 1909. Compared with the tabloid newspapers, these magazines were oriented more toward literature and paid less

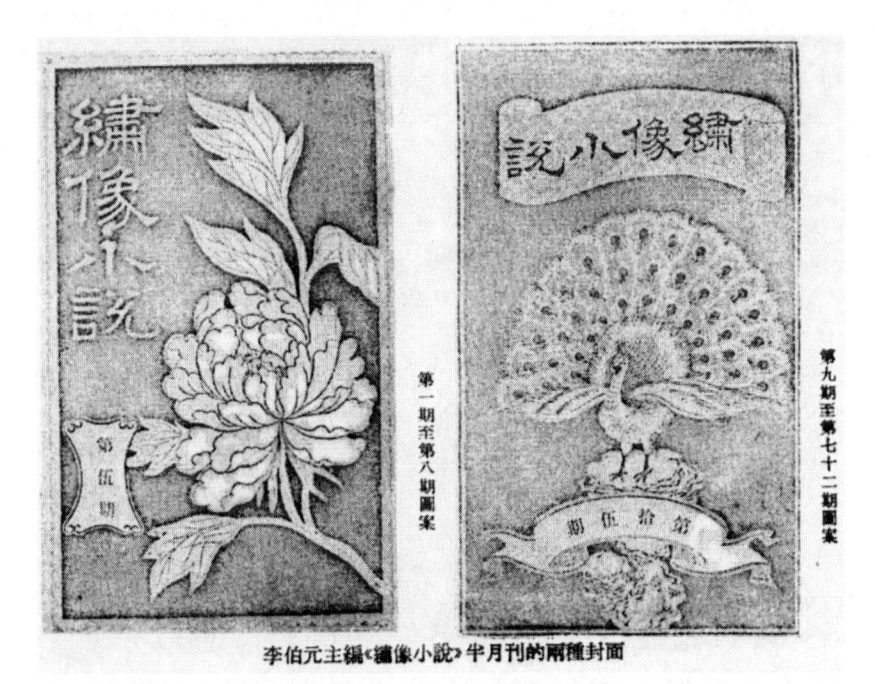

Figure 4 Sample cover pages of *Illustrated Fiction* (*Xiuxiang xiaoshuo*).
Source: Wei Shaochang, ed., *Li Boyuan yanjiu ziliao* [Li Boyuan research material] (Shanghai: Shanghai guji chubanshe, 1980), 17.

attention to courtesans, theatres, and other such pleasures. Yet they were essentially extensions of the tabloid newspapers – the same people produced them, they focused entirely on entertainment, and they employed the same satirical style in dealing with political content.

The permissive Shanghai political environment had much to do with the tabloids' success. Since the Qing government had little jurisdiction over Shanghai's foreign concessions, where almost all of Shanghai's presses were located, the city enjoyed a degree of journalistic freedom that did not exist elsewhere. The government tolerated periodicals so long as they did not call for its overthrow. This did not prevent the state from keeping a watchful eye over the press and from subtly pressuring its editors, a fact of which Li Boyuan and others were keenly aware.[23] Nevertheless, even though the Qing government enacted laws in 1906 regulating the print industry and introduced new press laws in 1908 censoring newspapers and journals, the central and local authorities had insufficient resources to enforce these laws. Tabloids hardly caught the authorities' attention, mainly because, in the eyes of the establishment, they were insignificant.

In the late Qing and Republican eras, forty-six tabloids were published in Shanghai.[24] In the late Qing era, some tabloids ran for as long as thirteen years, whereas others lasted only a month. At any given time between 1900 and 1910, roughly ten tabloids were published daily in Shanghai. On the eve of the 1911 Revolution, however, the tabloid press disappeared almost entirely from Shanghai and reappeared as a significant presence only in the early 1920s.

There are several possible explanations for this disappearance. First, two of the most important tabloid personalities, Li Boyuan and Wu Jianren (Figures 5 and 6), had passed away by 1910. Second, the tabloids' reckless pursuit

Figure 5 Portrait of Li Boyuan.
Source: Wei Shaochang, ed., *Li Boyuan yanjiu ziliao* [Li Boyuan research material] (Shanghai: Shanghai guji chubanshe, 1980).

Figure 6 Portrait of Wu Jianren. *Source:* Wei Shaochang, ed., *Wu Jianren yanjiu ziliao* [Wu Jianren research materials] (Shanghai: Shanghai guji chubanshe, 1980), 3.

of profits cut into quality, damaging their reputations. In the earlier years, they were indeed risqué, but they still maintained an aura of propriety. In the years leading up to 1911, they became overtly obscene and their stories were often apocryphal. As a result, they had many run-ins with the International Settlement authorities, who, motivated by Western religious moral precepts, often banned the papers and fined and jailed the editors. Finally, the tabloid press may have lost its initial freshness and readers may have become bored with satirical attacks on officials who by then had already been totally discredited. In a broad sense, the tabloids had exhausted their usefulness and novelty, and they lost their niche in the periodical market.

The Tabloid Community

The tabloid community consisted of the publishers, writers, editors, and contributors who produced the tabloids, as well as the tabloids' consumers – its regular readers and subscribers. Included among the consumers were occasional and casual readers of tabloid newspapers, magazines, and literature, along with audiences of dramas adapted from such literature. To be sure, the ideas, criticisms, and viewpoints expressed in the tabloid press spread beyond the tabloid community, as many other people heard their stories, jokes, and opinions in teahouses, brothels, workplaces, and homes.

Members of the tabloid community belonged mainly to the low and middle ranks of the literati. I define these literati to include all those who had received a substantial traditional education, regardless of whether they had earned a degree. They were a subset of the late Qing educated ruling class, a product of the government examination system. I exclude from my definition the elite literati who already occupied positions of power and influence in Qing officialdom, or who held other positions of political and intellectual prestige. Also excluded are those who were mainly educated in new-style schools with Western curricula.

The low- and middle-ranked literati were therefore sub-elites who were outside the normal circles of power. As a social group, they faced certain challenges in the late Qing. Their responses to the dramatic political changes stemmed from shared interests and outlooks. The tabloid community coalesced around its tabloid press and the literature published by tabloid writers in other presses. Thus, the voices of this community were specifically those of the low- and middle-ranked literati.

Editors, Writers, and Contributors

The publishers, writers, and editors of the tabloid press, often playing multiple roles simultaneously, formed the active core of the tabloid community. Besides

Li Boyuan and Wu Jianren, those rising to prominence in tabloid circles included Sun Yusheng, Ouyang Juyuan, Gao Taichi, Zhou Bingyuan, Zou Tao, and Shen Xizhi. Except for Ouyang Juyuan, who was younger, and Zou Tao, who was a bit older, all belonged to the last generation of literati born in the 1860s and 1870s who grew up in the 1880s and 1890s. Many, including Li, Sun, Gao, Ouyang, and Zou, had a *xiucai* degree, while others, such as Wu Jianren, had no degree at all. Many tried, but failed, to pass the provincial government examination for the *juren* degree. I call them "tabloid literati." Caught up in China's rapid transition, they were born too late to have earned prime civil positions in officialdom, but, unlike their younger contemporaries, they were born too early to have had access to a formal Western-style education. Determined to earn a living and a reputation, these early pioneers broke with traditional literati career patterns and transformed themselves into modern professional writers.

Li Boyuan was born in Shandong Province into a literati-official family with ancestral roots in Changzhou, Jiangsu Province. At sixteen, he completed his study of *The Four Books* and *The Five Classics*, the canon of a Confucian education. Under the guidance of his tutors, he then ventured into textual criticism. As a well-rounded literatus, Li excelled in the "eight-legged essay" required for Qing exams: poetry *(shi)*, rhapsody *(fu)*, verse *(ci)*, prose, calligraphy, painting, and seal carving.[25] He was knowledgeable in phonology, epigraphy, and textual criticism, as well as in the study of enunciation in verse singing. He demonstrated all of these skills throughout his career, along with a flair for writing novels and folksong verses such as *tanci*, which "orthodox" educators regarded as "low and frivolous."[26]

At the age of twenty, Li Boyuan returned to Changzhou, sat for the county-level government examination, won first place, and received the xiucai degree. In Nanjing two years later, he failed the provincial-level examination for the juren degree. It is not clear whether he retook the exam, but we know he never received that degree.

In Changzhou, where, as in many other towns in the Jiangnan region, literati of various ranks were concentrated, Li distinguished himself in literati circles. He was very quick of mind, sharp in word, and unrestrained in personal style. Many anecdotes about his literary brazenness circulated around town. Once, at a drinking party, a member of the Hanlin Academy composed an impromptu poem in which he made a mistake in the thirteenth rhyme, and Li pointed out this mistake right away. Everyone at the party was awestruck and expressed admiration for his knowledge of rhyme patterns in poetry.[27]

In the eyes of the townspeople, however, Li Boyuan was not a traditional literatus, certainly not in appearance. He was slightly built and effeminate.

Although it was still unusual at the time to see young people in town wearing glasses, Li wore a pair of hawksbill tortoiseshell glasses to correct for nearsightedness. He eschewed some traditional gestures of respect toward his elders, failing, for instance, to remove his eyeglasses when encountering older literati, as was the custom at the time. He also tried to learn English from a foreign missionary living in town, which was rare among the literati.

When Li Boyuan was born, Wu Jianren was just about to mark his first birthday. Wu was born in Beijing to a prominent literati-official family with ancestral roots in Foshan, Guangdong Province, where he grew up. The family's prestige had peaked at the time that his great-grandfather, an academic in the Imperial Academy, held various prominent official positions in many parts of the country. At the age of seven, Wu began his formal studies at home, with private tutors. At twelve, he entered the prominent Foshan Academy *(Foshan shuyuan)*, where Liang Qichao, a famous intellectual and reformer, had also been educated. In 1882, when Wu was sixteen, his father died while serving as a low-ranked official in Zhejiang Province. A year later, Wu Jianren, like Li Boyuan, had to leave home for Shanghai to earn a living.

Through his hometown connections, he found a job as an office clerk at the Jiangnan Arsenal, the official enterprise established by Li Hongzhang and Zeng Guofan, leading late Qing statesmen, in their efforts to modernize China's military. At first he worked as a scribe, copying office documents; later, he drew blueprints of machinery. In his spare time, Wu composed poetry and other texts in classical styles, developing his skills as a writer. At the age of twenty-five, he began publishing short literary pieces in Shanghai newspapers to supplement his income. At thirty-one, in 1897, just after Li Boyuan started *Fun*, Wu left the Jiangnan Arsenal to become a full-time editor and writer for one of Shanghai's early tabloids. He worked for five different tabloids during the next five years.

Sun Yusheng and Gao Taichi were, respectively, five and three years older than Wu Jianren. As with several other tabloid literati, they worked first as editors and writers for Shanghai's mainstream newspapers. After a brief stint with *Shenbao*, Sun became chief editor of *Xinwenbao* in 1896, a job he held until 1904. While still working for *Xinwenbao*, he became publisher, editor, and writer for *Anecdotes* in the summer of 1898 and for *Grove of Laughter* in 1901. Gao joined *Shenbao* as a writer at the age of twenty-six and later became its chief editor. He then became chief editor of *Zilin hubao*, the Chinese version of Shanghai's English newspaper, the *North China Daily News*. In November 1897, Gao founded the tabloid *Pastime (Xiaoxianbao)*, a supplement to *Zilin hubao*.

Surrounding this core of tabloid editors and writers were dozens of contributors who wrote for the tabloid press. They came from diverse social and intellectual backgrounds yet shared a love of literature and displayed similar attitudes toward reform. Among the well-known literati who wrote for *Fun* were Qiu Fengjia, a *jinshi* degree holder and educator; Pan Feisheng and Qiu Shuyuan, editors of various newspapers in Hong Kong and Singapore, respectively; Li Genyuan, who later joined the United Allegiance Society *(Tongmenghui)* in Japan; Xi Xifan, a rich Shanghai comprador; and Pang Shubo, who worked briefly for *Fun* and came to Shanghai from Suzhou with Ouyang Juyuan in 1898, when both were twenty years old.

Contributors to *Illustrated Fiction* and *All-Story Monthly* were just as diverse. For example, bestselling author Liu E first serialized his *Travels of Lao Can (Laocan youji)* in *Illustrated Fiction;* he made his living as a medical doctor, merchant, comprador, and official. Lian Mengqing, a journalist and friend of Liu E, also had his novel serialized in the same magazine. Bao Tianxiao often translated novels and published stories in *All-Story Monthly* while working as editor and writer for the mainstream newspaper *Shibao* and several other magazines. Zhou Guisheng, who co-edited *All-Story Monthly* along with Wu Jianren, had received a formal new-style education and was among the first in China to translate English literature into Chinese. Wu was responsible for Chinese works in the journal, while Zhou was in charge of translated literature.

Some tabloid magazine contributors did not write for the tabloid newspapers. Bao Tianxiao was one of those. He had a low opinion of these papers, regarding them as mere entertainment with little concern for political matters, and he worked only for major papers such as *Shibao*.[28] Zhou Guisheng, however, did publish his translated works in the tabloid papers.

Readers and Circulation

In the early years, tabloid readership consisted mainly of refined literati and merchants. Even Wang Kangnian, a jinshi degree holder who published China's early reform papers, was asked by many of his sophisticated friends outside Shanghai to purchase *Fun* for them.[29] Li Boyuan described the readership of *Fun* in the early years as made up of literati, merchants, and people from the world of entertainment, such as courtesans and opera performers.[30] In his novella *A Shanghai Swan's Tracks in the Snow (Haitian hongxueji)*, Li gives a further sense of *Fun*'s readers. They included owners of small and middle-sized businesses; accountants and managers; scholars and professionals such as journalists; employees of foreign businesses and banks; and leisured gentry and sojourners from the provinces. Courtesans did not constitute a large readership because most were illiterate,[31] but, as Catherine Yeh notes, their patrons tended to be tabloid readers.[32]

After 1900, the tabloids gradually expanded their readership by devoting a larger proportion of their pages to more diverse topics. At the same time, their style displayed less literary flair and refinement. Not surprisingly, reading tabloids became a common pastime for urban Shanghai residents as the habit of reading newspapers took root in the everyday lives of the literate public. Tabloid readership expanded to include people of middling literary abilities such as young students, small merchants, and shop clerks. For the most part, the readership was male, as the tabloids' content reflected male perspectives and catered to male pleasures and concerns.

The tabloids' content also reveals that they catered to a readership of low- and middle-ranked urban literati. Articles about the fairness and efficiency of government examinations and about the training of literati appeared frequently. Interactive literary activities, such as exchanging poetry about courtesans and prostitutes, with whom readers admitted involvement, also strongly points to this readership: high-ranked literati would never have openly admitted such a thing. All tabloids serialized works of fiction, on which newspaper sales depended; literati were enthusiastic readers of fiction.[33]

Although it is impossible to cite exact sales estimates, there does exist fragmentary evidence of the tabloids' popularity. Many tabloid literati confirmed Li Boyuan's claims that *Fun* sold well. In fact, Li was so confident of *Fun*'s popularity that in 1899, within two years of its initial appearance, he decided to reprint all the previous issues as a book. About a month and a half after *Splendid World*'s debut, Sun Baoxuan, a literatus from a prominent family of officials, wrote in his diary that the paper sold quite widely.[34] *Grove of Laughter* also sold very well; its editor reported that a man came to the office one day to buy sixty copies of the previous day's issue to mail out of town.[35]

Some scholars have also noted the popularity of tabloids. Naito Konan claims that as early as 1899 *Fun* had surpassed *Shenbao* in terms of daily print production.[36] Tarumoto Teruo observes that by the early 1900s, most successful tabloids sold as well as *Shenbao*.[37] Various estimates suggest that at its peak *Fun* sold between seven thousand and ten thousand copies per run.[38] This is a significant number, considering that it was not until 1901 that the major paper *Xinwenbao* reached a circulation of a little over ten thousand, surpassing *Shenbao*.[39] Still, daily production fluctuated greatly because most readers in the late Qing bought newspapers and magazines from vendors, not through subscription. The papers sold best when they offered something special, such as popular "flower elections" and hot novels. It is also worth noting that the actual tabloid readership was larger than the number of copies in circulation as purchasers would share their copies with others. Joan Judge estimates that, on average, each newspaper copy had about fifteen readers.[40]

Although the primary market for tabloids was in the Shanghai and Jiangnan areas, distribution was nationwide.[41] By 1904, *Fun* had about seventeen distributors in various cities. By the end of 1902, *Splendid World*'s distribution network extended to twenty-three large cities, including Beijing, Tianjin, Nanjing, Anqing, Hankou, Suzhou, Hangzhou, and Guangzhou, as well as to other more remote places throughout the country. Likewise, by April 1901, *Grove of Laughter* had a national distribution network of twenty-two cities and locales.

Unlike the newspapers, the tabloid magazines from the outset targeted a broader readership of various overlapping social groups, including literati, officials, reformers, students of new-style schools, entrepreneurs, merchants, and women.[42] One literatus-merchant said that his only hobby was reading fiction, and he praised *All-Story Monthly* for publishing more Chinese than translated fiction and for appealing to a diverse readership by offering more than ten genres of fiction.[43] One family recounts how three generations, including the grandmother and children, were engrossed in each issue of *Illustrated Fiction*.[44] Gu Jiegang, a distinguished historian, recalls reading *Illustrated Fiction* as a student in Suzhou in the late Qing.[45] Another scholar reported that *Illustrated Fiction* had a mass *(dazhong)* readership in urban centres.[46] Although reaching a mass market may have been this periodical's intent, people of rudimentary literacy did not constitute a significant part of its audience. Its early issues tried to appeal to women and readers with less-developed literary skills by using popular forms of storytelling such as tanci and local ballads, but these forms disappeared within a year.

Both *Illustrated Fiction* and *All-Story Monthly* had essentially the same readership, most of whom belonged to the rank-and-file literati. According to Xu Nianci, who lived in Shanghai at the time, 90 percent of those who purchased novels in 1908 were literati.[47] Since the rank-and-file literati were the most numerous of the literati, it is likely that they read serialized fiction in these two major journals.

Although no sales data are available for these two magazines, it is safe to assume that they had to sell at least enough to sustain their operations. In the 1910s, it usually took a minimum of three thousand copies for publishers to cover the costs of publishing books and magazines.[48] Since there was little inflation over the years, the two magazines must have sold at least that many copies per issue. As with the newspapers, the magazines' readership was probably wider than sales and subscriptions would indicate. Although the tabloids (which hereafter refers exclusively to tabloid newspapers) gained a large readership in the Jiangnan region, the magazines reached even more readers and had a larger distribution network.

Besides those in Shanghai, *Illustrated Fiction* had a network of eighty-seven distributors in cities and towns throughout China as well as in Tokyo, Yokohama, and Singapore. These distributors included bookstores, drugstores, and even a few government-funded institutions such as schools and military hospitals. Similarly, within one year of its debut, *All-Story Monthly* expanded its distributors to seventy-seven in forty-two cities and towns, including Tokyo. It also inserted mail order forms in many issues, offering discounts for orders of either six or twelve months.

The works of tabloid literati also reached audiences through books and other periodicals besides the tabloid press. Li Boyuan's novella *China Today (Zhongguo xianzaiji)* was initially serialized in *Shibao*. Wu Jianren's novel *Strange Events Eyewitnessed in the Last Twenty Years (Ershinian mudu zhi guaixianzhuang)* was first published in Liang Qichao's *New Fiction (Xinxiaoshuo)*. Some of their bestselling novels were reprinted as books many times over. Shanghai publishers reprinted Li Boyuan's *Officialdom Unmasked (Guanchang xianxingji)* many times, and his death in 1906 led to a dispute among publishers over the copyright. The Beijing newspaper *Patriotic Daily (Aiguobao)* serialized the novel, with added commentaries, at the turn of the century.[49] China's first new-style drama troupe, established in 1907, adapted it as a comedy, which it staged in Shanghai, Beijing, and Tianjin in 1908.[50]

Combining all the readers of newspapers, magazines, and books with the audiences of theatrical performances, the tabloid literati commanded a significant nationwide readership. Moreover, in contrast to the mainstream press, the tabloid press readership was more socially diverse and included people with both high and low literary abilities. To be sure, there was considerable overlap between readers of tabloids and readers of the major Shanghai papers; the literati, in particular, read both. Although papers such as *Shenbao* attracted a national audience of high-ranked literati, including government officials, tabloids were more popular among rank-and-file literati and had a more regional readership. Some reform papers, such as *Shibao*, also featured a "gossip column," containing news items that were "infectiously interesting, and usually true, but not quite fit for publication in the newspaper proper."[51] As a result, the paper may have succeeded in capturing some of the tabloids' readership. Nevertheless, urban residents of low literary abilities, if they read newspapers at all, would have been more likely to read the playful tabloids than the formal mainstream papers. Moreover, the tabloids were effective in communicating with an audience that otherwise had no interest in national politics. By making politics entertaining, they helped inform people who would not have sought this information elsewhere.

The Crisis of the Literati

The tabloid community was more than a social entity; as a producer of meanings, it was also a cultural entity. Reading and writing were interactive social, communal, and dialogic processes that produced and interpreted texts, and that shared and influenced thoughts and emotions. Writers wrote to satisfy readers' tastes, while readers formed opinions and consciousness by interpreting those texts. The meanings constructed by members of the tabloid community depended largely on their positions in the broader social relations of power.

Members of the tabloid community as a whole came from diverse social and economic backgrounds and possessed a range of values, politics, and dispositions. Yet most of them, as rank-and-file literati, had similar social backgrounds and similar interests and experiences. What they shared were exclusion from the ranks of power and anxiety over the systemic changes taking place in society. The reforms most particularly affecting the literati occurred in the educational and imperial examination systems, through which they earned privilege and ruling-class status. These reforms affected the entire literati class, to be sure, but the low- and middle-ranked literati suffered disproportionately compared with the elite literati, who were generally able to preserve their power and prestige.

In 1901, new-style schools began to replace the traditional tutorial system that for over a millennium had prepared literati for imperial examinations. This institutional change reduced the literati's position in the power structures of learning. They gradually lost employment opportunities as teachers, and their education was devalued. In 1905, by imperial proclamation, Empress Dowager Cixi ended the thirteen-hundred-year-old imperial examination system. This institution had not only supplied the Chinese bureaucracy with highly educated literati-officials but had also produced educated local elites who helped the state maintain social order and Confucian orthodoxy.

The phasing out of traditional education and shutting down of the imperial examination system set adrift an entire class of low- and middle-ranked literati, who found it impossible to anchor their social and political worth in traditional ways. Many felt that their educations had become useless and saw their social and economic status deteriorate sharply. Others, such as the tabloid literati, seized new opportunities in the print market and succeeded socially and economically. At the same time, they were anxious and uncertain about the future of the nation, their families, and themselves.

The members of the tabloid community shared these experiences, and the similar positions they held in the social hierarchy led them to assume similar political outlooks. The rank-and-file literati had their own reasons to be cynical, resentful, and even defiant. On the one hand, they resented the Qing state and its officials, and blamed them for their own declining position in society, for the internal crises afflicting China, and for China's declining position in the world. On the other hand, they resented the political and intellectual elites who took advantage of new opportunities brought about by reforms to increase their wealth and prestige.

The tabloid press both reflected and moulded these new political outlooks. It shaped new political identities for community members who aimed to salvage, if not enhance, the power and influence they were losing. At the heart of this political outlook lay a strong anti-establishment and populist disposition.

Themes and Plan of This Book

An examination of the tabloid press and community is significant because it tells us a great deal about an important yet quite neglected social stratum of Chinese society in the late Qing: the low- and middle-ranked literati. Historians of this period know much about the political and intellectual elites because information about them is so readily available. There have been numerous studies, for example, of Liang Qichao, Kang Youwei, Zhang Zhidong, and Zhang Binglin. Historians know little, however, about the low- and middle-ranked literati, who remain an amorphous group in this period although the latter made up the majority of the well-educated population.[52]

The thoughts, sentiments, and discourses of the tabloid community took the form of what I call "aesthetic populism." This populism consisted of ideas and rhetorical styles that appealed to "the people" and that opposed various segments of the political and intellectual establishment whom the tabloid community believed failed to serve the interests of the common people. Members of the tabloid community criticized the Qing government and officials, opposed the revolutionaries, and challenged the views of elite reformers who had become the new political aristocrats. This populism played an active role in shaping public sentiment and perception in the final years of the Qing.

This populism was aesthetic because it manifested itself in a particular kind of entertainment literature with distinctive ways of seeing, representing, and interpreting the Chinese state and society. It was expressed through literary tastes rather than street demonstrations. The chief characteristic of this aesthetic was "merry laughter and angry curses" *(xixiao numa)*, a phrase that tabloid writers themselves used to describe their satirical representational style of literature.

Recent scholarship defines populism as an antagonistic relationship between an oligarchic class and a subordinate class.[53] The former is an amalgamation of political, economic, and cultural elites. The latter is a heterogeneous coalition of people, coming from anywhere in the social hierarchy, who have a variety of unmet grievances and who feel disenfranchised and resentful of their circumstances. Their frustrations move them to discredit the oligarchic class and to charge it with corruption and malfeasance. These feelings arise in the first place because certain social changes threaten their livelihoods and security, depriving them "of their rights, values, prosperity, identity and voice."[54] Moreover, normal institutional channels are unable to resolve these problems. A "populist rupture" then takes place when the aggrieved coalition crystallizes and sets in motion oppositional actions.[55]

Populism thus involves what Francisco Panizza calls an "aggregation of discontents" that seeks to change the prevailing political discourse and to construct a new popular identity. To accomplish this, populism requires leadership to articulate the demands and frustrations of the aggrieved coalition. This leadership may be intellectual, political, or some combination of both, and it may or may not actually include members of the aggrieved coalition. The relationship between the leadership and the aggrieved coalition is, to a large degree, educational because people may at first be unable to identify explicitly what it is they lack. The role of the leadership, then, is "to awaken a dormant identity."[56] Reading is one way for people to awaken, for it gives them the chance "to formulate the unformulated."[57]

This conceptualization of populism describes well the situation in late Qing China. Growing animosity existed in the tabloid community toward the political and intellectual elites. The former coalesced into a disenfranchised group of people who felt increasingly resentful of the establishment. The resulting antagonism took the form of outright opposition, "passive" grudges, and appropriation of the ideas and discourses of the powerful and privileged.

The tabloid literati – publishers, editors, and writers – played a leadership role in developing aesthetic populism. Through their published works, they altered the discourse of the times, gave voice to festering discontents and resentments, and helped steer the identities of the anxious and aggrieved tabloid community. The tabloid literati certainly did not belong to the establishment yet they were themselves elites in a sense, belonging to China's ruling class. They were able to speak out publicly and shape public opinion through their writings; some of them enjoyed literary reputations as bestselling authors. Nevertheless, they had neither the political power of officials nor the intellectual prestige of, say, Liang Qichao, a leading intellectual and reformer.

Speaking in the name of "the people" became fashionable in the late Qing. Both elites and non-elites adopted the Enlightenment ideal of the will of the people as a basis for the legitimacy of the state. They all promoted, in varying degrees, populist ideas supporting the rights and power of the people. Liang Qichao was a leading advocate of popular sovereignty in a constitutional Chinese state. Despite their support of the people, however, members of the political and intellectual establishment never placed themselves among the people. They spoke to them, led them, and regarded themselves as their representatives – but they were not *of* them. Tabloid literati, in contrast, saw themselves as belonging to the powerless people. They saw themselves as educators of, and spokespersons for, the people. Yet they also saw themselves as having no political or intellectual clout, and complained that nobody wanted to listen to them.

In an age before modern electronic media, the tabloid newspapers and magazines were instrumental in assembling, in one forum, the voices of the rank-and-file literati, and consequently in creating a subversive culture. In doing so, they sparked something unprecedented: sustained popular participation in national politics took root among the rank and file. The tabloid press helped shape a public consciousness that delegitimized Qing rule, preparing the ground for the public to accept, and even welcome, the collapse of the dynasty. It also articulated unique versions of those rapidly developing Chinese twins, nationalism and modernity.

I base my analysis on five of the most popular tabloid newspapers (*Allegories, Anecdotes, Fun, Grove of Laughter,* and *Splendid World*) and two tabloid magazines (*Illustrated Fiction* and *All-Story Monthly*). My source materials also include novels, essays, and short pieces written by tabloid writers and published as books or in other periodicals. I examine six dimensions of the late Qing Shanghai tabloid press and community, devoting one chapter to each.

Chapter 1 shows how amusement and entertainment became the leitmotifs of the tabloid press and united writers and readers in a tabloid community. The chapter also points out how this seemingly benign culture both revealed the weakening of the Qing state's control of society and nurtured an attitude of defiance toward the state.

Chapter 2 shows how tabloid writers and readers constructed a critical discourse that vilified Qing officialdom. For over a decade, anti-Qing condemnation appeared daily in the press and countless works of fiction depicted corrupt, inept rulers and officials. The chapter analyzes how this critical discourse eroded the symbolic power of the state and became a cultural foundation of the 1911 Revolution that brought down the Qing Dynasty.

Chapter 3 describes the nature of nationalism as a discourse, a sentiment, and a movement in the tabloid community. It shows that nationalist sentiments were anti-imperialist but not anti-foreign, and analyzes the populist attitudes of tabloid writers involved in nationalist movements. It also shows how the writers simultaneously appropriated and challenged Liang Qichao's discourse on citizenship.

Chapter 4 investigates how the tabloid community responded to the challenge of Western political ideas and ethical values, which were gaining legitimacy in China. It shows that the community shifted in its attitude toward reform. Whereas many members heartily embraced reform in the early years, in later years they expressed doubts and worries about it. Unlike intellectual elites, especially those who had received a Western-style education and who were much more likely to adopt Western views on politics and ethics, they believed in fundamental Chinese ethics and wanted only moderate reforms.

Chapter 5 explores how the tabloid community questioned the changing political and social power structures that accompanied the shifting structures of knowledge. It shows how members attacked both so-called reformers who worked within the system for economic and political gain, and revolutionaries who were interested only in acquiring power.

Chapter 6 illustrates how market forces played a major role in developing tabloid populism and aesthetics. It begins with an analysis of the late Qing literary market, examining the relationship between the tabloid press and the rise of fiction, as well as between reader and writer. The chapter then explains how these market forces nurtured populism and shaped tabloid aesthetics.

The Conclusion of this book highlights the process in which the tabloid press and community emerged and thrived. It also summarizes two major findings. First, the press and community developed a distinctive aesthetic populism in the late Qing. Second, the rank-and-file literati in the community played a leading role in this development. The forces that united the rank-and-file literati and enabled them to create aesthetic populism are identified, and the historical significance of tabloid culture as a subversive force that contributed to the 1911 Revolution is discussed.

To understand this late Qing tabloid phenomenon, we begin in the next chapter with an inquiry into how the tabloid community first came into being, and what bound members of the community together.

1 Community of Fun

Making fun, or playing *(wan)*, was a catchword and central theme in the tabloid press. For Li Boyuan, "thousands of forms and transformations exist in heaven and earth and in between, all of which are truly and merely a playing game."[1] Seeing himself as "playing with life" *(wanshi)*,[2] Li chose as his pen name "Master of Fun" *(Youxi Zhuren)* and described his daily work for *Fun* as "using humorous styles and writing playful words."[3] Other writers also regarded their writing as "playful words," such as Sun Yusheng when he remarked that he had "playfully established *Grove of Laughter*."[4] Not only writers but also readers believed that fun was the essence of life. As one reader wrote in verse, "Living for a hundred years one is a passing visitor, having fun when you can, the night is still young."[5]

Fun they had indeed, mainly by playing with courtesans and with words. The booming business of prostitution was one of the premier attractions of Shanghai, at least for men who could afford it. Literati at all levels and from all occupations who congregated in the city as permanent residents, sojourners, and visitors, made up a large part of its clientele. A guide to entertainment in Shanghai, apparently written by Li Boyuan, counted 230 courtesan houses with 1,109 courtesans in the International Settlement. One report in *Fun* also mentioned over 200 courtesan residences, with over 1,000 courtesans, located in the area around Fourth Street.[6] These courtesans served growing throngs of literati, providing a perfect theatre for literati to enact the traditional liaison between what was commonly called "the talent and the beauty *(caizi yu jiaren)*."

To be sure, playing with courtesans was not the sole preoccupation of the literati. After all, the reputation of a literatus relied foremost on how well he wrote poetry and rhapsodies. With the advent of newspapers, literati found an unprecedented opportunity to show off their talents. As early as the 1870s, papers such as *Shenbao* lacked sufficient space to publish all the literary work submitted, and had to publish special periodicals to provide an additional outlet.[7] Tabloids provided space not only for the more established literati but also for those who were unable to publish in major papers. Thus, the combination of an intense public interest in courtesans and a large number of literati keen to play literary games helped the tabloids maintain a wide and devoted following. A shared appreciation of Shanghai as a unique city of fun, its variety and scale unsurpassed anywhere else in China, created another connection between readers and writers.

In this environment, a community centred on the tabloid press came into existence. The tabloid literati, the active core of the community, built around themselves social networks for fun, fame, and business. This community of readers and writers, the late nineteenth-century equivalent of today's Internet chatrooms and blogospheres, created a cultural craze that glorified the pursuit of fun and pleasure.

Flowers, Leaves, and Fragrances
Referring to himself, Li Boyuan proclaimed: "This master of fun has made the flower election the number one subject of the paper ever since its beginning."[8] This was not a mere boast. Immediately after publishing *Fun*, Li announced in June 1897 a plan to sponsor periodic public "flower elections" (*huaxuan*) in which readers would nominate and select the city's best courtesans, or "flowers." Shortly thereafter all the tabloids held these highly popular flower elections, and the pool of contestants expanded to include even the women and girls who attended the courtesans. Along with the flower elections came the male connoisseurs, female celebrities, poets, fundraisers – and, of course, troublemakers.

The First Flower Election in *Fun*
No one in 1897 had ever heard of a flower election sponsored by a newspaper, although such elections had already occurred in Shanghai's concession areas. Small groups of Shanghai literati had organized private courtesan competitions in the 1860s, 1870s, and 1890s; some had even published their results in *Shenbao*. It was Li Boyuan, however, who, via *Fun*, first turned such an event into a public spectacle.[9] Stressing the importance of knowing who was who in a city teeming with courtesans, Li asked his readers to nominate their favourite "flowers"; he promised to rank them fairly and to publicize the results the following month.[10]

Within a couple of weeks, the paper received over a hundred nominations. Each day, *Fun* published a selection of readers' letters and poems about courtesans, and Li and his readers carried out extensive dialogues in the tabloid debating every detail of the election process. One reader provided a list of criteria for evaluating courtesans, including character, beauty, literary ability, social skill, musical talent, and drinking capacity. The reader also suggested disqualifying courtesans who were the lovers of actors or carriage-drivers, or who had jealous temperaments. Li responded that the reader was being too restrictive. Lamenting that truly exceptional courtesans were hard to find in his day, Li informed readers that he would consider all candidates, and that courtesans need not worry that he would exclude them.[11]

Other readers, worried about the feasibility of electing the best courtesans, complained that the elections would be biased and untrustworthy. After all, how could it be possible to select the best of the two or three thousand courtesans scattered among hundreds of brothels? Others charged that the paper was being too frivolous and that Li lacked a moral conscience. Li strove repeatedly to defend himself in the pages of *Fun*.

Many readers, however, sent in poems and letters of praise regarding the elections and eagerly offered advice. One letter proposed holding flower elections just as the government held examinations: one contest for general excellence, like the government examination for civil officers; a second contest for courtesans who were musically talented but not beautiful, analogous to the government examination for military officers; and a third contest for those who distinguished themselves in literary talent, virtue, or loyalty to their patrons, similar to the specially arranged government examinations.[12] Suggestions, comments, and poems kept pouring in to *Fun*, and Li regretted that the paper could publish only one letter a day due to limited space. To accommodate readers, he had to postpone the date for announcing winners from an original date in July to early August.

All those involved became increasingly aware of the high stakes of the flower election; not surprisingly, many heated controversies ensued. One such controversy involved Jin Xiaobao, a highly regarded courtesan. She sent Li a message declaring that she did not wish to be a candidate in the election because she was ashamed to have her name associated with courtesans involved in sexual relationships with lowly clients such as actors and carriage-drivers. Li made Jin's message public a few days after he had already published some derogatory comments about her, and chided her for her arrogance. In response, one of Jin's patrons rebutted Li's comments and defended Jin.

Another reader, Xu Renjie, then jumped into the fray. He ridiculed those patrons who lavished extravagant praise on certain courtesans, pointing out that one so-called literate courtesan candidate knew only how to read calling cards for parties, and that another's paintings were actually done by her patron. Without directly naming Jin Xiaobao, Xu attacked her, suggesting that she threatened to withdraw only because she feared losing the election.

Xu then mocked all of Shanghai's courtesans, claiming that, without exception, they contrived their beauty by dying their hair, powdering their faces, painting their eyebrows, tightening their waists, and wearing high-heeled shoes. For Xu, courtesans like Jin made it difficult for Li Boyuan to host the election, a joyful activity not to be missed in such a fun and prosperous place as Shanghai.[13]

Rumours flew about who the finalists would be. Li helped spread these rumours, perhaps even starting some himself to fuel the anticipation. Readers scoured the paper for clues about prospective finalists; they drew up lists ranking their guesses and argued about the fairness of the rankings. Li deepened the suspense by telling readers they were off the mark.[14] Two weeks after announcing the winners, he published an article titled "Wrongly Reporting the Winner," in which he described the scenes of exhilaration and disappointment when messengers delivered the news to the courtesans:

> That day when the outcome of the flower election was about to be announced, courtesans, like those literati who were about to hear the outcome of their [government] examinations, were anxious and restless. They secretly sent their messengers to ask about the outcome. On hearing that a courtesan named Sibao won first place, the messengers first informed Wang Sibao of Puqing Alley; then Jin Sibao, of Shangren Alley; then later, Hong Sibao, of Baihua Alley, and lastly Zuo Sibao, of Qinghe Alley. The four courtesans, after suddenly hearing the news that they had won, were all thrilled and looked triumphant. Right in the middle of the frenzy, the newspaper came out, and it was Zhang Sibao of Xihuifang Alley who won first place. Wang Sibao, without reading the paper and mistaking Zhang for Wang, still insisted that she had won. Jin and Hong were also in doubt. A patron of Zuo Sibao arrived dejectedly and said, "What a *zuo*, what a *zuo!*" Another client said, "Zuo is very good, how could she not be as good as those non-Zuos?"[15]

Zuo was the surname of the courtesan, and the character *zuo* also means "mistake." Thus, the patron's and client's remarks served as humorous double entendres.

The final list of winners included 140 courtesans: 3 in the first rank, 30 in the second, and 107 in the third. Among the three courtesans in the first rank were the winner, Zhang Sibao, a sixteen-year-old with nine nominations, and the nineteen-year-old runner-up, Jin Xiaobao, with seven. The third, a seventeen-year-old courtesan, also had seven nominations. Li embellished the announcement with a long poem for each of the three first-rank winners, elaborating on their talents and beauty, and a short poem for each of the 30 second-rank courtesans. At the end of the issue, he also published the names of those who did not make it to the final list. Accompanying the final list was a celebratory preface and poem by Yuan Xiangpu, who had helped determine the final rankings. Yuan, a retired county magistrate then in his seventies, was known for his playful literary works, many of which appeared in *Shenbao*, and was reputedly a connoisseur of Shanghai's "flower world." In his poem, Yuan described himself as "having rambled in 'flower bushes' for over fifty years" and simply wanting to "win smiles from flower seekers since with the final list these seekers could now easily find flowers."[16]

Just one week after announcing the winners of the first election, Li produced another list of 39 courtesans based on previous nominations, chosen for their talent in singing and playing musical instruments. Three were included in the first rank, 18 in the second, and 18 in the third. Li claimed that this second list was essential because it gave courtesans with musical talent but who lacked physical appeal a chance to win.[17] Dubbing this list "winners of martial arts" and the earlier list of 140 courtesans "winners of letters," Li jokingly compared his elections to the hall of fame selections of Beijing opera actors who excelled in martial arts and to the government civil service examinations for men of letters.

The flower election craze showed no sign of letting up even after it was all over. In fact, just the opposite occurred. On the very day the list of 140 courtesans was announced, Li received three letters from readers complaining that Jin Xiaobao, the runner-up in the first rank, surpassed Zhang Sibao (the first-place winner) in terms of beauty and musical talent, and claiming that Jin should have won instead. The letters charged that Jin missed the top position merely because of some love affair she had been involved in, and that Li had therefore made a poor choice. Li immediately refuted the charges, claiming that he based the outcome solely on the number of votes and on readers' letters of nomination. He even appealed directly to Jin Xiaobao herself, saying that Jin knew how fair his judgment had been. Li asserted that he cared little about courtesans' love affairs, arguing that one does not make moral judgments in the world of courtesans as one would in the world of literati, and that the wrongs of courtesans were not important to public morality.[18] While defending the election results, he also pointed out – perhaps only to stoke the fires – that Jin Xiaobao had lofty aspirations, and that she had not spent any time with men she thought unworthy. As a result, more people ended up denigrating Jin than admiring her.

Numerous complaints came from patrons who were disappointed because their favourite courtesans were ranked too low or did not make the list at all. In a long letter to Li Boyuan, a patron who had been temporarily living in

Beijing requested that he reconsider his choices and include in his final list a courtesan named Lin Daiyu. The patron explained that he had known Lin for fifteen years, and that because of her literary and musical flair and her skill in understanding and communicating with her patrons, his circle of literati-officials all agreed that she was the best courtesan in Shanghai. While pleading his case for the courtesan, the patron wrote that while he was away in the capital he "was unable to forget about this event for even one day," that he "had no way to relieve himself from boredom and loneliness, and his only solace was to read *Fun* every day." He informed Li that his circle of literati-official friends in Beijing all treasured the paper and circulated it among themselves.[19] Within a month, this patron again wrote to *Fun* about Lin Daiyu.[20]

Besides patrons, a few courtesans themselves complained about being ranked too low on the final list. Li again told his readers and courtesans that the flower election was merely an opportunity to have fun, that they should not take the matter too seriously.[21] His words were hardly convincing, for the "price tag" of the ranked courtesans rose sharply. To quell complaints and arouse readers' interest, Li announced a plan to invite several dozen like-minded connoisseurs of courtesans to a meeting in order to choose courtesans from the final list and rank them once again. To justify this plan, he explained that he would model this re-ranking after the practice used in Chinese government examinations for the *jinshi* degree, in which those who had passed the examination were then reexamined at the imperial court and re-ranked for official assignments.[22]

Most readers reacted to this decision with delight, and submissions of prose and poetry extolling individual courtesans' beauty, talents, and charm poured into the paper. Enticing his readers to send in even more poems, Li wrote numerous poems himself and challenged others to compete with him for literary excellence. Sometimes he wrote poems anonymously or under different pen names to create a foil to which readers and other writers could react. In one case, he wrote a set-rhymed verse *(ci)* under a pen name, extolling the fun and pleasure to be had in brothels. A few days later, a matching verse from a reader appeared in the paper. Next to that verse, Li added a comment pronouncing the earlier verse to be elegant and tasteful, whereas the current one was merely quite good.[23]

Li Boyuan also asked readers to contribute literature – in the form of poetry, prose, prefaces and postscripts, couplets, and brief biographies of courtesans – to make the flower election a lasting memory. Works with titles such as "Ten Beauties of Shanghai," "Dreamy Verse of Courtesan Quarters," and "Teased by Carnal Desire" filled the pages of *Fun*. One veteran of the "flower field," with a pen name of "Master of the House of Joyous Flowers," wrote many poems paying tribute to the top courtesans; he also wrote a foreword to a booklet published by Li Boyuan that listed the names of the 140 courtesans.[24] Within two weeks of announcing the election results, the paper received so many literary contributions that Li decided to compile them into an anthology titled *Records of Shanghai's Fragrances*.[25] A month later, he again asked his readers to contribute brief biographies of winning courtesans, planning to compile them into a book called *The History of Flowers of the Erotic River*.[26]

The first flower election generated unprecedented public interest and contributed greatly to the rapid expansion of *Fun*'s readership during the publication's first two months. According to Li, he received more than two hundred letters of nomination.[27] He claimed that the day *Fun* announced the final list, all five thousand copies of the tabloid's first run were sold out before noon. Three thousand extra copies were printed to meet the demand, and on each of the next three days Li's office was crowded with people who came to purchase the day's issue.[28]

Flower Elections as a Fad

Fun sponsored more flower elections in succeeding years. Following its footsteps, other tabloid papers also made flower elections a recurring event. In 1901, the writers of *Allegories* organized more than a dozen such elections, proffering a goal of restoring the honour of courtesans at a time when the quality of their services had eroded and their reputations had been tarnished. Modelling it after the *Fun* election, *Allegories* held an election that produced two winning lists, one for general excellence, the other for musical talent.[29] It also held a small-scale flower election every month and asked readers to complete a dated nomination form (included in each issue) with their personal information and comments about their courtesan's looks and musical abilities.[30] The paper also sponsored a flower election during the Chinese Moon Festival, using the same dated nomination forms as in the monthly flower elections.[31] The tabloid *Pastime* held flower elections as well. The glut of elections sponsored by the newer tabloids prompted Li Boyuan to mock one of them for lacking taste and sophistication in both literary and "flower" fields, and to dismiss its elections as merely "the meddling of a mediocre guy."[32]

Repeated flower elections pushed writers to find new gimmicks in the hunt for fresh names and rising stars. Li Boyuan's second list of 39 courtesans in 1897 was one such gimmick. In 1899, Li for the first time sponsored a "leaf election" in *Fun*, which featured young female attendants to courtesans, aptly dubbed "leaves" attached to "flowers," as the candidates. This election produced a final list of 138 winning "leaves" consisting of 3 in the first rank,

35 in the second, and 100 in the third. A year after *Anecdotes* began publication, Sun Yusheng sponsored a flower election for child courtesans. Some patrons nominated nine-year-old girls, and one of the final winners, hailed for her singing, was only eight.[33] The following year, Sun held another election for child courtesans in which the sole criterion was physical beauty.[34]

In 1900, Li lowered the age range for his flower elections; previously limited to sixteen- to twenty-year-olds, they now featured thirteen- to eighteen-year-olds. At the same time, he tightened other criteria for candidates, excluding those who had been child courtesans, those who had married previously, and those with children.[35] The next year, however, in *Splendid World*, Li announced plans for a flower election specifically for child courtesans aged nine to thirteen.[36] The editor of *Allegories* had his own strategy to enliven the elections in his paper; every Sunday he visited three different brothels to evaluate their courtesans, and he published the results weekly, hoping his readers would follow suit.[37]

Regular flower elections created a community whose pastimes included nominating courtesans, participating in election decisions, contributing poems, and locating courtesan nominees using information provided in the tabloids. Many patrons continued to send in nominations several months after a flower election had ended. Letters of nomination mainly came from within the city, but many also came from other cities and locales, including Hangzhou.[38]

Choosing winners was usually a collective act. The night before the winners of the March 1900 flower election were announced, Li Boyuan invited several fellow literati and many highly ranked courtesan nominees to a party at a fine restaurant. He asked the men to evaluate and rank the courtesans. After several rounds of drinking and much discussion, Li gazed at the courtesans, as would a portrait painter working with a live model, then composed a poem for each of the thirteen would-be winners. Shortly thereafter, Ouyang Juyuan also wrote twelve poems about the first twelve winners.[39]

Some patrons confessed an addiction to flower elections. When Li decided to hold a leaf election rather than a flower election, several readers wrote letters pleading with him not to do so.[40] One reader wrote:

> I have no aspiration in my life other than to enjoy courtesans. In recent years, I have had a hard time finding fine courtesans on my own. How fortunate it was for me that you have been holding a flower election every year, and, based on the results of your elections, I searched for the top courtesans, and I have never been disappointed with them ... Yesterday in your paper, you mentioned that you did not want to have a flower election this year because of the lack

of talented courtesans in Shanghai. I am very concerned with this, and have to say a few words to you ... Your elections have so influenced the fame of courtesans that they also depend on you.[41]

Another reader's letter detailed his enthusiasm for tracking down all the "leaves" recommended in *Fun*. He had visited all the places frequented by courtesans and their young female attendants, such as gardens, well-known restaurants, and a horse racetrack. At these places, he carefully observed and compared them with one another. He also arranged dinners with some of the nominated "leaves" so he could talk with them, hear their voices, watch their manners, and evaluate them. After all this work, he distributed a list of his favourite "leaves" and nominated one as the first-place winner.[42]

Patrons contributed poems and biographies about the winners. Submissions were often so numerous that Li Boyuan had to apologize for publishing only the best among them. Sun Yusheng planned to publish an anthology of biographies of Shanghai's winning "flowers."[43] Many patrons were eager to have their works published, and this would give them a brief moment of literary fame and elevate their worth in the eyes of courtesans.

Other readers looked for like-minded men through the tabloids. One asked to meet Li Boyuan. According to his self-introduction, he had been a patron of Shanghai's courtesans for about twenty years, and whenever he heard of an excellent courtesan, he would seek her out, stay with her for a month, and then write about her. He invited Li for a drink to discuss this writing project; he had already written over twenty volumes *(juan)*, and planned to write thirty.[44] This reader certainly found the right person to consult.

Readers eagerly sought out famed courtesans. Before Xie Guixiang won a 1900 election, she received only two or three calls a night to attend patrons' drinking parties, and was able to stay at each place for a long time. Men saw her as an "ordinary flower" because apparently she lacked a radiant look. The night after her victory, she received fifty to sixty calls, and on succeeding nights she received thirty to forty calls per night. With such a hectic schedule, she attended five or six parties in the time "it takes an eye to blink"![45] For many, including officials and merchants, lists of winners became guidebooks for finding concubines. Zhang Sibao, the top winner in Li Boyuan's first flower election, became the concubine of an imperial minister's son.

All tabloid writers were experts on and avid patrons of courtesans. In the early years of *Fun*, Li Boyuan showed up daily at the Zhang Garden teahouse, chatting and laughing with an entourage of courtesans. One contemporary described the scene as resembling an ancient master scholar lecturing to his disciples seated around him. Because Li was such a celebrated customer, the proprietor instructed waiters not to charge him for his tea and refreshments.[46]

Many winners of flower elections were also the writers' favourites. One eighteen-year-old winner called herself a disciple of Li Boyuan, for he had taught her to improve her singing skills; he loved listening to her sing while sitting beside her at restaurants and teahouses.[47] Li also became very fond of a certain seventeen-year-old, Xie Guixian, and was frequently seen at her residence, where he held banquets for his friends. Not surprisingly, Xie made it to the top in the first flower election of Li's new tabloid paper, *Splendid World*, rising overnight from obscurity to stardom.

Sun Yusheng "discovered" Li Jinlian, an obscure courtesan who had been living in a brothel. Sun came to regard her highly, and affectionately called her "lotus flower," from her name, "golden lotus." Li Boyuan was also infatuated with her.[48] Sun, Li, and Shen Xizhi, founder of *Allegories*, then gave her a makeover. They secretly helped her move to a new residence in a nicer area, changed her name to Li Pingxiang, and named her new abode "the chamber of heavenly fragrance," which they wrote at the top of the entry gate. When Li Boyuan held the second flower election in *Splendid World*, he made Li Pingxiang the top flower.[49] She was said to have become so famous and desirable that patrons often crowded inside and outside her residence.[50]

In the preface to his bestselling *Dreams in Splendid Shanghai (Haishang fanhuameng)*, Sun Yusheng proudly told readers that the novel was based on over ten years' experience as a veteran of brothels. In the novel, Sun modelled the character Gui Tianxiang after his own concubine, Sushi. Sun had taken Sushi from a brothel when he was thirty-six, and she died of illness a few years later.[51] When Sun was around forty years old, he became fond of another courtesan and pursued her with lavish gifts.

The Voyeuristic Community

Flower elections may have actively engaged only the most devoted participants, but the tabloids' exposure of Shanghai's erotic quarters surely entertained many voyeuristic readers. To further entice such readers, the tabloids devised a range of ingenious strategies. Perhaps the most brilliant was the "Four Buddhist Warrior Attendants" *(sida jingang)* campaign that made four courtesans household names. Sun Yusheng described the origin of the campaign's name. Every day in the late afternoon, customers began filling up the Zhang Garden teahouse. Courtesans often arrived in groups, and four of them – Lu Lanfen, Lin Daiyu, Jin Xiaobao, and Zhang Shuyu – always sat at a round table near the entrance. Observing this striking scene, Li Boyuan imagined them as statues of the Four Buddhist Warrior Attendants who guarded the Buddha statue in Buddhist temples.[52]

Li and his fellow writers then orchestrated a relentless media campaign in 1898 to promote the four courtesans. In March, Wu Jianren serialized in *Pastime* his novel about the four courtesans. In the summer, he published the novel as a four-volume illustrated book called *The Wonder Book of Shanghai's Famous Courtesans – the Buddha's Four Warrior Attendants (Haishang mingji sida jingang qishu)*. In the fall, Li Boyuan, along with Ouyang Juyuan and Pang Shubo, who was then working with him at *Fun*, enlisted the four courtesans to spearhead a fundraising campaign to establish a suburban cemetery site for the exclusive use of Shanghai's courtesans and prostitutes. To help solicit donations, promoters circulated photos of the "Four Buddhist Warrior Attendants." The campaign continued for six months, generated a large literary production, and ended with the purchase of the cemetery site. In the process, the reputations of the four courtesans came under intense scrutiny because some were accused of embezzling funds.

Fun honoured donors in the paper, and Li Boyuan published an anthology of selected poems about the campaign. Patrons wrote elegies, eulogies, and epitaphs for imaginary courtesan funerals. Ouyang Juyuan and Pang Shubo together wrote a ten-act dramatic script about the fundraising and published it in a booklet. Even the *Tiannan xinbao*, the Chinese newspaper in Singapore published by Qiu Shuyuan, featured a major article about the four courtesans.[53] A year later, Li Boyuan himself expressed surprise at how quickly the fame of the four courtesans had spread.[54]

Beginning in 1898, the tabloids used photos of courtesans as an effective gambit to sell papers. Li Boyuan reported that many readers were asking him to print in the paper photos or portraits of courtesans. Citing the difficulty of doing so, Li instead sold courtesans' photos separately along with the paper.[55] He ordered ten thousand photos of each of the top-ranked courtesans in a flower election, but these sold out in a matter of days and he had to order several thousand additional copies to meet the demand.[56] The *Fun* office also compiled a booklet titled *Pictures of and Poems for a Hundred Beauties in Shanghai*.[57] In addition, Sun Yusheng sold photos of top-ranked child courtesans with a caption on each photo.

The community loved to pry into courtesans' lives. News of courtesan activities, love affairs, scandals, and suicides filled the daily pages of the tabloids. In 1898, the editor of *Anecdotes* advertised to recruit one or two persons to report on courtesan news.[58] Writers and readers expressed their opinions and kept a vigilant eye on the state of the "flower field." Soon after the 1897 election, a third-ranked courtesan named Zhu Ruchun married the son of a wealthy provincial official. In less than a year, the marriage broke up and she returned to the Shanghai courtesan business. This news prompted various reactions. Some criticized the courtesan for marrying in the first place, some wanted to find out who was responsible for the breakup, and others simply made fun of her.[59] When Lin Daiyu and Lu Lanfen, two of the well-known Buddhist Warrior Attendants, fought over one patron, Li Boyuan wrote numerous reports describing how they verbally attacked each other and suggested that the patron in question come out publicly and settle the dispute himself. In the style of a catechism, Li wrote of a conversation about the case with an imaginary guest. The guest asked why the two courtesans fought in public if they wanted to keep secret their relationship with the patron. Li replied:

> In a profound love, lovers cannot forget about their love for one second; if they know that someone else is stealing their lover, even if they do not wish to overtly express their anger, their hearts cannot help it … Love creates jealousy; jealousy creates fun; and who else but Lin and Lu, the two amusing people, could produce such a fun thing?[60]

Readers took sides, argued, and gave advice to the courtesans. The debates continued even three months after the event.[61]

Love affairs between high-profile courtesans and opera singers attracted much public interest, and writers squeezed all they could out of these stories. One such case involved Gao Caiyun, a Beijing opera star, a man who always played the female role. Gao was immensely popular among women, especially courtesans, because of his handsome face and remarkable acting skill. A rich and socially prominent Shanghai man filed a lawsuit accusing Gao of having a long-term affair with his concubine, Gu Cailin, a former courtesan. Gao attempted to force him to relinquish her. Between April and May 1899, when the trial took place, Li Boyuan studiously followed all developments in the case, eventually publishing the entire court transcript. He then wrote numerous articles mocking Gao and Gu for their shabby and shameful physical appearance during their incarceration, chastising them for their illicit relationship, and applauding their imprisonment.[62]

In the end, Gao was sent to prison, where he eventually died. Li published a *tanci* script recounting both the affair and the trial. *Allegories* also serialized a fictional account of the affair, occasionally accompanied by illustrations, one of which was subtitled "Lascivious and violent, Gao Caiyun transgressed the law." Shen Xizhi, the paper's editor, wrote an introduction to the story that Li Boyuan soon published in *Fun*.[63]

For the voyeuristic community, patrons were just as interesting as courtesans. Some patrons with an exhibitionistic bent published their love letters; others chose to settle their disputes with courtesans in public letters designed to pressure the courtesans and elicit the public's sympathy. Many more offered opinions on how best to appreciate courtesans, commenting on their beauty, manners, and musical and social skills. For these men, playing with courtesans was not merely for sexual gratification. In fact, one became respected and distinguished in the "flower field" only with refined cultural taste and sophisticated appreciation for courtesans. Comparing two courtesans, Zhang and Jin, Li Boyuan wrote:

> To evaluate a courtesan is like evaluating a painting. In the Yuan dynasty, there was a competition for artists, and the given theme was "A house is behind the clouds." One artist painted a chimney from which cooking smoke rose to the clouds. Another artist, who was even more imaginative than the first, painted a few vegetable leaves that floated along mountain streams, with the multitude of mountain peaks half veiled by clouds. Both paintings implied the existence of a house without actually painting it, a representation that embodies the art and beauty of implication and reservation. The courtesan Zhang's manner is more reserved and enigmatic [than Jin's], and thus more intriguing. The courtesan Jin is almost perfect, except that she is a bit artless in manner. Appreciating courtesans is also like tasting food. As enchanting and appealing as a mint cake with the taste of purity and freshness, it may not be to everybody's liking. However, well-stewed pork in soy sauce, with a strong taste and inviting aroma, can easily get everybody jumping at it.[64]

Sun Baoxuan wrote to convey his unique understanding of the pleasures of keeping company with courtesans:

> I have sojourned in Shanghai for a few years, and have had many friends with whom I have frequently gotten together ... we often have banquets in brothels and usually have courtesans perform for us ... those who do not understand us think that we are there just for sexual pleasure; I say that we are not there only for sexual pleasure, rather, we are there for the pleasure of friendship. Rarely have people talked about this as I have, and few really have understood what I meant.[65]

At one point, Li Boyuan even planned to identify four male patrons to star as counterparts to the "Four Buddhist Warrior Attendants."[66] Perhaps for the sake of the men's reputations, he did not carry out the plan.

Wordplay and Other Pastimes

If making courtesans playthings affirmed writers' and readers' sense of virility and masculinity, then playing with words affirmed another aspect of the literati's identity. Their wordplay was intricately connected to their "flower-play." Community members displayed keen interest in and attention to literary quality. The tabloid papers provided them with an avenue to distinguish themselves from fellow literati with wit, creativity, and literary prowess. Poetry in particular served as the touchstone of one's sophistication as a literatus. Tabloid community members used courtesans as poetic inspiration and devices in literary games. Many became word-epicures, caring only for words for the sake of words. Artistic creativity consisted of little more than set phrases, hackneyed expressions, and banal literary extravagances.

The culture of fun went far beyond "flowers" and wordplay. The fetishizing of fun as a cultural practice was emerging; having fun became glamorous and legitimate in the modern age. Countless writings praised Shanghai's culture of fun and pleasure for its unique blend of new and traditional entertainment. The community was introduced to new pleasures in the form of foreign cuisine, Western-style fashion, deluxe modes of transportation such as horse-drawn carriages, and activities such as strolling in public gardens. Traditional forms of entertainment, such as debauchery, gambling, opium smoking, and theatre-going, became more glamorous and daring. The press provided daily reminders of these activities, prodded their readers to participate, and produced a growing experiential consciousness of fun among community members.

Literary Games

Selecting a pen name was a starting point in displaying one's literary flair. Writers and readers who contributed work to the tabloids all had playful pen names, and many had multiple names. Li Boyuan had more than a dozen. Sun Yusheng's pen name was "Born from a Stone in the Rapids of Shanghai" *(haishang laishisheng),* a name that echoed his alternate pen name "Sounds of Jade" *(yusheng).*[67] Naming offered infinite playful possibilities and identities. Readers chose names such as "Wanderer of the World," "A Garrulous Person," "A Retired Scholar in the Clouds," "A Person with Occasional Success in Riddles," "Snow Eating Poet from the South Sea," and "Flower-Loving Man."[68]

For writers, the title chosen for each anecdote needed to be playful as well. Writers usually assembled each news item into pairs that they called "couplets." They constructed these couplets to be stylistically symmetrical, with equal numbers of words and with a semiotic resemblance. Some paired titles in *Fun* were in four-character style, such as "Talented Scholar with Five-Character Poem" and "Loyal Minister with Eight-Legged Essay." Other paired titles were in seven-character style, such as "Absent in Wedding, Bride Worried Greatly" and "Fake Ship Ticket, Buddhist Priest Fell into Trap."[69] Some paired titles in *Grove of Laughter* read as a two-character pair, such as "High Officials" and "Narrow Avenues."[70] *Anecdotes* had titles such as the four-character pair "Lady, Spare His Life" and "Playboy, Happy at Heart."[71]

Playful verse, prose, and rhapsodies appeared daily in the tabloids and in each magazine issue. In the early months of *Fun,* Li Boyuan regularly listed the names of contributing authors and apologized because limited space prevented him from publishing all of their work. In two such apologies, he mentioned that he had received twenty-seven and thirty-nine submissions, respectively, many of which contained multiple poems.[72] Because of the large number of poems submitted for publication, Li decided to establish as an outlet the *Shanghai Literary Society Monthly (Haishang wenshe yuekan).*[73]

The courtesan was a major motif in the works of literati. Not only did Li Boyuan, Sun Yusheng, Ouyang Juyuan, and others write verses on the subject but they also encouraged readers to follow suit, writing their own poems and discussing them at tea- and wine-drinking parties. Readers idealized some courtesans and belittled others who failed to live up to their standards. One reader, responding to a biography of a courtesan published in the previous day's paper, wrote ten seven-word, four-line poems for that courtesan.[74] Another reader wrote ten four-line poems about the "ugliness" of some prostitutes, defining ugliness as being too old, too tall, too fat, too dark, and having overly large feet and breasts, discoloured hair, moles and facial pockmarks, or only one eye.[75] Another reader, from Hubei, wrote ten four-line poems, each of which also ridiculed the ugliness of prostitutes with particular bodily defects such as protruding foreheads, watery eyes, missing arms, and deafness, as well as those who were hunchbacked or crippled.[76]

There were, of course, poetry competitions, which attracted a great many participants. Scholars today have taken note of one poetry competition in particular because one of the winners was Zhou Shuren, prompting speculation about whether it was not actually the famous writer Lu Xun.[77] In another poetry competition, readers assembled a collection of names, each referring to a certain tonal pattern for singing verses, and then composed poems in which each line contained one of those names. The names referred to short poetic phrases such as "clump of flowers," "spring from heaven," "shining moon in a dark yard," and "boating at night." Some readers composed poems with restrictions on rhyme or use of characters. One poem depicted a scene in which a young girl, sitting hidden behind a wall screen beside a secluded creek, wrote throughout the night a long love letter to her faraway lover. The two opening lines of the eight-line poem read:

> The screen wall zigzags six times and the creek meanders in nine angles.
> A letter the length of a *chi* [33 centimetres], written until the fifth section of night, was sent west of the Liao River.[78]

These opening lines conformed to the required rhyme because in Mandarin Chinese both the word "creek" *(xi)* in the first line and the word "west" *(xi)* in the second line end with the same sound. Another requirement was that the lines should use the words for the numbers one to ten, as well as the words for "hundred," "thousand," and "ten thousand." The two measure words "*chi*" and "*zhang*" (3.3 metres) had to be used also.

Other readers wrote playful prose that showed off their literary skill and imagination. Some parodied classical prose to make fun of the contemporary world, using, for example, the famous "Nan Pavilion Preface" *(Nanting xu)*, written by Wang Xizhi in 353 CE, and Tang poet Du Mu's "The A Fang Palace" *(Afanggong fu)*.[79] Some were vulgar. One wrote an elegy for his broken chamber pot, personifying the clay pot as his favourite concubine. When "she," a beautiful and intimate companion, crashed to the floor and broke into pieces, his heart also broke. He felt lonely at night without "her" at his bedside.[80] Another reader ridiculed henpecked husbands for allowing their women to rule over them, for allowing femininity *(yin)* to rule over masculinity *(yang)*. The prose vividly described how wives beat their husbands – "lashing their bodies with bamboo, fists striking their waists, nails scratching their faces" – and the resulting physical appearance of their husbands: "Blood and bruises on their faces, cracked skin and minced flesh, chestnut-like bumps on their heads, pain in their buttocks." It mocked pathetic husbands who kneeled at the feet of their wives while begging for mercy, who endured the shame of having servant girls laugh at their meekness, and who enjoyed endless pleasures at night with their wives while secretly worrying about their fate the next day. The reader concluded that these husbands were "puny men of letters" who lacked the physical strength to fight the evil females – but it was still worth paying the price of "one hundred lashes" to have a beautiful wife.[81]

Besides poetry and prose, other literary games enjoyed popularity, especially at drinking and gambling parties. Games required rules, and the more sophisticated the rules, the more challenging and fun were the games. At a so-called winter relief party *(xiaohanhui)*, one person initiated a rule for composing couplets in which the last word of the first line and the first word of the second line, when combined, must be the name of a material used in Chinese medicine. Using this rule, the players produced about ten couplets.[82]

In order to facilitate merrymaking at parties, writers, including Li Boyuan and Sun Yusheng, designed games themselves. Li devised a set of cards with a poem written on one side and instructions on the other. Players would use each card for one round of drinking. Those who failed to find the right answer to the question implied by the poem would pay a penalty. Sun designed another game requiring each player at a drinking party to compose a four-line poem. Each line had to be a set phrase taken directly from four types of literary sources, without adding or missing a single character. Sun's four categories included names of poetic styles *(qupai)*, titles of Beijing opera scenes, phrases from the *Book of Odes*, and phrases from poems by famous poets. The entire poem also had to exhibit coherence and grace. The penalty for players who failed to compose such a poem was to drink another round.[83]

Many readers also contributed drinking games, and one reader created such a long list of drinking rules for parties that it required four installments to print.[84] Other drinking games had few rules and required players to be more spontaneous and creative. In one game, a player began by composing a short poem, and the next player had to come up with a poem based on clues in the previous one.

All tabloids regularly sponsored riddles, some on a daily basis. Players were numerous and games would occasionally last ten days or more. One riddle in *Grove of Laughter*, for example, asked four questions about women in Shanghai's brothels, including how many were courtesans, how many were prostitutes, how many had small feet, and how many played a double role as prostitute and attendant to a courtesan. The riddle designer deliberately played on ambiguities in the categories and the impossibility of finding a definitive answer. In the ten days after the riddle was first published, forty-two answers appeared in the paper. The players offered many playful solutions and clever jokes based on their own definitions of the four categories. The editor commented on each player's "playful words," evaluating their literary sophistication and "playfulness."[85]

Solving riddles often required a familiarity with classical literature along with playful flair. Riddles sometimes took the form of short poems and phrases. One reader connected thirty-two first names of Shanghai courtesans to lines of poetry extracted from the works of famous ancient poets. Another composed a riddle in which the reader had to find a single character that logically matched a four-line poem. The matching character took the form of a complex character containing three individual characters as its components, and the lines in the poem connoted the simpler component characters.[86] Solutions to some of these riddles were merely a single character, while solutions to others were more complicated. The answer to one riddle in *Fun* included phrases from such classical works as *Chronicle of Zuo*, *Book of Changes*, and *The Four Books*, the pattern names of verse, titles of *kunqu* opera, and the names of famous Beijing opera actors.[87]

Wordplay was competitive. All tabloids and magazines regularly sponsored competitions in poetry, prose, and riddles, for which they often printed specially designed entry forms in the papers. The press awarded winners small prizes such as cash, theatre tickets, cakes, cigarettes, painted fans, books, inkstones, fragrant soaps, and cotton towels. One issue of *All-Story Monthly* contained a list of answers to sixteen previously published riddles, along with the name of each winner. The first person who mailed in the correct answer to a riddle became the winner and won a small prize. Forty-five readers solved the thirteenth riddle on this list, and the winner received a box of envelopes. The same issue also listed solutions to another set of eighty-four riddles published in the previous issue.[88]

In one riddle competition, *Grove of Laughter* offered prizes ranging from books, fragrant soaps, and towels to body oils.[89] Most participants came from Shanghai, but many also came from other cities and towns in the Jiangnan area. At one time, *Grove of Laughter* presented awards only to residents of Hangzhou, Suzhou, and Ningbo.[90] The papers also often offered small gifts to readers whose poems were accepted for publication. In one case, six winning readers each received a group photograph of four top courtesans from a recent flower election and a box of mooncakes.[91]

Other Kinds of Leisure
Writers and contributors talked about Shanghai's cultural environment with awe and admiration, emphasizing its modern flair. One writer described the city's scenery in the first section of a rhapsody *(qu)*:

> Shanghai, the most bustling place; visions become blurry; eyes become fuzzy; every street crisscrosses. Steel-wired carriages; leather-canopied carriages; fast as wind and electricity. Three-way intersections, Chinese and foreign police; patrolling, with clubs in hand.

Each of the verse's next six sections describes one kind of fun: visiting courtesans for entertainment, going to bordellos for the "real thing," attending storytelling performances, eating fine dinners of Western cuisine, attending operas, and playing in gardens.[92]

Fourth Street and the surrounding vicinity was one of the most commercial hubs of the International Settlement, and descriptions of the area appeared regularly in the papers. Teahouses, opium dens, restaurants, theatres, storytelling houses, brothels, hostels, and shops of all kinds lined both sides of the street; most of them boasted indoor plumbing and electric lights. One reader wrote a short whimsical piece introducing over fifty restaurants and teahouses and their best dishes.[93] Li Boyuan described it as the most prosperous street in Shanghai:

> Carts and carriages pass through it like flowing water, horses like swimming dragons, men and women walking to and fro like weaving cloth. On the street, one's eyes are dazzled by colours, and one's mind is drunken-like and lost. Even if one's heart harbors hatred and worry, one throws them away and forgets all. Who knows how many thousands or tens of thousands are spent in one night? It's truly China's big playground."[94]

One contemporary eyewitness described this night scene on the street:

> Electric lights were sparse, and gaslights, their tubes twisted in all kinds of shapes, hung in the shop fronts that were separated from each other by inches; at night hundreds and thousands of gaslights, covered with colourful glass, burned simultaneously; they were so numerous that they seemed like stars in the sky.[95]

Another writer described a street performer narrating a story about a child courtesan leading a man and his friend into a brothel where they ate and drank. The two heard a commotion next door and police arrived to quell a fight among some gamblers. As background to his narration, the storyteller mimicked the sounds of Fourth Street: people opening and walking through doors, people talking and laughing and arguing, horse-drawn carriages driving past, music coming from teahouses, the soft voices of child courtesans soliciting customers, and the voices of women and children.[96]

So captivated was Li Boyuan by this ambience that, three and a half months after *Fun* commenced publication, he moved his office to an alley off Fourth Street, just to be close to the action. He informed friends and readers that they could now conveniently stop by his office to chat about news and to buy the paper. When for an undisclosed reason he moved again a year and half later, the new location was also in an alley off Fourth Street.[97] Fourth Street was certainly the place to be. *Grove of Laughter* had its office on a street that intersected Fourth Street, *Allegory* in an alley off Fourth Street, *Anecdotes* in an alley off Third Street, and *Splendid World* in an alley off Broadway *(Damalu)*, another of the heavily commercialized streets in the International Settlement.[98] In 1900, at least six other tabloid newspapers were located in the same alley as *Grove of Laughter*.[99]

Beyond Fourth Street and the concession areas, newly designed public gardens decorated the urban space of Shanghai. Numerous articles portrayed the chrysanthemum shows and music parties in various Shanghai gardens. One such garden was Zhang Garden, "another world where music flows through banana leaves and cranes dream under thousands of bamboo trees."[100] A reader enumerated ten kinds of fun one could have in the garden, including playing pool, watching films, and watching fireworks displays. Another reader described how he "went visiting friends one morning, but after going to more than ten houses he found no one at home; arrived at Zhang Garden and saw all the friends whom he could not find earlier, sitting there, chatting and drinking tea. Isn't this fun?"[101]

By 1899, many readers wrote about their new experiences moving about the city. It had become fashionable for courtesans and their patrons to ride together in horse-drawn carriages that circulated along Shanghai's major commercial streets. In the summer, they took nightly excursions to Shanghai's famous gardens, often not returning until dawn. The excursions became so popular that Li Boyuan thought it necessary to advise readers of the risks of staying in the gardens past midnight; they could catch cold or even get pneumonia from the cold and damp air. Li noted that his concern was warranted because many patrons and courtesans were frail and in poor physical condition.[102] Readers sometimes wrote about these garden outings with courtesans, recounting the joy of flirting with these women along with sympathy for their low social status.[103] The fashion of riding in horse-drawn carriages, often with courtesans, served a purpose – having as many people as possible see the occupants amusing themselves. It was therefore a new way of identifying oneself; it was ultimately a statement about self.

The tabloid community celebrated life by stressing those leisure activities that gave Shanghai its reputation as a "playground." One reader playfully glorified the extravagances and vanities of Shanghai residents in a poem titled "Singing Songs for Whoring, Gambling, Eating, and Dressing."[104] Drinking for pleasure was an incessant interest. Another reader sighed that only alcohol could bring him pleasure, more so than even his wife and children.[105] Yet another described the best and the worst drinking situations – the worst being when "neighbours are crying, somebody is talking about depressing matters, a drinking partner is called away, or the liquor has run out just when the drinking has begun."[106] Numerous prose pieces bore titles such as "Singing for Drinking" and "Rules for Drinking."[107]

In the earlier years of the tabloids, articles about the joy of opium smoking appeared, with titles such as "Introduction to Smoking Opium" and "List of Shanghai Opium Dens."[108] The papers provided information about opium houses in the International Settlement, including opium prices, available grades, and services provided to customers. By 1899, however, the papers began denouncing opium smoking.[109]

As for gambling, another popular pastime in Shanghai, readers and writers had mixed feelings. On the one hand, they approved of gambling in such prose essays as "On Things Used for Gambling" and in countless local-style ballads such as "Ten Ballads on Catching Sparrows at Brothels."[110] On the other hand, they criticized the mayhem that ensued from gambling. Several articles supported the police who arrested gamblers in a brothel.[111] Many other articles warned readers about the dangers of gambling and the personal ruin that could result from gambling addiction. In one article, Li Boyuan warned readers to watch out for a certain unnamed gambler, revealing his tricks at the gambling tables. Two days later, he exposed that gambler, giving away his place of origin and the names of the brothels he frequented; he warned readers that the gambler could change the tricks he used, and that they should beware of playing with strangers.[112]

Articles on theatrical performances appeared frequently in the tabloids, discussing the ups and downs of the storytelling business, the rise of *kunqu* opera, and the new-style dramas *(xinxi)* performed in theatres.[113] As readers and writers showed great interest in these types of entertainment, the papers began to treat as stars opera performers, local verse singers, and storytellers. News, gossip, and criticism followed the stars' performances and private lives. Readers and writers wrote biographies of and poems for them, sometimes responding to each other's works.[114] Sun Yusheng wrote biographies of *kunqu* and *qinqu* opera stars. Some papers reported criminal cases, such as one involving an actor who tried to marry a married woman, and civil trials, such as the case of a theatre owner who sued an actor for breach of contract. Many other articles were conventional reviews of shows. When tabloids began to format their content into columns in 1901, they included one column for the theatre world. Such a column in *Splendid World* provided daily schedules for city theatres and featured critical reviews of performers. For example:

Jin Yaoxiang from Suzhou area performed *pinghua* and was very funny.[115] As soon as he started to talk, the entire audience began to laugh wildly, and so he is highly valued. He came to Shanghai once every three years, and was always scheduled to perform in Yu Garden at noontime, and in the Concession in the afternoon and at night ... What was most magical about him was that every day he told the same story in all three performances, yet each time he rattled off jokes without repeating a single word. Consequently, the audience never tired of his storytelling. One day, the storytelling-house was so crowded that it did not even have spare standing room, so Jin was carried onto the stage on someone's shoulder. Once on stage, Jin promptly said, "all performing artists are afraid of dead ends *(zoutou wulu)*; only the artists of pingtan can prosper by walking on heads *(zoutou)* and still not have a way out *(wulu)*."[116] On hearing the joke, the audience let out a roar of laughter.[117]

With so much attention placed on performers, it was not surprising that the tabloids began to sponsor "opera actor elections" modelled after the popular flower elections. *Allegories* periodically held such elections. Consequently, the papers became instrumental in making and breaking the reputations of theatrical performers, just as they had of courtesans. Sun Yusheng revealed how he had helped Wang Xiaonong, a Beijing opera actor whom he admired, rise to stardom in Shanghai. Initially, Wang's deep voice received little appreciation from Shanghai audiences and he left the city after performing for six months. When Wang returned to Shanghai to try his luck a second time, Sun's friend Zhou Bingyuan happened to be hosting an election for Beijing opera actors in his tabloid, *Pastime*. Sun made sure that Wang became the first-place winner, and Wang rose instantly from obscurity to stardom. Their mutual admiration came full circle when Wang wrote a playful and elegant essay of appreciation, publishing it in the same paper.[118]

While writers and readers wrote and conversed about having fun, they also indulged in fun themselves. They thus became both the subjects and the objects of their texts, unifying everyday life and the literature about that life. The relentless pursuit of fun and pleasure in the press did not occur without some controversy, however. In the early years of the press, editors and writers often had to defend and apologize for their papers in a social environment in which the orthodox tradition denounced such hedonism. By the early 1900s, such sensitivities, apologies, and defences all but disappeared, revealing more about the public's attitudes toward fun and pleasure than about the writers' attitudes. The readers clearly began to take for granted the publication of "frivolous matters" and legitimized the pursuit of fun. The shift in attitude testifies to the power of the tabloid press in creating a community built on sharing both literature and similar attitudes toward fun.

Social Networks

Writers and readers of the tabloid community formed many kinds of social circles. They organized literary societies, interacted socially with tabloid advertisers and other businessmen, and established networks of friendships. These social interactions helped participants build literary fame and, of course, make money.

The wordplay in tabloids not only enabled members of the community to display their literary egos but also provided opportunities for them to join the exclusive social circles of literary societies, many of which the tabloid literati themselves established. Li Boyuan first "discovered" Ouyang Juyuan because of his contributions to *Fun*, including prize-winning poetry. Ouyang became a regular tabloid writer soon thereafter. Within months of *Fun*'s founding, Li announced plans to establish the Art and Literary Society *(Yiwenshe)* and invited literati to join. The society eventually claimed a membership of forty.[119] Li then established two more societies, the Calligraphy and Painting Society *(Shuhuashe)* in February 1899 and the Shanghai Literary Society *(Haishang wenshe)* shortly thereafter. The latter sponsored one of Li's literary competitions[120] and at different times even published its own journal, *Literary Society Monthly (Wenshe yuekan)*, and paper, *Literary Society Daily (Wenshe ribao)*, both of which used *Fun* as an operational base.[121] Sun Yusheng and Gao Taichi organized the Poetry Society *(Shishe)*, and published many members' poems in Sun's paper. Zou Tao also organized a poetry society through his paper, *Amusement.*[122]

Tabloid writers and contributors constituted the core of these societies. Membership extended beyond Shanghai, even including some members of the Imperial Academy.[123] It was through these literary connections that writers cultivated relationships with many influential people. Li Boyuan had personal contact with Wen Tingshi and Dong Kang, both members of the Imperial Academy. Wen, best known for his poetry, attended a Chinese New Year dinner at Li's home in 1900 and participated in his flower elections in 1901.[124] Dong Kang, known as a collector and bibliographer of rare books, appeared often as guest of honour at Li's parties. Li's good friend Sun Baoxuan had close relatives among the top echelon of Qing officialdom. Sun's father and brother served as high-level court officials, and his father-in-law was the brother of Li Hongzhang, a leading statesman in the late Qing. Li supposedly wrote his novel *The National Incident of 1900 (Gengzi guobian tanci)* with insider information from his high-profile contacts.[125]

The literati circles often met in teahouses and restaurants and held parties in brothels, combining work with play. In May 1898, Li Boyuan attended a banquet in his honour at the residence of Jin Xiaobao, the famous courtesan. It was hosted by a prominent Japanese businessman, and at least seven other star courtesans from various flower elections attended. Guests included Dong Kang, Japan's consul general in Shanghai, Ouyang Juyuan, and several other Japanese writers of Chinese poetry. At the banquet, the Japanese businessman and Li Boyuan composed poems extemporaneously and dedicated them to each other. Li later published the poems and wrote two pieces of prose commemorating the occasion.[126]

In one of his novels, Wu Jianren vividly portrayed one meeting at the House of Dazzling Flowers, the residence of a famous courtesan; the conversation provided perfect material for the next day's paper. While using the real names of the courtesans in attendance, Wu disguised the writers' names, although readers could easily guess their identities from the clues he provided. The papers frequently reported such parties, listing names of participants, literati and courtesans alike, accompanied by poems that the literati had written. Sun Yusheng recalled that socializing usually began after nine or ten o'clock at night, after the day's work had ended. Then his friends, including Wu Jianren, Zhou Bingyuan, Gao Taichi, Li Boyuan, Shen Xizhi, Yu Dafu, and several others came to the *Grove of Laughter* office to drink wine or listen to music. "It is really like a club," Sun reminisced.[127] Missing from his account was the presence of courtesans who provided the music. On another occasion, a literatus known for his poetry invited six other literati, including Sun Yusheng, to a party with ten courtesans at the residence of one of the courtesans. Pointing out that "poetry, wine, and playing with women are something that has no end," Sun promised to publish the poems written at the party.[128]

The literary societies facilitated interactive activities among their members. Writers contributed work to each other's papers and magazines, and participated in each other's sponsored activities. When Qiu Shuyuan sponsored a poetry competition, one literatus responded with a poem; he in turn invited two other literati, including Zhou Bingyuan, to contribute.[129] Another literatus challenged eleven others to respond to his poem in *Grove of Laughter* while thanking some of them for recommending a certain courtesan as his concubine.[130]

These literati circles helped the tabloid literati build fame. The writers commended each other's literary excellence in their papers and displayed readers' praise for their work. Thus, Wu Jianren wrote of *Fun:* "[Li] started *Fun* and created a fresh and different style in our country's newspaper business. No fewer than ten newspapers followed the example [of *Fun*] and imitated its style, but none could surpass its excellence."[131] Li Boyuan was acclaimed as "protector of flowers," "king of the flower kingdom," and "master of poetry."[132] Wu's reputable literary friends wrote introductions to his novels, hailing him with language such as "trying continuously without end until his words awed readers,"[133] "the giant of the literary world," "the master of fiction," and "having achieved the greatest literary fame."[134]

The celebrity status of the writers is seen in the attention paid them and in the stories told about them by their contemporaries. Wu Jianren was depicted as speaking with humorous irony, making listeners roll with laughter at his jokes as he remained composed and expressionless.[135] Wu was a known alcoholic, often replacing meals with drink. After drinking, he would often talk passionately about politics.[136] Sun Yusheng had a reputation for loving cats and for acting out roles from Beijing operas, which he enjoyed immensely. Zheng Yimei recorded one of Li Boyuan's legendary escapades. According to him, Li and a Daoist friend playfully exchanged clothing one day and went out for a drink. After drinking, Li took his friend to a brothel. On the way, the friend realized Li's intention and refused to go, but Li, in the Daoist's gown, pushed him along. Their squabble in the street attracted a number of passersby and made quite a comical scene, as it appeared that a Daoist was forcing a man to go to a brothel. Embarrassed, the friend eventually released himself from Li's grip, while Li continued alone to the brothel wearing the Daoist's gown.[137]

The extent of the literary circles in which Li and Wu travelled was most apparent at their funerals. The record shows that fourteen well-known literati wrote poems and couplets to mourn Li's death and praise his literary achievements.[138] Many more friends wrote short biographical essays about him. According to one contemporary writer, several hundred people attended Wu's funeral, and several hundred more were broken-hearted at the loss.[139] Unlike traditional literary clubs for literati, which were entirely private and hidden from the public, these tabloid-centred societies solicited members from the public and sought public recognition by operating completely and purposively in the public eye.

Besides forming literary circles, tabloid writers deliberately cultivated relationships with local merchants and business establishments. During Chinese New Year and other major festivals, they published expressions of goodwill in articles and poems, often directly addressing specific Shanghai businesses and merchants with wishes for good luck and prosperity in the coming year. Li Boyuan was particularly creative in engaging the business community. Within a month after initiating *Splendid World*, he featured a dated blank nomination form on the front page each day, inviting readers to use it to recommend any worthy person or business. Readers responded well, and several recommendations appeared in the paper daily under "Letters from Readers." In one issue, a reader praised a hairdresser's haircuts; in another, a hostel was praised for its clean and pleasant setting. It is likely that the owners of some small businesses recommended themselves, but this did not seem to matter much.

Six months later, Li Boyuan announced plans to publish an anthology titled "Unrivalled in Shanghai," featuring personally selected nominations of special people and businesses in Shanghai. He noted that nominations published in the paper thus far had established the reputations of many businesses and people. Li encouraged more submissions covering a wider social range. He suggested that nominees could include dutiful officials, artisans with special skills, scholars with learned specialties, and merchants and businesses that provided special goods and services. He promised to publish all nominations in his paper, even those not chosen for the anthology.[140] The nominations indeed appeared in a new column, also titled "Unrivalled in Shanghai." In contrast to earlier years, when *Fun* catered mainly to literarily sophisticated readers, these columns suggest that by 1901, more ordinary urbanites had become regular readers of the tabloids.

By publishing readers' recommendations of local businesses, Li ingratiated himself with Shanghai's business circles and made his papers important to them. One of the few photographs of Li Boyuan, taken around 1904 at a party, shows clearly his special relationship with such circles. For this photo, Li posed in the centre amidst eighteen prominent Shanghai businesspeople, among whom were executives of a Japanese-owned silk factory, owners of silk and textile factories, major pharmaceutical and textile merchants, and several large real-estate investors.[141]

While writers worked hard to develop good relationships with business patrons, the reverse was also true, as can be seen in the many published notes from writers to business owners and merchants expressing thanks for gifts or invitations to banquets. Gifts included products of merchants' own firms, along with calendars, newly published books, service guides, tea, dietary supplements, and pastries and candies. Thank-you notes always praised the merchandise. In one note, the editor of *Allegories* thanked two merchants and praised the books they had sent him, one on spiritual healing and the other on fortunetelling. In the next note, he thanked a business for a banquet invitation and apologized for not being able to attend because of a scheduling conflict.[142] The editor of *Grove of Laughter*, after receiving a hundred packages of tea from a tea merchant, recommended the beverage as beneficial for health and appropriate for the season.[143] The good feelings expressed in the papers veiled the cruder commercial relationship between writers and business owners.

Fun and friendships in the literary societies likewise masked the members' mercenary motives. Li Boyuan earned a sizeable income from the Shanghai Literary Society and the publication of the society's monthly. According to Zhang Chun, the society attracted literati nationwide and received submissions ranging between three thousand and fourteen thousand volumes *(juan)* per month during its operation. Contributors had to pay twenty *wen* as a "registration fee" for each volume submitted. Estimated revenue was about fourteen hundred or fifteen hundred *yuan* per month. As an added source of revenue, individuals who proposed a theme for each round of submissions often donated money to the society.[144] Even if Li Boyuan made only half of what Zhang estimates, his profit was still significant.

Members of the Art and Literary Society were skilled at calligraphy, painting, and stone carving, and through tabloids they provided customized services to their patrons.[145] Li Boyuan advertised his services as a painter and calligrapher, listing his prices for painting paper fans and for calligraphy of various sizes. Shen Xizhi provided similar services. Among the most often requested was his calligraphy, written in couplets onto scrolls and on namecards. He charged a half-yuan for each character on namecards. If a customer desired a special style of calligraphy, such as the *wei* style rather than the standard *kaishu* style, the charge per character doubled to one yuan.[146]

From the very beginning, writers' newspaper businesses served also as publishing houses. The papers came in handy for many literati who could not find publishers for their work, especially their collections of rhapsodies, verse, and prose. Li Boyuan used *Fun* and *Splendid World* to advertise and publish these works, along with brief introductions highlighting special literary and artistic features. Publications included various anthologies of poetry, calligraphy, paintings, and engravings, all of which Li collected from his friends and acquaintances and from submissions. He sold these publications and shared the royalties with the contributors. At times, Li's newspaper office functioned as a bookstore, displaying and selling work by his friends and fellow literati. Correspondence between Li Boyuan and Liu Juqing reveals a mutual sense of cooperation in selling each other's works in their respective cities. Li advertised a collection of Liu's engraved calligraphy in *Splendid World* and sold the book from his newspaper office, whereas Liu sold Li's novels in Nanjing.[147]

Conclusion

Pursuing fun and pleasure in wordplay had deep roots in Chinese literary tradition. Literati throughout history distinguished themselves with poetry and entertained themselves through word games. Neither was the tradition of infatuation with courtesans new; it reached its most celebrated moment in late Ming Nanjing, when well-known literati and famed courtesans exchanged poetry and acted out real-life dramas about love. The late Qing culture of fun differed from this tradition, however. Whereas in the past the pursuit of fun was largely a private matter enjoyed by the privileged few, the late Qing culture of fun engaged a large literary public. Unlike in the past, when indulging in fun was considered immoral, irresponsible, and a deviation from the Way, the late Qing culture of fun lay beyond the control of the state and increasingly became legitimate in the public eye. Tabloid community members unapologetically championed the new culture of fun, breaking state taboos and values, thus making fun a form of popular resistance. The grandeur of China's *fin de siècle*, in which nothing sacred remained intact, originated precisely in the public's pursuit and legitimatization of fun; it was through this new culture of sexuality and recreation that the state first began to lose its grip on the public.

Since the beginning of the Qing, the politics of the body and of sexuality constituted an important control mechanism for the state, mainly by maintaining public morality and social order. Control of sexual behaviour played an important role in a legal code that regulated such things as chastity in widowhood, loyalty in marriage, and entertainment. In 1656, a literatus in the Jiangnan area organized a flower election and was beheaded for this by the Qing government.[148] Yet by the late Qing, the government was not even able to eradicate prostitution, especially in urban centres such as Shanghai and Beijing. Its regulations forbidding officials to visit brothels were reduced to mere jokes as some officials took prostitutes as concubines. By 1905, the Qing government even tacitly legalized prostitution by taxing prostitutes and imposing various regulations on brothels.[149]

In the wake of this growing official tolerance, the tabloid community no longer debated the legitimacy of prostitution on moral grounds alone. Writers such as Li Boyuan and Sun Yusheng openly supported prostitution on the grounds that it was vital to the city's commerce. For Li, sojourners in Shanghai – literati, merchants, artisans, and students – saw the city as a playground with brothels that also served as meeting places, banquet locations, and business offices.[150] Sun drew on historical and current evidence to argue his case. Historically, he said, prostitution in commercial centres had always helped to attract merchants. He argued that the current government, despite its policies on gambling and opium smoking, tacitly approved of prostitution because it too wanted to benefit from the resultant commercial growth. Sun further noted that his readers, learning of a rumoured plan by the British concession authority to forbid unlicensed prostitutes to enter teahouses, had threatened to boycott the area.

The culture of fun was hedonistic and, to the state, sinister. It insisted on an attitude toward life in which the pursuit of fun and pleasure was the essence, if not the ultimate purpose, of living. Yet for the Qing state and Confucian society, the purpose of life was to fulfill one's duty to the state and to the family. The idea of a pleasure-oriented existence inevitably encouraged individuals to neglect these duties. The traditional Chinese idiom *"wanwu sangzhi"* expresses the danger that self-indulgence in material things such as objects of art could lead to neglecting one's duties and purpose. More overtly threatening to the state, the attitude of play and fun evoked a passive but direct challenge to state authority. As Yeh also points out, literati had traditionally assumed an attitude of playing in order to distance themselves from the state. This age-old practice had long been a signifier of literati resistance to state power, and their late-Qing contemporaries no doubt recognized both the sign and its meanings.[151] Another Chinese idiom, *"wanshi bugong,"* captures succinctly what such an act entailed. The word "wanshi" means "to play with life," and "bugong" means "to have no respect"; joining the terms suggests that a life that accentuates playing and fun leads to disrespect for authority and established moral values.

In her study of Shanghai's theatre culture, Meng Yue provides a perfect example of how well the Chinese idiom of "wanshi bugong" describes late Qing reality. Meng observes that 1870s and 1890s Shanghai fostered an exuberant and "festive" theatrical atmosphere in which theatre managers, performers, and audiences alike engaged in "chaotic," "dangerous," and "unruly" activities that were forbidden and prosecuted elsewhere in China, due to either traditional norms or state policing.[152] As discussed above, tabloids played a key role in engaging the reading public with Shanghai's theatre performances, and many of their readers indeed indulged in theatre-going. The tabloids' celebration of the pursuit of pleasure, in this case expressed in theatre-going, no doubt threatened the establishment.

In the beginning, the tabloid papers, by focusing on matters of pleasure and fun, seemed merely to represent a community that rejected orthodox moral values and endorsed liberal attitudes toward sexuality and fun. This changed at the turn of the century when politics came to garner considerable attention in both papers and magazines. The massive tabloid literature that once exposed the quarters of courtesans and brothels now began to dwell on exposing Qing officials. This challenge to the moral ideologies of the state thus spearheaded a more serious challenge to the political legitimacy of the Qing.

2 Officialdom Unmasked

The 1911 Revolution that brought about the demise of the Qing Dynasty was neither bloodless nor peaceful.¹ The Chinese public certainly knew what was happening as the mainstream press followed events closely. People smelled the gunpowder and were well aware that the Qing Dynasty was collapsing. Yet it is also known that the 1911 Revolution produced almost no public fuss, especially in the Jiangnan region, in the sense that informed rural and urban folks apparently showed no regret for or resistance to the fall of the dynasty.² City markets functioned as usual, theatregoers attended plays, and people went about their daily routines without missing a beat. As Bao Tianxiao observed in his memoir, "from the Wuchang uprising to the abdication of the Qing, the people of Jiangnan were nonchalant, treating [these events] as no big deal, just like changing sitting positions in a mah-jong game, or going to a different restaurant, or sleeping overnight undisturbed, and getting up the next morning hearing that the dynasty had been replaced."³

This image of a calm and dismissive urban public, standing ready to accept the Qing's fall, offers an intriguing puzzle. What explains this reaction? Why did the public so easily accept the Qing's collapse? After all, the Qing Dynasty had ruled China for more than two and a half centuries.

One explanation lies in the prevalence of anti-Qing discourse in the waning years of the dynasty, a discourse that centred on bashing officialdom. This new critical rhetoric turned the political establishment into a public spectacle and helped shape a political consciousness in which the awe and authority of the Qing government evaporated. The tabloid press spearheaded this critical discourse. Li Boyuan's *Fun* initiated the trend in making officialdom a central motif in discussing China's problems, a motif that became the most critical issue in the tabloids. Li's bestselling novel *Officialdom Unmasked (Guanchang xianxingji)*, first serialized in *Splendid World* in April 1903, was the first work of its kind to expose, ridicule, and condemn the evil world of officials. Following its publication, the public was inundated with many other novels and literary works targeting officials and officialdom; more than a dozen novels appeared with the word "officialdom" in their titles.⁴

At first, in 1897, *Fun*'s condemnation of Qing officials was minimal and its complaints general. One writer used five rhymed characters to describe Qing officials' code of conduct: bribery, concealment, falsehood, evasion, and sleep. The writer explained that Qing officials advanced their careers through bribery; concealed unfavourable information from both superiors and subordinates; pretended to be virtuous and upright; evaded their obligations; and did no real work, as though they had sunk into a deep slumber at their jobs.[5] This was the extent of writers' early criticisms. The "palace coup" of 1898, however, which the mainstream newspapers highly publicized, helped arouse interest in national politics and whetted the public's appetite for knowledge of what was taking place behind the scenes of officialdom.

Sensing this change, tabloid literati began publishing more political humour and criticism. By 1899, almost every issue of *Fun* contained at least one or two items aimed at Qing officials and government policies, and its tone became increasingly acerbic. The criticisms still tended to be general, however, rarely attacking specific people. As mentioned in the Introduction, it was not until the Empress Dowager committed herself to reform in 1901 that writers became truly audacious in criticizing the Qing government and its policies. New tabloids appeared featuring serialized novels attacking officialdom, including *Official Careers Unmasked (Guantu xianxiang ji)* in *Grove of Laughter* and *National Incident of 1900 (Gengzi guobian tanci)* in *Splendid World*. Li Boyuan promptly changed his pen name from "Master of Fun" in *Fun* to "Chief of the Southern Pavilion" *(Nanting tingzhang)* in *Splendid World;* this new name hinted at his role as a dissident, similar to those literati in the South three centuries earlier who had criticized the Ming Dynasty.

Writers now began to lash out at the Qing court and its policies, and to reveal the names of targeted officials. Discussions of officialdom occupied more space than ever in the daily tabloids. Beginning in January 1902, *Allegories* had two columns: "Jokes about Officialdom" *(Guanchang xiaohua),* which mocked Qing officials, and "Satire on Current Affairs" *(Shishi fengwen),* which focused solely on political and social news. By 1903, tabloids began to branch out from the previous focus on officialdom by discussing a broad range of issues, including constitutional reform and political rights. By 1904, five of the seven columns in *Splendid World* were devoted to either political or social criticism, and even the non-political columns occasionally contained political barbs. It is safe to say that some kind of attack on officials appeared every single day in the tabloid press. The scope and depth of these criticisms increased until the end of the Qing Dynasty in 1911.

Benefiting from the more open atmosphere at the turn of the century, the tabloid magazines also assumed an unbridled critical stance from the outset.

Illustrated Fiction published a significant body of serialized fiction, tanci, drama, and ballads that portrayed the state, officials, and their representatives as the chief culprits. Each issue contained five to ten serialized stories about everything from Chinese contemporary society to recent Western political history, in forms ranging from visionary novellas to translated Western and Japanese fiction. Fiction about Chinese society mostly focused on the state and Qing officials; titles included, among many others, Li Boyuan's *A Brief History of the Enlightenment (Wenming xiaoshi)* and *Living Hell (Huodiyu)*, and Ouyang Juyuan's *Idle Talks (Fupu xiantan)*. Serialized fictional stories in *All-Story Monthly* were even broader in scope than those in *Illustrated Fiction* because they specialized in a dozen new genres.[6] Still, much of the fiction in *All-Story Monthly* followed the tradition of *Illustrated Fiction* by focusing on political and social criticism of contemporary China. Novels targeting the government and its officials included *Officialdom Unmasked – Continued (Houguanchang xianxing ji)* and *A Brief History of Chinese Evolution (Zhongguo jinhua xiaoshi)*. *All-Story Monthly* also published shorter pieces in its sections, such as *Mockery (Jitan)* and *Miscellaneous Notes (Zalu)*, that ridiculed the political establishment and lamented the sufferings of the people.

In the muddled and precarious decades of the 1890s and 1900s, targeting officialdom as the biggest obstacle to China's future, over all other domestic and foreign problems, was not as banal as one might think. In no time in Chinese history had writers dared to write about living rulers and officials in this way, much less turn them into public spectacles. It was the ingenuity of the tabloid writers that posed the moral degeneration of officialdom as the quintessential issue facing China. For them, this degeneration was more consequential to China's well-being than any of its policies. For Wu Jianren, it did not matter which political system China adhered to if politicians lacked moral integrity. If leaders were morally corrupt, Wu argued, how could they make any political system work, and how could they build a strong nation? Stressing the absence of moral leadership, the tabloid community also criticized the government's inability to lead China out of its dire domestic and international situation.

Moral Degeneration

To understand how the tabloid press attacked the morals of Qing officials, it is helpful to consider the imagery used in their stylistically vivid narratives. In fact, one can best understand the countless anecdotes, essays, tanci, ballads, dramas, short stories, and serialized novels as visual representations, as cartoon-like anecdotes, caricatures, sketches, portraits, and pictorials. In the style of "merry laughter and angry curses," writers utilized wit, slapstick humour, and biting satire to elicit readers' laughter and contempt.

Comics

The tabloid press devoted special columns to mocking the moral misconduct of Qing officials using humour and satire. *Splendid World*'s satirical columns included "Grove of Mockery" *(Fenglin)*, "Playful Talk about Current Affairs" *(Shishi xitan)*, and "Funny Spirit" *(Huajihun)*. Comical stories occasionally appeared in other columns, such as "A Glimpse of Officialdom" *(Guanchang yiban)* and "Stories of Current Affairs" *(Shishi yanshuo)*. *Grove of Laughter* featured columns such as "From *Grove of Laughter*" *(Xiaolin benzhi)*, "Official Careers Unmasked" *(Guantu xianxing ji)*, and "Funny News" *(Xiaohua xinwen)*. *Allegories* featured columns titled "Diary of Playful Talk" *(Xitan riji)* and "Jokes on Officialdom" *(Guanchang xiaohua)*. Likewise, burlesques and caricatures filled the novels serialized in *Illustrated Fiction* and *All-Story Monthly*.

All tabloid writers were skilled at making fun of officials. Wu Jianren produced a large body of humorous and sarcastic work ridiculing officials, some of which are compiled in *Complete Collected Works of Wu Jianren* under the section titles "New History of Laughter" *(Xinxiaoshi)*, "New Collection of Popular Jokes" *(Xinxiaolin guangji)*, "Sarcastic Words" *(Qiaopihua)*, and "Humorous Talk" *(Huajitan)*.[7]

Countless anecdotes portrayed officials, from ministers to magistrates, building their careers through bribery and deception and by currying favour with their superiors. These anecdotes portrayed officials using their careers as an avenue to riches and spending time in their jobs doing nothing but plundering the people. Wu Jianren asserted that "local officials who extort people are just like robbers."[8] Two such anecdotes follow, one from *Fun* and the other from *Splendid World*:

> Prefect Wen of Henan was summoned to present himself to the Empress Dowager and the Emperor while the imperial rulers were returning to the capital after the Boxer Uprising. Before the interview, to ensure he would not run into trouble, Wen delivered some white gold to the head eunuch, Li Lianying. When Wen came out of the interview, he went to visit Li, and Li's Pekingese dog barked at him. Li bent slightly forward toward the dog and the dog jumped right into his arms, wagging its tail. Wen, bowing to the dog, said, "Brother Dog, I am now a member of your family. Uncle Li took care of both of us, so the next time you see me don't bark at me again."[9]

A regimental commander ordered a battalion officer to search for bandits in the countryside. When the officer returned empty-handed, having captured no one, the commander was angry and dismissed him from his position. The commander then assigned the battalion officer's lieutenant to report on the campaign. The lieutenant reported imprudently, "Our troops captured nothing, but actually we did capture a few pigs and sheep, several chickens and ducks. All of them are now in confinement at the camp. Let me, your subordinate, bring them to you, my superior, so you can judge and punish them as you wish."[10]

With vivid brushstrokes, the writers portrayed officials as arrogant, pathetic, lustful, despicable, and clownlike. In one account, a member of the Grand Secretary was obsessed with his résumé. Every time he met a new visitor, he would immediately recite his résumé and then gesture to end the meeting.[11] Another man from Suzhou with the surname Han bought an "alternate" official position in Zhejiang. After waiting more than twenty years to obtain the position and earning no income in the meantime, Han used up his family wealth and resorted to digging up the garden of his ancestral home in Suzhou, in search of hidden treasure.[12] Still another story mocked a county magistrate who took advantage of government sales of official titles:

He has three sons ... He buys for his eldest son an official post as a county magistrate, and, to make sure that the son knows well his work once he has the job, the magistrate takes the son with him whenever he conducts his official business, and provides his son with detailed guidance in dealing with daily routines and with court cases. As for his second son, he orders him to learn financial management from those financial consultants and assistants in the county government. However, for his third son, he does not buy an official post for him, nor does he ask him to learn a particular profession; instead, he allows him to hang around with the gatekeepers of the county government to learn their common manners. What kind of future will he have? Friends and relatives are all puzzled with this arrangement, and occasionally someone asks the magistrate about it. The magistrate sighs, "In the future, when the eldest son takes the job of a magistrate, the second son gets to manage the finances for the county government, and the youngest becomes a guard at the gate. Since there will be one common ambition from the top to the bottom and since there will be one union of the brotherhood, there is no way that the family's fortune will leak out."[13]

According to another satire, purchasing official titles became such a well-organized enterprise that it was run like a business. If a magistrate's title sold for ten thousand *liang* of silver, the aspiring magistrate would put up four thousand liang and his prospective subordinates, such as legal assistants and accountants, would make up the rest collectively.[14] Once the titled magistrate got the job, he would divide his future "profits" with his staff in proportion to their contributions, or investments. If for some reason he lost his job, the whole group would chip in to get his job back.[15] In another satirical piece, a petitioner suggested that the government establish a company to sell official posts, as this would make the operation more efficient.[16]

One news item in *Splendid World* told of a provincial judge from Guangdong who claimed to be moral and upright, even refusing to have a concubine. Yet he impregnated a married woman whom the judge's family had hired to comb the hair of its female members every day. As the woman approached labour, the judge offered her husband three thousand *yuan* to find a new wife. The husband demanded twenty thousand liang of silver, however, and threatened to sue the judge if he received anything less.[17]

In their typically imaginative way, the writers also likened officials to animals, and officialdom to the animal kingdom. One piece told the story of a snake wanting to become an official. The snake was confident about climbing to a high position because, like real officials, it had a sharp and narrow head and a slippery body, well suited for poking around in the world of officials.[18] Another piece ridiculed bookworms, who, like officials, read many books but knew nothing about protecting the kingdom. Another compared officials in the capital to starving cats that moved to Beijing to earn a living. The cats defended their move by reasoning, "We heard that the capital is the ultimate place for one to get what one wants by using one's power. Thus we thought that there must be a lot of mice there." The story's association of officials with mice was intentional, since for many Chinese mice represent wickedness.

When writers were unable to find cases of outright wickedness, they captured instead officials' humorous and embarrassing moments:

Yesterday afternoon, Li Lianying wanted to drink soda water from Holland to quench his thirst and to calm his nerves. Not knowing the trick of opening the bottle, the popping cork hit him right in his eye. Feeling excruciating pain, he threw the bottle to the ground, and the noise of the shattering glass could be heard from far away.[19]

Of all the strategies tabloid writers used to mock Qing officials, none was more hilarious and trenchant than the link they created between the corruption of officials and the vice of prostitutes. In fact, prostitutes and officials were the two most exploited social groups in the tabloids. Countless humorous stories demonstrated that both groups were morally corrupt, despite differing from each other in every other respect. When seeking promotion, officials would ingratiate themselves with their superiors using the same disgraceful trickery that prostitutes used to charm their customers.[20] Wu Jianren likened district and county officials' reactions to bribes from local gentry to prostitutes' responses to gratuities from patrons. Both groups displayed pleasure or displeasure based on how much money they received.[21] Officials were portrayed as even more depraved. In some stories, officials resorted to befriending courtesans of higher-ranked officials, begging the women to speak on their behalf for a job or promotion.[22] In one allegorical novel, a character said bluntly, "Officials would not be officials if they had not associated with prostitutes."[23] Officials were not even as fortunate as prostitutes – prostitutes could at least choose or reject their patrons, but officials had no such liberty. Moreover, officials had to pay frequent bribes to earn promotions, while prostitutes needed to pay only a one-time fee to settle into a brothel.[24] Likewise, Li Boyuan found it ironic and amusing that officials viewed themselves as morally pure *(qingguan)* in the same way that courtesans viewed themselves as virgins and "sing-song" girls *(qingguan)*.[25]

One story in *Fun* featured a man who came to Shanghai for the first time. Standing on Fourth Street, he sees courtesans constantly riding around in carriages, their drivers acting like officials' drivers, with the words "Official Business" written on lanterns on the front of the carriages. The man asks someone to explain what kind of official business the courtesans are involved in. A bystander replies, "The general who is responsible for collecting taxes from brothels has an army of courtesans. He brings them to inspect various brothels, restaurants, and to manage other affairs." The man has a sudden revelation: "Any woman who wants to become an official should come to Shanghai."[26]

Although most of these sarcastic anecdotes withheld the names of the officials involved, readers could still recognize individuals through other information that the stories did provide, such as the officials' titles, locations, and associates. *Splendid World* contained a news story about a certain unnamed ministry official who arrived in Shanghai to bring a courtesan named Chen back to Beijing as his concubine. The story suggested sarcastically that no one wanting to get involved in railway or mining ventures should miss the chance to visit this official.[27] This seemingly innocent notice made obvious the ministry official's identity, and mocked both him and anyone wanting to meet him.

Officials were active patrons of prostitutes. One anecdote depicted a commotion at a brothel in Suzhou, which attracted over a hundred spectators. An official from Zhejiang along with his team of men had forced a courtesan to kneel before him. While the official banged on a table and cursed angrily, the courtesan and the madam of the brothel knelt and begged for forgiveness. Apparently, the courtesan had not answered the official's call the previous night.[28] An even more farcical story featured a provincial commander in Nanjing who often drank with courtesans. One day, a team of thirty or forty armed men broke into the brothel. Assuming that they were bandits, the commander quickly hid under a bed. As he was dragged out from under the bed, he kowtowed repeatedly, begging for his life. Suddenly one man from the team, a soldier in the commander's own troop, recognized his leader and immediately knelt before him, pleading for his life.[29]

The tabloids could even drag the Emperor playfully into dealings with prostitutes. In one column, the Emperor issued an edict to announce the winners of a flower election that ranked prostitutes based on patrons' votes. The edict praised the winning prostitutes as learned and talented people, invaluable to the government. The Emperor bestowed special titles and favours on the top prostitutes in the list of winners. While the edict was obviously fictitious, the winners were actual Shanghai prostitutes, some of them well-known courtesans.[30]

Just as flowers and bird painting had once been a distinctive genre of traditional Chinese art, satire involving sex and politics now became a distinctive genre of sarcasm that targeted officials. The link between sex and politics, between the female body of prostitutes and the political body of Qing officials, created a heightened sense of moral chaos: prostitutes represented disorder in society and officials represented disorder in the state. The humorous and sarcastic textual renditions of Qing officialdom were so powerful that the literary devices gave the texts the visual qualities of comic strips and cartoons. Like cartoons, which employ stereotype, exaggeration, and symbolism in the service of both comedy and contempt, tabloid texts depicted officials as moral villains of almost limitless depravity. While political cartoonists use symbols as visual shorthand to convey meanings beyond the images themselves, tabloid writers too left a ruminative afterthought among readers that went well beyond the anecdotes about the absurdities of officialdom. The tabloid press excelled at imparting a visual quality to its written texts, thus enhancing its representational and interpretive power in the minds of its readers.

Sketches, Portraits, and Pictorial Stories

Just as artists draw quick sketches, detailed portraits, and illustrations for stories, tabloid writers depicted, in brief as well as elaborate narratives, the activities of the Empress Dowager, the Emperor, officials, and the Qing government. In every issue, news about the rulers and officials appeared side by side with columns about the daily activities of courtesans and prostitutes.[31] Just as they wrote countless biographies of courtesans and stories about scandals in Shanghai brothels, tabloid literati reported on the Empress Dowager's delights and dislikes, and on quarrels at her court. They wrote brief biographies of grand officials that described eccentric habits and career paths as well as corrupt behaviours. The tabloid press made rulers and officials into celebrities, just as they made courtesans into stars. *Splendid World* had one column – "China in Dreams" *(Menghualu)* – that focused on rulers and the inner court. Other columns about officialdom included "Collected Talks" *(Tancong)* and "Occasional Talks on Current Affairs" *(Shishi outan)*. Reports in those columns were supposed to be informative and factual, not necessarily funny.

The Empress Dowager Cixi's activities often included receiving gifts and bestowing favours. One news item in *Splendid World* reported that Cen Chunxuan presented her with a basket of mountain peaches; she in turn rewarded him with ten *jin* of dates from Shandong.[32] During celebrations, officials and members of the imperial family would rack their brains trying to think of gifts to please Cixi. Countless reports listed who contributed what to whom, and who was awarded what from Cixi. Examples from just one issue include: (1) A provincial governor sent his staff to Beijing to present Cixi with forty pots of plum blossoms, and the delighted Empress Dowager ordered that the pots be placed around her quarters in the Summer Palace; (2) Ma Yukun was awarded a belt with an imperial jade seal, a four-character calligraphy brushed by an imperial ruler, a jade scepter *(ruyi)*, and eight pieces of silver bullion; and (3) Prince Qing contributed to Cixi's coffer over 100,000 jin cash, while Prince Zhen doubled this amount. A longer news item revealed the significance of these gifts, recounting how a prince had sent Cixi presents for her Longevity Day *(Wanshoujie)*. The eunuch in charge asked too much money for the favour of presenting the gifts to Cixi on the prince's behalf. Angered, the prince yelled: "Even though you do not bring them inside, the inside still can't take away my title as a prince."[33]

Everyone feared the Empress Dowager Cixi. Tabloid writers reported that she removed Minister Wang from his position on the Grand Council because he offended her by using the wrong words in a memorial.[34] Another account detailed how Li Lianying, the Empress's trusted eunuch, lost his position. As the story goes, someone discovered explosive powder in the imperial palace.

Furious, the Empress Dowager shouted at Li Lianying, "What do you think you are doing? How could you have had no idea about this?" and demanded that he investigate the incident right away. Li arrested four suspicious eunuchs in the inner court and had them beaten to death for the crime. When Li reported his success to Cixi, she retorted, "This time it is you with whom I am angry. If it had been someone else, he would have had to ask himself how many heads he has on his shoulder" (implying that she would have beheaded anyone else). Li Lianying kowtowed repeatedly and pleaded with the Empress, "I have served you, my ultimate ancestor, for several decades, and I cannot even begin, in a short time, to recount the kindnesses you have shown me. But now your humbled lackey indeed has too great a load on his shoulders; in addition, I am getting old, and have a failing leg. I just beg my ultimate ancestor again to bestow your benevolence upon me." Cixi replied, "You are just making this up as an excuse for yourself." Li Lianying could not utter a word in reply. Cixi decided, "All right, I will take away some responsibilities from you." Li's position as general head of the inner court ended the following day, yet he continued to receive annually ten thousand liang of silver from the Empress.[35]

Tabloid writers missed no chance to stress Cixi's femininity and vulnerability. In one account, Cixi was seen on her Longevity Day wearing shoes with soles more than five inches high, adorned with two pearls as big as dragon eyes and brightly coloured jewels and tassels.[36] Another related how Cixi caught a cold after viewing embroidered silk screens in the rear hall of the Cining Palace. A story about Cixi's escape from foreign troops that had entered the capital to suppress the Boxers described her as appearing pathetic and pitiful. In this story, when Cixi's entourage approached one locale, the county magistrate thought it was a trick and closed the town gate, preventing their entrance. They proceeded to another county. The weather was cold and Cixi did not have enough clothing to stay warm. This county magistrate, kneeling before the Empress, asked whether Han-style clothing was adequate; Cixi, with tears in her eyes, replied, "It has come to such a mess today, how could anyone even care if it is Han or Manchu style?"[37]

Another story exposed the Empress Dowager's extravagance. It detailed the luxuries of a newly constructed building, *Fozhaolou* (Under the radiance of Buddha), in the imperial residence. In the hall of this building, the walls and ceiling around the imperial canopy were decorated with images of peaches, and images of birds were carved into the canopy columns. These decorations alone reportedly cost about 150,000 jin cash. The report concluded sarcastically, "There are seven grand engineering achievements on earth. After this building, the number has increased to eight."[38]

Each of these individual anecdotes offers a snapshot of the inner court and officials. Together, the picturesque sketches and stories paint an elaborate portrait of the Empress Dowager as a ruler who cared more about her own material comfort than anything else. While writers put her in the spotlight, revealing intimate and often humiliating details of her character and life, they were even bolder in exposing Qing officialdom. Rarely did they say anything favourable about officials, and *never* anything positive about officialdom.

Gossip about officials was so detailed and expressive as to approach the effect of a graphic representation. *Illustrated Fiction* actually did illustrate some embarrassing episodes involving officials, interchanging textual and visual images to aid readers' comprehension and amusement. The four images shown in Figures 7 to 10 illustrate exactly their textual stories.

At work, officials apparently did nothing but drink, smoke, play, and scheme to make financial profit. One writer reported that when Wenti worked in the prefecture of Kaifeng, in Henan Province, he would lie in bed the entire day, smoking opium and allowing no visitors. At the time of the Boxers, when the Empress Dowager's entourage arrived in Wenti's area, things suddenly got very busy. To avoid disturbance, he locked the gate to his residence and put up a sign saying, "Morgue, do not enter."[39] Another writer named a four-circuit official in Nanjing who loved to gamble and who would bet over one thousand jin cash in a single round of mahjong.[40] Yet another revealed how officials fought over the distribution of money using verbal abuse and physical violence. Officials at both capital and provincial levels shared the profits accruing from document fees collected when the government sold officials' titles. In 1902, however, the government stopped selling the titles and profits dwindled. Officials in Anhui Province quarrelled over a share of the diminished profits and resorted to violence during a meeting; a group of over twenty officials beat the opposing officials. The conflict had a precedent, as thirty-seven officials in Zhejiang were already involved in lawsuits over profits.[41]

Cases involving officials who demanded gifts and bribes from subordinates appeared regularly in the tabloids. One anecdote recounted the greed of a provincial Henan official without revealing his name. This official travelled to a county in the province, and the magistrate presented him with a cash gift. The provincial official rejected the gift outright, seemingly in the name of moral respectability. In fact, however, he considered the amount of cash inadequate. The county magistrate tried a second time to offer a cash gift, doubling the amount presented. It was not until the third offer that the provincial official accepted the gift, after overhearing the magistrate angrily saying to a guard that this would be his last attempt. The official later boasted of his

Figure 7 Bribing an official with his accountant in the doorway.
Source: *Illustrated Fiction* [*Xiuxiang xiaoshuo*], vol. 35 (Shanghai: Shanghai Commercial Press, 1904).

Figure 8 Frightened official meets with Westerner.
Source: *Illustrated Fiction* [*Xiuxiang xiaoshuo*], vol. 71 (Shanghai: Shanghai Commercial Press, 1906).

Figure 9 Officials smoking opium in Nanjing.
Source: Illustrated Fiction [*Xiuxiang xiaoshuo*], 71 (Shanghai: Shanghai Commercial Press, 1906).

68 Merry Laughter and Angry Curses

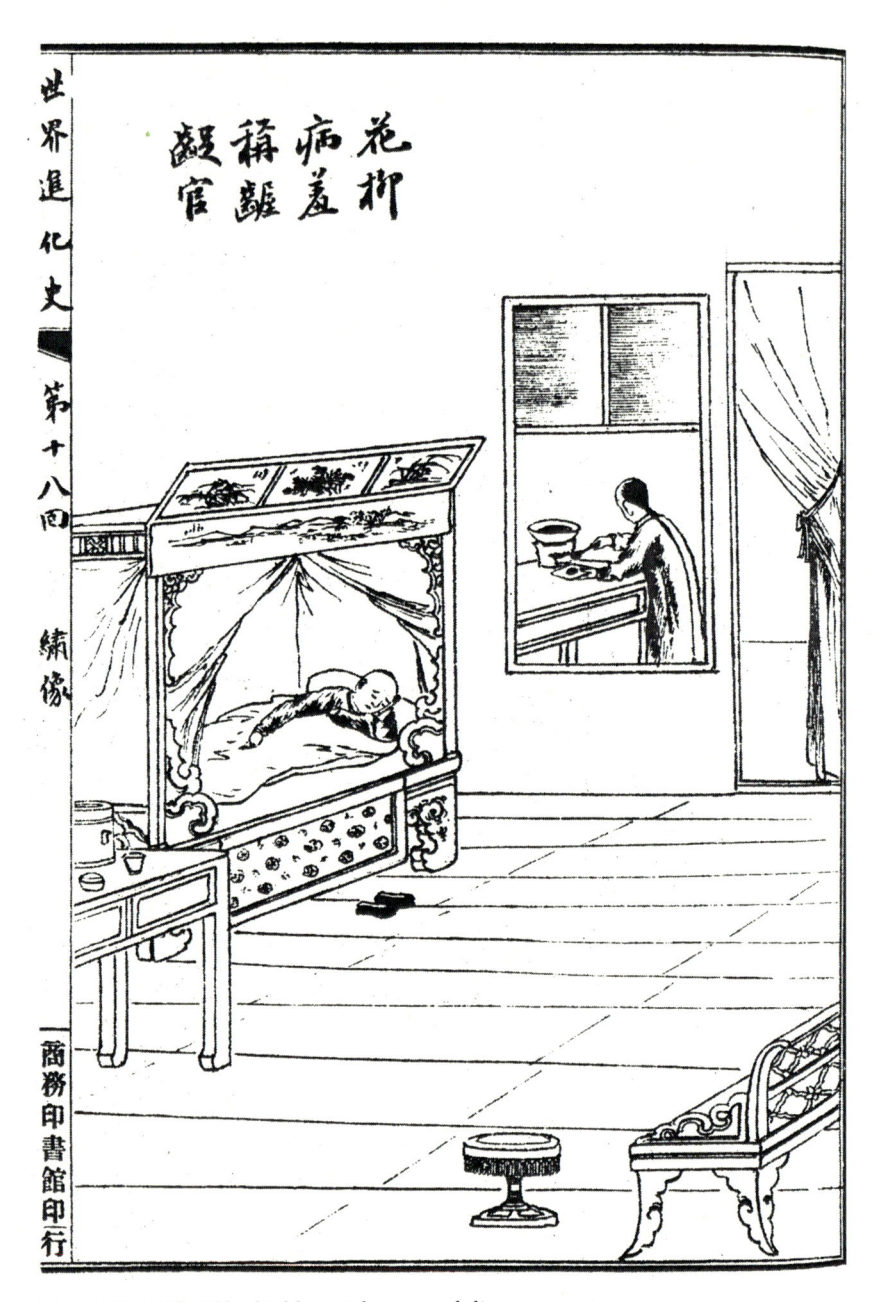

Figure 10 Official bedridden with venereal disease.
Source: Illustrated Fiction [*Xiuxiang xiaoshuo*], 70 (Shanghai: Shanghai Commercial Press, 1906).

acumen in accepting the cash at just the right time. In later reports, writers revealed the names of officials involved in nefarious activities, including the superintendent of the Tianjin Circuit[42] and the military governors of Fujian and Zhejiang.[43]

At times, writers went beyond sharing anecdotes by providing analyses of the corruption. One writer stated bluntly that among all careers, that of an official was the most heinous and disgusting, for officials made money through cheating instead of honest work. The writer went on to analyze how officials in the capital and those in the provinces differed in their corrupt strategies. In the capital, ministers, princes, and grand literati relied on their own prestige and power to attract talented people, who then had to provide bribes for their patronage. In the provinces, officials extorted money by controlling local politics, influencing the legal system, and meddling with educational reforms and new industrial and commercial ventures. The same writer noted that many provincial power brokers were actually members of the Imperial Academy; unable to succeed in the capital, they took to the provinces in search of better money-making opportunities. Some of those grand literati used their prestige and connections to raise funds for new commercial and industrial ventures. Once they got these funds, and knowing nothing about business, the writer observed, they simply squandered the funds for personal pleasure, performing no real work.[44]

One story related a conversation between a guest and a member of the Hanlin Academy. The latter was overjoyed on hearing that the government had decided to provide subsidies to officials at his level. The guest then asked him, "Money or wife, which is more important?" The academician replied that money was of course more important, reasoning that "without money, how can one support a wife?" The guest then asked him to compare money and achievements; the academician again chose money, explaining: "As the popular saying goes, 'It is all for money that one travels thousands of *li* to take an official post.' What is the purpose of getting a promotion, if it is not for money?" The guest pushed further, asking him to choose between money and parents. At this point, the academician said to himself, "The Emperor rules the country through filial piety. But for us this piety is for lip service only. Money, of course, is more important than parents, but I cannot admit this openly." So the academician replied that the two were equally important. Just then someone arrived to inform the Hanlin academician that the government had cancelled the subsidies. Seeing the academician's joy suddenly change to fear and dread, the guest understood the priority he gave to money over parents.[45]

Tabloid writers had no reservations about attacking officials. Ouyang Juyuan put it bluntly in his preface to Li Boyuan's *Officialdom Unmasked:*

Nobody under heaven is more despicable than a thief, but a thief robs you once and officials steal all the time. Nobody under heaven is more hateful than a foe, but you know what the foe has done to you and you don't know what the officials have done to you. I wonder if these were ever of concern when the bureaucratic system was initially set up. Is it possible that officials do not have human properties, so that they can behave like this? The state is weak, but the officials are powerful; the country is poor, but the officials are rich. Officials shattered all pieties and officials ruined all virtues.[46]

One essay echoed this sentiment regarding officials' immorality, observing that they lack even a sense of shame. Those administrators who had lost their jobs because of corruption still regarded themselves as worthy. When they returned to their homes, local administrators and literati still treated them respectfully. Lamented the writer, "The officials are all shamelessly connected to each other."[47]

Tabloid writers paid particular attention to officials at the provincial level and above, frequently featuring biographical sketches and spotlighting moments of frailty and weakness, idiosyncrasies, and character flaws such as arrogance and cruelty toward subordinates. Officials such as Yuan Shikai, Zhang Zhidong, and Li Hongzhang did not escape the writers' critical attention.[48] One article compared a provincial governor to Li Hongzhang, pointing out a shared habit of swearing at their subordinates.[49] Another piece reported that Zhang Zhidong began to have problems with his legs before the infections in his mouth healed. Zhang had to be helped when walking out to meet guests, which exempted him from the ritual of kowtowing.[50] An article by a reader criticized the general of the Beiyang army for using his forty-ninth birthday as an excuse to accept "donations." Officials from the Bureau of Commerce donated various gifts, including a jade scepter that was worth five hundred jin. The author complained of officials' extravagance at a time when countless people from various provinces were suffering from natural disasters and hunger. The author did not name the general, but it was obviously Yuan Shikai.[51] Another writer published short sketches of six top officials in Jiangxi Province, each of whom had a peculiar specialty. Among them were Jiang, who was skilled at fawning over his superiors; Fu, who was fond of eight-legged essays; Wu, who was chummy with his carriage-driver; and Gu, who indulged his concubines.[52]

Tabloid literati carefully observed personnel changes that took place in the top ranks. They traced officials' career moves, their promotions and demotions; followed closely those on the fast track; and observed who recommended whom and for what position. In order to detect the way the political winds were blowing, the literati particularly followed the rise and fall of officials known for their attitudes toward reforms. When Liang Dingfen, a supporter of reform, became prefect of Hubei, tabloid writers repeatedly reported his activities in this new job.[53] Rumours later surfaced that he was being considered for promotion and that Zhang Zhidong would someday employ him.[54]

What interested writers most, however, were the dirty secrets and the nepotism that lay behind personnel changes. Their articles painted colourful pictures of networks of officials involved in bribery, and of family alliances and other personal relationships. One report explained how Cixi promoted an official named Chen to the position of general commissioner of grain transportation. To get this job, Chen paid tens of thousands jin cash to a certain eunuch to speak to the Empress on his behalf. Having received so much money from Chen, the eunuch tried hard to secure him this job; in fact, this was the third position he found for Chen, who deemed the first two to be unsatisfactory.[55] In another story, a prefect ingratiated himself with an opera actor who was a favourite of a member of the Grand Secretariat; he got a promotion through the actor's intervention.[56] One writer revealed how Xia, the governor of Shaanxi, arranged jobs for his relatives; the writer provided the names of these relatives and their positions.[57] A similar report recounted how an official in Baling county, Hunan, got his job through his relationship by marriage to another official. As in the other cases, the report omitted the official's name, but the person's identity was clear since he was in charge of county police and militia forces.[58] More intriguing was a report showing how one governor, who had complete control of all officials in the Beiyang military establishment, tried to extend his powers in the South by placing his men in various important posts there. Although unnamed in the report, the official was clearly Yuan Shikai.[59]

Writers spared no ink in revealing the infighting at court and among top-ranked officials, all struggling for power and influence. Many anecdotes revealed the tense relationship between the Empress Dowager and the Emperor; one read: "At meals, the Emperor serves the Empress Dowager 'mountain game and sea delicacies' *(shanzhen haiwei);* only after the Empress gives the Emperor something with her chopsticks can he eat."[60] Another related how Cixi had the heir apparent's teacher beat him with a stick forty times for failing to listen.[61] Dramatic plays depicted the heir apparent whining pathetically to his trusted assistant about the impending loss of his title due to Prince Qing's opposition.[62] Two pieces in the same issue of *Splendid World* revealed the political strife at court.[63] The first was in Suzhou dialect:

> Little prince, someone has said that you have already arrived in Ningxia, others said that you still remain with the Empress Dowager and the Emperor, and that the three of you have talked about sharing power. Alas, nobody knows what really has happened. I heard from a friend who came here from Henan that you are now in the same boat as Li Lianying, and that you two are sitting on the same hot rocks.

The second piece was in Beijing dialect:

> As of today, nobody cares to mention Lu Chuanlin anymore. It has been heard that he currently does not relate well with the Empress Dowager or with the Emperor who take only 30 or 40 percent of whatever he says seriously. Whenever important issues arise, the grand secretary Rong acts quickly to press him and to warn him with such words as, "Hey, old codger, do not mess up our business! If you ever make trouble for us in front of the Empress Dowager and the Emperor, you must not want to live long." On hearing these words, Lu did not dare to utter a word, and he resorted to letting others take control. All of you, think about it. Isn't he pathetic and pitiable?

One story described how Zhang Zhidong, a top Qing statesman, skillfully and deviously crushed his enemy as if he had, to use the Chinese idiom, "borrowed someone else's knife to kill one's enemy" *(jiedao sharen)*.[64] Another told of Jiang Fengqing, the alternate superintendent of the Jiangxi Circuit, who initiated impeachment proceedings against Zhou Hao. When the superintendent, Fu Chunyi, got wind of this, he relayed the news to Zhou, whose protector, Hu Fu, vowed to prosecute everyone who went along with the impeachment plan.[65]

The foregoing is just a small sample of the moral and ethical criticisms that the tabloids levied against officials. Such criticisms revealed to readers that the political establishment was far less moral than it professed to be. They successfully cultivated a perception and understanding of contemporary politics that saw moral decay as the central problem of Qing officialdom, thus striking a blow at the Qing's legitimacy to govern. In Chinese political culture, a regime's mandate to rule relies on its moral authority, and officials are often more important than political institutions.[66] Public perception of the moral degradation and malfeasance of Qing officials, fostered by the tabloid press, no doubt eroded the regime's power.

Inability to Govern

Tabloid literati repeatedly warned that the key problem was not a lack of solutions to China's crises; rather, it was the absence of anyone in a position of power who could lead China out of the chaos. Immediately after the abrupt end to the Hundred Days' Reform, Li Boyuan complained that no one in China understood Western knowledge well enough to carry out reforms.[67] One writer mapped out the political forces at the top. He explained that the term "reformers" *(weixindang)* had become widely known to the public after the 1898 reform movement; all who disagreed with the reformers were lumped together as conservatives *(shoujiudang)*. According to this writer, this terminology did injustice to those so-called conservatives, because none of them truly followed and upheld traditional values and ethics. Instead, the writer identified four political groups in China: evildoers, who deceived the ruler and oppressed the people; ignoramuses, who regarded themselves as learned and virtuous but knew nothing about solving China's problems, and even when under fire from Western cannons could not tell whether the attack would cause a mere itch or severe pain; persons without a nation, who cared only for their families' fame and fortune, forgetting the nation entirely; and persons without opinions, who had no advice to give the ruler and were capable only of blindly following others.[68]

Officials were either unwilling or unable to carry out reforms. One anecdote, written in Beijing dialect, described four officials who opposed the government's decision to abolish the use of eight-legged essays in examinations:

> Yesterday, I overheard four officials in the capital talking among themselves, saying that they wanted to bring back the "eight-legged" essays. The four sent a formal petition to Wang Wenshao.[69] They wanted him to represent them, to tell the emperor that the "eight-legged" way is important for the great Qing dynasty. They reasoned: after all, didn't all of the virtuous ministers and good officials in the past and today get where they are via the "eight-legged" way? If now you want to throw it away, wouldn't you become a person who eats tangerines, but who forgets the Dongting Lake?[70] We plead with you, Grand Secretariat, to bring it back. So all literati under heaven can be relieved and elated, and reformers will shut up.[71]

In a similar mocking tone, another anecdote told of Gang Ziliang, a grand secretary in the Grand Secretariat. During a trip to Nanjing, Gang had "big talks" with officials in charge of various divisions of the Jiangsu provincial government. Gang reportedly told the military official, "Of what use is the manufacture of guns and cannons? It is enough to use bows, arrows, swords, and spears to fight the foreigners." To a superintendent of a new-style school, the grand secretary said, "New-style schools merely train traitors to China."[72]

As late as 1907, tabloid writers continued to believe that readers would find humour in officials' stubborn refusal to think critically about Chinese Learning. One anecdote told of a Qing minister who incessantly read books of Chinese Learning, even during meals. He exhorted his subordinates to study these books: "The teachings of the sages are as immutable and timeless as the rivers on the earth and the sun and moon in the sky." Even if they mastered only a small part of the sages' words, he insisted, they would become better officials. While the subordinates all submitted to the minister's will, in private they laughed at his pedantry. Once, a subordinate preparing to take a long trip visited the minister to say good-by. The minister, offended by what he thought was the subordinate's flippant and undignified manner, asked whether he had been studying hard at home. The subordinate, half rising from his seat and lowering his head, said, "I don't deserve to be regarded as a diligent student since your humble subordinate has only read the Three-Character Text *(Sanzijing)*."[73] As the Three-Character Text was a basic text for young children, the subordinate's response showed complete disrespect for the minister, and his body language made his sarcasm even more pointed.

Officials resisted reform for various reasons. One article summarized the shady paths that officials followed in climbing to the upper ranks, and argued that by the time they attained positions of power, these officials had already become corrupt, arrogant, and inflexible in their thinking. How could anyone expect such people to carry out reform, the author asked, especially if they consider Western learning a heresy?[74]

Another story vividly portrayed the prime minister as just this type of official: arrogant, deceitful, and unwilling to accept the New Learning *(xinxue)*. In this piece, a literatus from the Jiangnan area, well known for his literary achievements, went to the capital to become a tutor to the prime minister's grandsons. During their first meeting, the prime minister disrespectfully asked the literatus why he had not heard of him before, since the latter was supposedly well known in Jiangnan. Moreover, said the prime minister, all famous literati in the country are under my patronage and regard me as their boss. Wanting this job, the literatus suppressed his anger. Telling the literatus how to teach, the prime minister continued, "Nowadays, Western Learning *(xixue)* is especially meaningless and useless. I always hate to even hear about it, and

I will not let my sons and grandsons have this kind of learning." The literatus acquiesced, realizing that the prime minister was too deeply rooted in the Old Learning *(jiuxue)* to change his mind. The literatus was a promoter of the new Western Learning, and his pride was hurt. He became dissatisfied with the meals he was given and wanted to quit after only six months of teaching. Then the literatus heard that the government planned to send some officials abroad on a mission. He immediately asked the prime minister to help arrange for him to accompany the officials. Although the prime minister promised to help, he did nothing at all and the deadline passed. The literatus decided to quit his job. On hearing this, the prime minister remained silent for a long time and then said calmly to the literatus, "Being arrogant is the problem that all young scholars have. How can one be impatient in matters of life's opportunities and experiences?" Raising his voice, the literatus answered, "Teacher, although you are muddleheaded all the time, you are still able to get talented people to serve at your side. But if I stay here for another half year, I will be no longer alive." The prime minister laughed grimly but showed no sign of anger, saying only, "Such words, such words." The writer concluded: "Prominent court officials all have cultivated an etiquette of tolerance, and they will show no sign of anger even if others snap and spit at their faces. Like the immutable Tai Mountain, they are unable to even slightly change their guarded appearances and baneful practices."[75] Without saying so explicitly, the writer revealed how the cool composure of the prime minister betrayed his sense of self-righteousness, and how threatening this sense could be.

Officials at various levels worried about their job security. One story told of some county law clerks who, on hearing that the government was recruiting people with knowledge of foreign laws, began to worry that they would lose their jobs. Reading about the Emperor's edict promoting legal reforms, they complained that the government would eliminate their positions.[76] Reports showed that alternate officials waiting for jobs were especially anxious. One such official confessed: "It's not that I do not know that the New Policy and reform are good, but if the reform is carried out there will be no more jobs for me to have. So, I do not want to hear anything about it."[77] Descriptions of the anxieties of top officials caught up in these changes included even Minister Zhao.[78] Rumours spread of personnel reduction policies,[79] the abolition of the examination system,[80] and the future of the Hanlin Academy[81] well before any real changes took place.

In many ways, writers suggested that officials cared mostly about themselves rather than about China's future. Wu Jianren argued that whenever district- and county-level officials met, all they discussed was the profitability of various "unfilled" posts; they never discussed local politics or the lives of local people.[82]

One essay in *Grove of Laughter* observed that opposition to bureaucratic reform was stronger than support. The writer criticized opponents as conservatives who cared only for their own interests. He pointed out that the nation's power was concentrated in the hands of four or five lineage-related ministers *(zongchen)* who treated the nation's fate as their private toy.[83]

According to the tabloids, not only did officials oppose reform but they were also incapable of carrying out reform even if they wanted to. One character in Wu Jianren's novel, *Strange Events Eyewitnessed,* asked, "Officials themselves were opium addicts, so how could they carry out a policy forbidding opium smoking?"[84] Other articles complained that officials were unqualified for their posts. One noted that those provincial officials who had bought their posts varied so greatly in their level of literacy that the least literate among them had to ask others to write their official documents. Some even used the wrong characters, becoming confused by characters that sounded or looked similar.[85]

While some officials could not even master Chinese learning, others were either ignorant of or misunderstood Western Learning. One member of the Hanlin Academy told his friend one day, "The shape of the earth is round, this I already believe. But I wonder if the two lines – latitude and longitude – are hanging up in the sky or wound around the earth."[86] In the following story, another academy member, regarding himself as well schooled in Western Learning, demonstrated his "knowledge":

> In 1898 ... on a hot summer day, a certain academician in the Imperial Academy went to his friend's house to have a chat. Since he was quite fat, the minute he sat down he was already sweating as though he had been soaked in the rain. So, he took a book from his friend's desk and used it to wipe the sweat from his face. The friend stopped him and said, "This is a book." The academician glowered, replying, "When Westerners go to restrooms, they always bring newspapers with them to read there. After they finish, they use the newspapers to clean themselves up. You are really a headstrong conservative, and you don't even know it!"[87]

Another article asked how Cen Chunxuan, governor-general of two provinces, could be respected by the people, given his method for halting continuous drought. Cen's idea of firing cannons into the sky came from the West, where some believed that rain could be induced by exploding gunpowder.[88]

Many tabloid discussions complained of problems in newly established new-style schools. One essay written in 1899 criticized officials who proposed closing such schools, but also blamed those officials who wanted to keep the schools open despite their failure to find qualified teachers.[89] Another article pointed out that officials operating the new-style schools often knew little about Western Learning, having secured jobs merely through their connections. The article proposed that the government find ways to guarantee the recruitment of competent officials for these schools.[90]

Tabloids portrayed Qing officials as useless, especially when it came to dealing with foreign powers. In his *A Brief History of Enlightenment (Wenming xiaoshi)*, Li Boyuan told many stories of local officials who were submissive to foreigners. These officials feared offending foreigners living in their own counties, since any conflict would result in reprimands from their superiors and even dismissal. Local officials thus strove to please foreigners, even if it meant going against the wishes of locals who protested foreigners' infringement on their interests. At the time of the Boxer Uprising, an article reported a meeting of a grand secretary and several ministers at which none of those present had any idea what to do about the crisis.[91] Even the Empress Dowager was supposedly afraid of foreigners at this time.[92]

Many articles reprimanded the failure of imprudent, greedy, and reckless Qing officials to protect Chinese economic interests from foreigners. One article quipped that inept Qing officials worked to annihilate the nation by giving away many prime Chinese mines to foreign companies in exchange for nothing.[93] Another told the story of a foreign company that relentlessly explored mines in Hunan and attempted to bribe Beijing officials for mining rights to all of Guizhou Province. The writer worried that the company would get the deal since Beijing officials were greedy and corrupt.[94] Yet another report showed one Qing official's lack of concern over China's enormous foreign debt stemming from war indemnities. Going against the traditional moral aversion to debt, the official reasoned that it was better for China to owe money to other countries than vice versa. After all, why should China not use the resources of other countries?[95]

Li Boyuan described the government's call to establish a constitutional polity as a joke. Writing in 1906, he explained that even ten years earlier, the concept of a constitutional polity was unheard of in China. To work on reform, ignorant top officials had to rely on those who had studied abroad and acquired a *jinshi* degree after returning. These returnees, using new terms such as "policies" *(fangzhen)* and "purposes" *(mudi)*, suggested that a constitutional polity was good. While those inside and outside the court, from grand council members to scholars of current affairs, all agreed on the desirability of establishing a constitutional polity, nothing actually happened. Only after a year had passed and many members of the grand councils had retired or been replaced did the government begin sending people abroad to investigate constitutional polities.[96]

Community Consciousness

As we saw in Chapter 1, the tabloid community came into existence with a zest for fun. In this chapter, we see that this community began to develop a critical discourse that exposed political corruption and morally unacceptable conduct among officials at all levels, and that demanded a change in such behaviour. This interactive community thus established a new relationship between society and literary representation. A community consciousness took shape, making socially engaged political activity acceptable. We can identify five main characteristics of this process.

First, public expectations and sensibilities gradually changed at the turn of the century. When tabloids first appeared, Li Boyuan had to defend himself for openly humiliating his targets, whose names he concealed but whose identities were apparent to readers.[97] In 1899, writers had to justify their exposure of officials' wrongdoings. By early 1900, however, the need to conceal identities disappeared as the public was no longer uncomfortable reading disrespectful and caustic tabloid texts. So many characters in the "news" and in fiction were prototypes of well-known Qing officials that readers probably entertained themselves by trying to identify individuals. When the government began to favour reforms, tabloid writers became even more daring in revealing the names of corrupt officials. At the same time, they became skilled in averting reprisals by not offending anyone whose power could reach them.

Second, tabloid community members took a keen interest in literature that entertained by mocking and criticizing officialdom. Sun Yusheng recalled that *Splendid World* reached the height of its popularity when it began serializing Li Boyuan's *Officialdom Unmasked* in 1903. Readers rushed to the tabloid's office to purchase each day's issue.[98] The novel's popularity led to its publication as a "pocket book" in 1904.[99] Like Li's novel, Wu Jianren's *Strange Events Eyewitnessed* enjoyed instant success and became tremendously popular.[100] Both Bao Tianxiao and Sun Yusheng observed that *Officialdom Unmasked* appeared at precisely the time when people wanted to hear about such matters.[101]

Third, people integrated politicians and political issues into their everyday conversations, especially in the form of jokes and humour. After all, what could be more amusing than talking about high officials as if they were lowly prostitutes? It is not hard to imagine that funny and provocative stories circulated widely, and that readers and their friends and associates shared their frustration with the establishment when they met at workplaces, teahouses, brothels, banquets, and family dinner tables. After telling a story featuring an official and a former prostitute, Li Boyuan specifically instructed readers that the story was good gossip material.[102] Certainly the often anecdotal, colloquial style of storytelling in the press was easily adapted for oral transmission within the community.

Fourth, bombardment with official-bashing literature helped shape the consciousness of tabloid community members. A commentator in *Strange Events Eyewitnessed*, speaking directly to "those who had not yet become an official," warned that if they still wanted a career in officialdom after learning of its evils, they would become worthless to him as readers.[103] A critical consciousness also grew out of the rapidly changing social and political context. Certainly, those who read about the elaborate wedding ceremony of Emperor Tongzhi in *Shenbao* in the early 1870s felt very differently about the dynasty than those who read about the construction of the Empress Dowager's luxurious summer palace in *Splendid World* in the early 1900s. Readers undoubtedly saw the Empress's luxury in the context of what they perceived to be China's general decline.

Finally, and most importantly, was the fact that readers actively and openly participated in public discussions. In various public forums sponsored by the tabloids – poetry competitions, letters to the editor, literary games and riddles, and everyday gossip columns – readers increasingly spoke out and found their political voices. Tabloids headlined articles written by readers in leading columns such as "Talk of Society" *(Sheshuo)* in *Splendid World* and "Opinions from the House" *(Benguan lunshuo)* in *Allegories*. *Splendid World* dedicated columns to readers' letters, including "Letters from Readers" *(Laihan)*, "Essays from Readers" *(Laigao)*, and "Selected Articles" *(Xuangao)*. In fact, many of the criticisms outlined above came from readers.

The voice of the tabloid community had become an activist voice. Community members protested injustice and demanded change. One article lamented the unjust fate of two poor people, one of whom was a cake vendor imprisoned for daring to sneak a glance at the Empress Dowager and the Emperor as they rode past in a procession in the capital. The other was a worker in the Forbidden City who was to be executed for inadvertently concealing a small knife on entering a hall.[104] Another writer argued that, in order to reform China's bureaucratic system, the law dealing with officials must be changed. Officials who violated the law ought to be punished thrice as severely as ordinary people. They should be ousted from their positions, their crimes written on their foreheads so they could never re-enter officialdom. The government should confiscate bribes and forbid officials to move around towns and counties with large retinues and carriages in pompous displays of power. Finally, when officials made incorrect judgments at trials, ordinary people should have the right to appeal, no matter how small their cases were. In this way, abuses of authority would not go unchecked.[105]

The community utilized the media to expose officials' misconduct. After all, there were no other channels for doing so, as people had no right to send letters of grievance directly to high-ranking officials.[106] The writer of an open letter to a military governor accused the governor of having little talent for this important post. The letter described the governor's career as a trail of vice and stupidity, and warned him of coming misfortunes. Although the governor's name was omitted, his identity was clear in the description of his career path.[107] One poem recounted a governor's plan to execute three Army Academy students who took weapons outside the school without permission. The poet criticized the governor for treating the students' lives as cheaply as those of dogs, and professed that "it is better to die than to have no freedom" *(buziyou wuningsi)*.[108]

Also appearing in the tabloids were reports of how reform-minded people adopted the idea of "organization" *(tuanti)* as a tactic, and how they put it into practice. According to one 1902 report, several hundred students boycotted the provincial examination held in Zhejiang. The report argued that the students were clearly enlightened *(wenming)*, that the organized will of the people was very powerful, and that there was therefore no need to fear the government.[109]

In some cases, such community protests may have actually contributed to the downfall of certain officials. On 18 June 1899, *Fun* published several couplets in the style of "bamboo-twigs" ballads *(zhuzhici)*.[110] The couplets ridiculed the superintendent of a new-style school in Nanjing for mismanagement. *Fun*'s editor wrote a note explaining that a friend had sent him the couplets with a request that he publish them. In his accompanying letter, the friend complained privately to the editor that the school was disappointing because it lacked substance, and that the superintendent was arrogant and hired more bad teachers than good ones; in addition, the superintendent was enamoured with Lin Jiangxue, the top winner in a flower election organized by *Fun*, and planned to marry her. Two days later, *Fun* followed up with a short report by the editor and an essay. The report revealed more damaging details about the superintendent. The essay bemoaned the fact that even though establishing new-style schools was the only measure remaining from the Emperor's comprehensive reform plan of 1898, authorities were not even carrying out this reform well.

Soon thereafter, *Fun* reported that Imperial Commissioner Gang had fired the superintendent.[111] A week later, the paper published an essay about how Gang had ordered the closure of the new-style school. While praising Governor-General Liu Kunyi for establishing the school, the essay blamed the superintendent's mismanagement for the closure.[112]

Although it is not clear whether *Fun* had any influence on the superintendent's misfortune, the paper did provoke the public. Some believed that the paper had gone too far in criticizing the superintendent. In defence, *Fun*'s editor published an open letter addressed to a certain Nanjing official – apparently the friend who had sent him the original couplets. As mentioned earlier, in 1899, the editor still felt uneasy about open confrontation and was again compelled to defend his paper as accurate and trustworthy. In this open letter, the editor claimed that *Fun*'s criticism accurately reflected the public's demand for justice. He added that the Nanjing official's own letter to him, along with another article from a reader defending *Fun*, accurately reflected public opinion *(gonglun)*. Besides, the editor claimed, *Fun* had no relationship with the superintendent and did not wish to get involved in politics since the paper was intended only for entertainment; nonetheless, *Fun* was determined to thumb its nose at hypocrites. The editor then noted that many people had sent in letters condemning the superintendent, but that he did not publish these as they were unsigned.[113]

In *Officialdom Unmasked*, first serialized in 1903, Li Boyuan implicated many top officials and eunuchs for wrongdoing, including Zhang Zhidong, Li Lianying, and Zhang Biao.[114] Some officials, including Zhao, an advisor to Governor-General Liu Kunyi, were forced to resign because of the revelations.

In particular, writers protested against officials who attempted to stop them from expressing themselves freely. Officials regarded late Qing journalists as "the dregs of the literati" *(siwen bailei)*, accusing them of causing trouble for the government.[115] One fictional account described how the military governor of Anhui bought the *Wuhu ribao* solely to prevent the paper from attacking him. He then changed the paper's name to *Anhui ribao* and converted it into a government newspaper.[116] Whenever Shanghai newspapers attacked him for wrongdoing, so the story went, the governor would respond by publishing news and essays showing how hard he worked and how much he cared for the people.[117] Although fictional, the story bore some semblance of reality. Since in Shanghai government papers could not compete with local commercial newspapers, officials did subsidize some commercial papers to speak on their behalf.[118]

In 1903, Wu Jianren quit his job as chief editor of the *Hankow Daily* to protest against the prefect of Wuchang, Liang Dingfen, who censored the paper and eventually converted it into a government newspaper under his own control. After leaving the *Hankow Daily*, Wu wrote an open letter to Liang, criticizing him for usurping control of the paper and for obstructing his free expression.[119]

When the Ministry of Civil Affairs imposed temporary regulations on periodicals in 1907, *All-Story Monthly* published two essays protesting both the regulations and the statutes. One essay accused the government of obstructing the free development of public opinion. It contended that with these statutes, "no one would dare to speak up about the government's failures in domestic and foreign policies. Officials would thus suppress the people more severely. No one would dare to discuss the harm the government brought to the nation. People also would no longer be able to speak about the injustices they have suffered and the problems they have faced."[120] The essay rebutted each of the regulations and statutes with detailed arguments. In particular, it condemned the first statute, which forbade the publication of anything that slandered the imperial court. The essay argued that since the imperial court was inseparable from the government, any wrong committed by the court would harm the entire nation. The second essay focused its criticism on the fourth statute, which prohibited the publication of any unauthorized news about China's diplomatic policies and events. The government wanted to keep its diplomatic dealings secret, the author reasoned, because "the dealings must be harmful for China, so the government does not want the Chinese people to know about it."[121]

Members of the tabloid community certainly understood the power of their pens. One writer said in a preface to *Officialdom Unmasked:* "Around 1900, the situation was chaotic and depressing. However, people like us did not give up and we were not afraid of being punished. We spoke and wrote, criticizing and demanding truth. Therefore, people like them [officials] did not dare repress criticisms. Who says lowly people cannot save the world?"[122]

Conclusion

The demise of the Qing Dynasty and the establishment of the Republic was a revolution. No less important than the revolution itself, however, was the failure of the late Qing state to effectively control both the content and the means of circulation of information, ideas, and critical opinions. For over a decade, the tabloid and other presses relentlessly excoriated the Qing government and its officials. The late Qing state confronted something unprecedented in its history: a significant portion of the literate masses – nationwide and particularly in Jiangnan – resisting inept, often corrupt rulers and officials through reading, talking, and writing. The tabloid community signified the first popular participation in national politics ever to take root among the low and middle classes of the educated, especially the traditionally educated. This segment of society might have been the only grassroots voice that could have rescued the Qing government; instead, this voice had the opposite effect.

In this chapter, I did not attempt to solve the problem of why the fall of the Qing Dynasty generated so little public sympathy. I intended only to identify some important clues that might help us understand how, by 1911, the attitude of the politically unaffiliated populace toward the Qing regime had changed from reverence to indifference and scorn. As the vanguard of Qing officialdom bashing, the tabloid press played a pivotal role in helping the public see the "true" colours of the regime. Its critical discourse on officialdom effectively eroded the symbolic power of the Qing government and its powers of persuasion.

This late Qing development echoes events in seventeenth- and eighteenth-century France. In his study of the forbidden bestsellers in prerevolutionary France, Robert Darnton shows that underground literature, including political slander, philosophical pornography, and utopian fantasy, worked to challenge the established values of the Old Regime and to undermine the foundations of monarchical legitimacy. While cautioning against making a direct link between this forbidden literature and the French Revolution, Darnton suggests, by examining the ways in which texts circulated and addressed their readers, that the subversive literature might have shaped popular perceptions of the monarchy and indeed created a breeding ground for social unrest and political change.[123]

Although the historical contexts of late Qing China and seventeenth- and eighteenth-century France differed greatly, both countries witnessed the emergence of a subversive popular literature in the years leading up to their revolutions. Compared with the French experience, the late Qing tabloid literature perhaps had a swifter, more direct effect in nurturing the rebellious environment leading to the 1911 Revolution. There is also a similarity in the subversive nature of both countries' literature: both challenged the legitimacy of the state by undermining its moral foundations. In France, erotic literature, scandalous polemics, and political slander eroded the moral reputation of the political establishment. In China, the tabloid literature, with its promotion of fun and prostitution and its criticisms of the moral failings of officialdom, weakened the moral authority of the Qing state.

Although there is no causal connection between these seditious forms of literature and revolutions, it is worth noting that successful revolutions are always vocalized before they are enacted. As unimposing as these tabloid literatures might seem in their criticisms, the damage they inflicted on the reputation of the state undermined the regime's ability to continue ruling. To be sure, the tabloid literati never published a single article, report, anecdote, or poem favouring the overthrow of the Qing government. After all, the late Qing state still sanctioned social and cultural privileges enjoyed by the literati class, and tabloid writers never explicitly stated that they wanted the dynasty to end.

In the next chapter, I discuss how Chinese nationalism manifested itself in the tabloid community and describe the community's attitude toward the Qing as the ruling dynasty.

3 Imagining the Nation

Modern Chinese nationalism emerged in the late Qing in response to China's encounter with a new and forceful imperialist world order and as a result of China's engagement with Western political philosophies that inspired alternatives to traditional Chinese polity. The Shanghai tabloid press articulated three important facets of modern Chinese nationalism: sentiments, discourses, and movements. Each facet defended China as a sovereign nation-state and provided Chinese society with an identity, or a national "We."[1] As this nationalism evolved, the tabloid community imagined the Chinese nation in relation to both Manchu rulers and foreign powers, and articulated the nature of citizenship in a modern Chinese state.

To help frame my analysis of the tabloid community and to better situate it in a broader intellectual context, I at times contrast the views of the tabloid literati with those of Liang Qichao, at the time the most prominent and influential figure among the intellectual elite and a major inspiration to Chinese nationalism. The tabloid press adopted a language of nationalism – its terminologies and expressions – that Liang Qichao and others, such as Yan Fu, for the most part introduced. The press also shared and appropriated many of the assumptions, attitudes, and policy preferences of the intellectual elite, yet also challenged and diverged from them in important ways.

Sentiments

Studies of late Qing nationalism have created the impression that Chinese of various political and social persuasions, threatened by foreign imperialist powers, had become obsessed with the question of China's survival as a nation and as a race. Some scholars have characterized the nationalistic sentiments of the first decade of the twentieth century as "anti-foreign," as "anti-imperialist," and as having "a strong sense of ethnic/racial identity."[2] There is solid evidence to support this view. One cannot overstate the barrage of emotion-laden nationalistic rhetoric that both leading and lesser-known intellectuals and writers produced from 1895 onward, filling the highbrow and popular presses. Lavish displays of such rhetoric appeared during the

Boxer Uprising, the Russo-Japanese War, the anti-American boycott, and the railway rights movement. During all of these episodes, broad segments of the population experienced a very real and heightened sense of urgency and crisis. One might conclude, therefore, that late Qing China was boiling over with nationalistic sentiment.

If one considers the sentiments appearing in the tabloid press, however, a more nuanced picture emerges. Prompted by the emotional response to China's crisis in her confrontation with foreign powers, the tabloid community, like Liang Qichao and many other educated Chinese, adopted an anti-imperialist stance. They shared the conviction that a strong Chinese nation-state was the only way China could defend herself against foreign aggression, and none of them was racially "anti-foreign." The tabloid community, however, differed from Liang Qichao in its views of ethnicity. The community showed little ethnic bias, whereas, in his early years, Liang evoked ethnic hatred toward the Manchus to promote his political agenda.

Attitudes toward Foreigners, Race, and Ethnicity

The modern press made possible the first widespread public dissemination of nationalistic sentiments in China during the Sino-Japanese War of 1894-95. In the provinces, the war drew a wide circle of informed and educated people into discussions about national affairs. Bao Tianxiao describes how educated people in Suzhou, people who had never before participated in such discussions, were shocked at the news of China's defeat by the Japanese and the postwar presence of Japanese concessions in the city. They began to ask why China was so weak and Japan so strong.[3] The nationalistic sentiments of the educated Chinese derived largely from anxiety about China's weakness and a sense of shame at her defeat.

The earliest issues of *Fun* expressed concern for the nation with lamentations and clichés about China's weaknesses and problems: "Nowadays, the nation is poor; the people are tired; and the scholar-officials are demoralized."[4] Anti-imperialist expressions first appeared in late 1898 when various tabloids began publishing news, commentaries, and essays about foreign military aggression and the scramble of foreigners for spheres of influence in China. One article in *Fun* reported that a large number of Russian soldiers had moved into Siberia, threatening Chinese territory.[5] In another article, Li Boyuan described how a Westerner compared China to a watermelon:

> Since Italy demanded Shamen Bay from China, various other nations began to follow it as an example. Yesterday, a certain Westerner, talking about China's current situation, even described Chinese as watermelon seeds. Hearing these

startling words for the first time, one fails to comprehend. But after thinking them over, one finds in them a fresh meaning. It is said that watermelon seeds have the most extensive market, even though they are not a necessity in everyday life. They are sold everywhere, in theatres, teahouses, and wine shops ... Since Westerners plan to divide China among themselves, they perceive it as a big watermelon; its land is like the flesh, its people like the seeds. Once the flesh is eaten up, the seeds scatter. The seeds are then either collected for sale or thrown out and abused; it is hard to know which fate is in store for the seeds. Alas, China is in danger now! It is hard to know if the Chinese are alert enough to have fear.[6]

Li made similar comments a few days later, likening China's fate to the foreign circus he had attended. Describing the dazzling performances, he remarked that if China resisted reform and clung to the old examination system and the ritual of kowtowing, she would meet the same fate as the circus animals – fettered and enslaved, kneeling and dancing to their masters' commands.[7]

The anti-imperialist voices grew louder, more acerbic, and more frequent. Writers directed countless cries of frustration at the foreign powers' infringement on Chinese sovereignty. On New Year's Day 1898, Li Boyuan repeated what one Japanese man had said to him:

China suffered only headaches when it was humiliated in the Sino-French war in 1884, and could recover with herbal medicine. By the time of the Sino-Japanese war in 1895, the ailment had already entered the flesh, yet it was still not without cure. But today, Germany occupies Shandong, Russia Manchuria, France, the Hainan island, and England eyes the Zhoushan islands. The illness is like tuberculosis, deep-seated and hopeless.[8]

In 1900, the chief editor of *Shenbao* dismissed news, reported by other Shanghai newspapers, that the Russian government was pressing the Qing government to accept a treaty with a border unfavourable to China. The editor of *Pastime* wrote more than a dozen articles ridiculing and humiliating the chief editor's silence about Russia's action, calling the editor "the poisonous semen of the Russian wolf."[9] Writers expressed anti-imperialist sentiments in the form of ballads and dramas to make their messages more accessible to readers with low literacy levels. One such ballad described the loss of Manchuria in the Russo-Japanese War, lamenting the people's suffering and the government's inability to protect them.[10]

Tabloid writers often used sarcasm and humour to express their feelings. One writer imagined a conversation between Mr. X and Mr. Y. In this piece,

Mr. X stated that China was now enlightened and improved because the government now dealt with foreign powers in a reasonable way. At the time of the Boxers, the government acted aggressively by secretly ordering generals in the East and South to attack foreign battleships. By the time of this article, however, Chinese authorities moved their battleships out of port to make room for foreign battleships, thereby maintaining peaceful relations with foreign nations. This policy of continuous retreat, reasoned Mr. X, showed that China had reached the zenith of its enlightenment. Mr. Y retorted that this enlightenment was actually a retreat, just like that of the Chinese battleships.[11]

Other writers expressed more concern about foreign economic and religious imperialism. One contributor wrote that most Chinese mines had fallen into foreigners' hands and provided a list of fourteen major Chinese mines owned or leased by foreign companies.[12] In his fiction, Wu Jianren also described how foreign goods saturated Chinese markets, leading to an outflow of silver from China.[13] Wu expressed his fear through one of his protagonists: "Right now, foreigners want to wipe out other people's countries. China has not yet been divided, and they already are building churches everywhere, proselytizing, wanting to spread their religions all over China. Can't you imagine what it would be like after [China's] division?"[14]

In *A Brief History of Enlightenment (Wenming xiaoshi)*, Li Boyuan portrayed many characters as frustrated with the injustices China was suffering. One character, discussing foreigners' freedom to do whatever they wanted in China, exclaimed, "If our people harmed [the foreigners'] cats and dogs, we would have no hope to keep our lives," implying that Chinese lives were of very little consequence.[15] At the end of a chapter about conflict between Chinese and foreigners, Li commented: "Dealing with foreign nations, China always loses. When foreigners violate Chinese law, China can do nothing about it; when Chinese violate the laws of foreign countries, they have no way to escape punishment."[16] In the stories Li told in his papers and novels, even some Chinese – those who had converted to Christianity, and to whom foreigners had given special privileges – dared to defy Chinese laws.

Most anti-imperialist sentiments in the press were rooted in an undeniable reality: foreign nations were indeed predatory and powerful. Moreover, if the Chinese government had been more competent, foreigners would not have been able to dominate China. While protesting foreign aggression, tabloid writers regarded the Qing government as the ultimate culprit. They attacked almost anyone in a powerful government position for contributing to China's weakness. Countless stories appeared in the press disparaging stubborn conservatives, supercilious and opportunistic reformers, and hypocritical and power-hungry revolutionaries – all of whom, according to the writers, harmed the nation while supposedly defending it.

Writers also mocked those Chinese whom they believed benefited from association with foreigners. Reporting that the Chinese government had to pay indemnities to foreign powers to settle the Boxer Uprising, one writer chastised compradors who delighted in the fact that their foreign bosses could use those monies to restart their businesses and make a fortune.[17] Another writer ridiculed those Chinese who acquired foreign citizenship and then scolded their own people from their new identity as "foreigners."[18] Arguably, the nationalistic sentiments in the tabloid press were a reaction to more than merely the rise of foreign powers. Writers used foreign aggression as a pretext to address domestic problems involving government policies, officials, and political elites – problems that the low- and middle-ranked literati knew had existed for a long time.

Tabloid writers adopted some of the same anti-imperialist rhetoric used widely in the mainstream press, albeit with a twist. In 1899, one writer noticed that using the term "400 million Chinese" *(siwanwan zhongguoren)* had become a popular way to describe the Chinese population as a whole.[19] In the tabloid press, writers also often used the similar phrase "400 million compatriots" *(siwanwan tongbao)*, a common metaphor indicating that all Chinese came from the same family. Tabloid writers adopted these terms to create a sense of a national We, but they also made fun of this usage. One writer, noting that the words *tong* and *nong* sound alike in Shanghai dialect, offered a witticism in which an audience, hearing speeches by reformers who incessantly used *tongbao* to refer to the Chinese people, wondered why they called the people *nongbao*, which means stupid and useless.[20] Another writer shared a similar witticism about the term *zhina*, a word widely used by the Japanese to refer to China. For him, this term's derogatory connotation brought shame to 400 million Chinese people because, when pronounced in the local dialect, *zhina* sounded like *zhuluo*, meaning pig. Foreigners were, he suspected, actually calling China a nation of pigs.[21] This joke was not entirely groundless since the term, as one scholar argues, reflected Japan's orientalist and imperialist treatment of China.[22]

By 1902, writers' nationalistic expressions began to reflect the vocabulary of Social Darwinism. Many wrote about the nation-state and the Chinese race in terms of a competition among nations and races. One writer explained how Chinese became aware of their racial and national identity in the context of "the other." In his view, Chinese came to comprehend the meaning of nation-state *(guo)* and race *(zhongzu)* only after becoming aware of foreigners' success in building their own nations.[23] The pages of the tabloid press frequently expressed fears that someday the Chinese race, and even the nation-state, might fail in this competition and become extinct. Another writer lamented that foreign powers had forced China to make concessions and pay war indemnities. Expounding on the strength of Western powers, the writer called for reform to enable China to successfully compete against them.[24] One allegorical tale compared China's fate to a competition among mice: one group of mice had been enslaved by another, yet after reform the enslaved mice won battle after battle, finally gaining independence.[25] The tabloid writers saw an inseverable connection between the survival of the nation-state and that of the Chinese race, a perception influenced by Liang Qichao and other intellectual elites.[26] In a rare move, *Fun* reprinted in its entirety one article from *Dagongbao* warning that the great Qing empire was facing collapse, with over 400 million Chinese in danger of enslavement. The article called for Chinese to fight against this tragic fate and save the race.[27]

Although anti-imperialist, the tabloid press showed few traces of antiforeign or ethnocentric sentiments. Anti-imperialist attitudes did not imply hatred toward foreigners simply because they were foreigners. In the tabloid press, awareness of Chinese racial identity in terms such as *tongbao* and "400 million Chinese" implied neither hatred toward foreigners nor any sense of racial superiority. Writers rarely used derogatory words such as *woren* (short Japanese) and *yiren* (barbarians) when referring to foreigners; instead, they made a conscious decision to employ neutral words such as *xiren* and *yangren* for Westerners and *riren* for Japanese.[28] Some writers insisted that many rural Chinese were still ignorant and backward because they called Westerners *yiren*.[29] Moreover, writers reacted strongly against the Boxers during and after that movement, denouncing them as ignorant barbarians and criticizing their brutality and encirclement of foreign legations in Beijing.[30] Writers supported the Qing government's suppression of the Boxers even as they condemned foreign soldiers for ruthless killing and plundering.

One writer went so far as to praise the foreign troops that controlled the capital in the aftermath of the Boxers. He reported that the foreign-controlled areas were clean because residents were required to wash the fronts of their houses to minimize dust, and to light road lamps at night for security. Once the foreign forces withdrew, these areas were no longer as clean and orderly as before.[31] Another writer admired the skill with which foreign soldiers in Shanghai practised their military drills.[32]

Tabloid literati also observed firsthand the efficiency of the foreign administration of Shanghai's international concessions. One writer suggested that

Shanghai officials adopt foreign administrative practices such as establishing a special bureau to provide physical examinations and licences for prostitutes.[33] Another writer, observing the bright lanterns and colourful banners displayed in the French Concession to celebrate a French national holiday, marvelled at how Western nations commemorated their culture and history, which helped them develop strength and courage. While praising the French celebrations as "terrific, terrific," the writer expressed a sense of deep shame that China, with a long, four-thousand-year history, had not yet devoted a single day to celebrating its people and history.[34]

Indeed, the lack of animosity toward Westerners was striking, especially in situations in which one would have expected a more hostile reaction. According to one humorous report, five or six drunken Westerners created a street disturbance when they visited a brothel. Cheering and yelling, they fondled several prostitutes, who scattered in all directions. In the rush, one prostitute accidentally knocked over a peddler's "smelly tofu" stand; oil and grease spilled all over her clothing. Gleefully, the writer described how bystanders clapped their hands and cheered loudly at the scene. He concluded, "Alas, Westerners also fool around," suggesting surprise that, like Chinese, they too can behave indecently.[35] Many expressed admiration for Westerners' public manners, as in one anecdote praising Western table manners and the practice of ordering no more food than they could finish. (The writers stopped short of glorifying foreigners, however.)

The tabloid press showed not only little sign of anti-foreign racism but also a total absence of hostility and ethnic superiority toward Manchus, in sharp contrast to Liang Qichao who, prior to 1902, was very anti-Manchu. As early as 1896, Liang criticized the Qing government for carrying out racial policies favouring Manchu over Han officials.[36] The failure of the Hundred Days' Reform of 1898 prompted his attack on the Qing government as an alien regime unfit to rule China. It was not until the turn of the century that Liang began to disassociate himself from this radical anti-Manchu position. By 1903, he had begun to articulate his concepts of "little nationalism" *(xiaominzu zhuyi)* and "great nationalism" *(daminzu zhuyi)*, proposing that the Han-centric "little nationalism" should give way to anti-imperialist "great nationalism."

Tabloid writers viewed the Qing regime as legitimate because it had ruled China in a traditional Chinese manner for over two hundred years. For these writers, ethnicity played no role. This was Wu Jianren's position when he argued that the Qing Dynasty conformed to the Chinese administrative model. Many writers even faithfully championed the cause of the Guangxu Emperor.

In 1899, when the Qing court debated the candidacy for heir apparent, Wu wrote several articles pleading with the court to reinstate the Emperor. When the Empress Dowager issued an edict ordering the celebration of the Emperor's thirtieth birthday, Wu Jianren organized an essay competition in his tabloid on the theme of the Emperor's longevity.[37] Li Boyuan also published a paean in celebration of the Emperor's birthday.[38] Although writers relentlessly criticized the Qing government and Qing officials, their attacks were never along racial/ethnic lines, and they did not want to see the end of the Qing Dynasty.

Writers condemned the revolutionaries in countless sarcastic anecdotes and critical essays. One writer, for example, criticized a group of radical students who used race and ethnicity as defining features of the nation. Other articles pitied hotheaded youths who wasted their lives on the revolution.[39] In his novel *Touring Shanghai (Shanghai youcanlu)*, Wu Jianren lashed out at those revolutionaries who "claimed to be patriotic and to care for the people ... Yet, they did nothing to strengthen China under foreign domination, and gave no thought to protecting hundreds of thousands of overseas Chinese. All they wanted was revenge for things that had happened three hundred years ago." Wu appeared to be implicating Sun Yat-sen's revolutionary group in this criticism. He even excused the Qing government for favouring Manchus in appointing officials, suggesting that nobody can completely abandon the impulse to favour people from one's own native place. He further argued against revolution on two grounds. First, he believed that foreign powers would use the chaos of a civil war between revolutionaries and government troops as an excuse to occupy China in order to protect their churches and businesses. Second, he saw revolutionaries as opportunistic, citing news reports that the revolutionary party had already promised one unnamed foreign nation twenty commercial locations in exchange for a promise not to oppose a revolution. He asked: "Would not the other nations also want twenty places?"[40]

Conspicuously absent in the tabloid press, therefore, was any analysis of race and ethnicity. Writers appear to have attached little importance to ethnic divisions in the construction of a national We. One even argued that the Miao people, an ethnic minority living primarily in southern China, were Chinese.[41] Curiously, when referring to China in the tabloid press, writers never used the term *zuguo* (fatherland), a word that bears an ancestral and ethnic connotation. Instead, they used the term *zhongguo*, or Middle Kingdom, a word with more of a political connotation.[42]

The Nation-State as the Salvation

In the 1890s, intellectual elites such as Kang Youwei, Liang Qichao, Yan Fu, and Tan Sitong played a major role in using Social Darwinism to articulate the idea of China as a nation-state in competition with the nations of the world. Liang Qichao, who once complained that the Chinese had not yet even given their country a name, used his prolific and provocative writing to popularize the rhetoric of China as a nation-state.[43] The late Qing press reveals how pervasive this rhetoric had become in China. Words such as *guo* (nation, country), *guojia* (nation, state), and *zhongguo* (China) appeared frequently in reference to the nation-state as the ultimate geopolitical community.[44] The "discovery" of the Chinese nation, according to many scholars, gradually but fundamentally changed the way Chinese thought about political allegiance. A collective commitment to the Chinese nation-state – a nation-state as a family with a shared paternity – slowly but surely replaced traditional loyalty to dynasty and emperor.[45]

Influenced by the intellectual elite, the tabloid community also reflected this shift of loyalty from ruler to nation-state. Although one writer could still, in 1898, pay lip service to loyalty to the Emperor,[46] by 1900, this idea had almost disappeared from the tabloid press, although some sympathy for rulers as victims of foreign power remained.[47] Although they said nothing positive about the Empress Dowager, writers did express concern for Emperor Guangxu and the fate of the dynasty, but only in the context of supporting Guangxu's reform policies and opposing the Republican revolution.[48] In contrast, countless appeals for a strong Chinese nation-state appeared in editorials, essays, and poems.[49]

Belief in a Chinese nation-state showed up in debates over local provincial autonomy. The majority of opinions in the tabloid press opposed local autonomy *(zizhi)*. As early as 1903, one writer claimed that some reformers supported local autonomy only because the state was incapable of building a strong China. Acknowledging that those reformers actually wanted to build a powerful and independent nation, the writer rejected outright the idea of local autonomy, pointing to the strength Germany derived from its union of twenty-six small states. He warned that "parcelized autonomy" *(fenzhi)* would mean anarchy *(buzhi)*, and that a divided China would provide foreigners with an easy opportunity to gain control. The central government, he railed, failed to unite the provinces into a collective whole; the state was the quintessence of China's future, yet, as matters now stood, it was also responsible for China's dire present.[50]

Although the tabloid community joined the elites in placing trust in the nation-state, they differed from them in some crucial aspects, to which we now turn.

Discourses

The nation-state question dominated the political and intellectual scene during the last two decades of the Qing Dynasty. What kind of polity should China have? What role should the people play in that polity? How could people be transformed into citizens of an "enlightened" Chinese nation? The tabloid community had much in common with Liang Qichao as far as China's polity was concerned, but differed with him over how to prepare the people for a constitutional polity and over the nature of the people's role in that polity.[51]

Transforming the People

Already in the 1890s, Liang Qichao recognized that a strong Chinese nation-state depended foremost on the people's willingness and ability to contribute to it. For Liang, one of the principal purposes of reform was to prepare the people for citizenship in the Chinese nation-state.[52] He first used the term *guomin* (citizen) in December 1898 in his new magazine, *Qingyibao*, published in Yokohama. In an 1899 article in that magazine, Liang defined guomin as people who regard the nation as belonging to them; he stressed the importance of a nation's people and viewed the competition among nations as essentially a competition among their guomin.[53] In February 1902, after *Qingyibao* ceased publication, Liang inaugurated a new magazine, *Xinmin congbao*, in which he refined his discourse on the people with his treatise *On the New Citizen (Xinminshuo)*, which was serialized intermittently for four years. In this treatise, Liang extended his idea of guomin to the concept of *xinmin*, or "new citizens" ready for a new Chinese nation-state.

Along with his ideas about new citizens, Liang articulated on various occasions the concept of *qun* (grouping or collectivity), a term first interpreted by Yan Fu in a Social Darwinist context. When Liang began articulating his ideas about the "new citizen" in 1902 and became increasingly enamoured of Western values of progress, individual rights, and freedom, he also began to question whether Confucianism could help achieve such a nation-state. For Liang, the strength of Western countries lay in their collectivity, whereas traditional Chinese ethical values took the individual rather than the group as the point of departure. Believing many traditional ethical values to be incompatible with collective ethics, Liang stressed the need to establish new ethical values in order to transform Chinese people.[54] The collective unit to which Liang appeared to refer is what Benedict Anderson would call an imagined community.[55] Liang totally disregarded the Chinese type of collectivity that was based on those Chinese ethical values inhering in social and familial organizations. Perhaps he also saw the Confucian emphasis on self-cultivation as evidence of the individual as the point of departure: "For the most part, Confucianism no longer fits the new world"[56] – a world constituted, as he saw it, by nations competing for power and wealth. *On the New Citizen* prescribed for China a new public morality or civic virtue *(gongde)*, borrowed from Western civic ideas of the common good and the well-being of the nation.[57]

Famous for his passion and frequent changes of mind, Liang adjusted his ideas about ethics. Whereas in the early part of *On the New Citizen* he abandoned traditional moral values, toward the treatise's end he stressed traditional moral values as necessary for Chinese to become citizens of a modern Chinese nation. In his 1905 *Reflections on Moral Education (Deyujian)*, Liang equated his idea of "citizen's morality" *(guomin daode)* with the traditional morality of noblemen.[58] This change occurred on his return from a trip to the United States at the end of 1903.[59] Liang reconciled this apparent contradiction by separating public morality from personal morality *(side)*. He saw the importance of individual morality as based on traditional values of self-cultivation, yet his sense of self-cultivation was no longer a traditional one that saw "sages and noblemen" as the ideal. For him, self-cultivation meant becoming a modern citizen *(guomin* or *gongmin)* according to public moral principles.[60] Liang's concept of public morality sought to strengthen group cohesion, as Zarrow points out, whereas his notion of personal morality aimed at shaping individuals for the use of the group.[61]

Tabloid writers also saw a need to "transform" Chinese people by preparing them for a modern Chinese nation. They adopted the term "guomin," which saw frequent use in Chinese presses after it first appeared in Liang Qichao's *Qingyibao*.[62] One writer discussed the difference between the terms "citizen" *(guomin)* and "national" *(guoren)*, arguing that the former accepted whereas the latter evaded their obligations to the nation. Praising Westerners and Japanese for acting as citizens in their respective nations, the writer blamed the Chinese for failure in this regard, which permitted China to be dominated by foreigners.[63]

Tabloid writers, however, never used the term *xinmin*, signalling a clear difference between them and Liang regarding the true meaning of citizenship. Like Liang Qichao, they saw moral education as crucial for transforming the people into citizens, but they differed from him in their understanding of what these moral values should be. Liang predicated his notion of public and private morality largely on Western civic values, for example, making freedom *(ziyou)* the core value of public morality.[64] The tabloid literati, however, largely adhered to traditional Chinese ethics. Chapter 4 will further discuss their perception of danger in new ideas such as freedom, and their call for the reinforcement of traditional moral values.

Following the tradition of Confucianism, Wu Jianren made little distinction between public and private morality. For him, cultivation of the individual in accordance with traditional Chinese ethics required the individual to act in the common good. Wu expressed this opinion through one of his characters in *Touring Shanghai:*

> *Gongde,* the catchword of the experts of the New Learning *(xinxuejia),* convinced me the least. How can we separate public and personal morality? The total of the personal is the public; if everyone is moral, and everyone treats each other morally, then doesn't that amount to public morality? ... The ideas of public morality, patriotism and *qun* are also discussed in *Daxue,* though the terms are used differently. Why make them something new and different?[65]

Wu also saw the values of patriotism and collectivity that Liang prescribed for the new Chinese citizens as necessary for the nation, but he saw these values in Confucian terms. Indeed, the tabloid writers did not really aim to transform people; they wanted instead to fortify certain traditional ethical values in people. Concerned mainly with the decline in traditional moral values in society, they linked national welfare to the everyday moral choices of the people.

Complaints and criticisms in the press and in literature about the total loss of morality helped create a widespread sense of social crisis. Nothing so bluntly described the allegedly pervasive moral decay in society than the short *zaju* play *All that Is Empty (Fengyuekong).*[66] The play featured a conversation about contemporary society between a main speaker, a clown, and his sympathetic listener, a rough and virile character. The play opened with the clown asking, "In today's society, is there anything that is not false?" He immediately listed an array of popular yet undeserved honorifics such as "loyal ministers, filial sons, righteous husbands, chaste wives, honorary temples and memorial arches." As for literati, he noted that they too held all sorts of titles, such as *xiucai, juren, jinshi, hanlin,* and *liuguan* (academy resident), but all they really did was "fool around with their writings to gain fame and success." The clown declared Shanghai to be the worst place of all, infested with superficiality, falsehood, and insincerity:

Those who have some kind of official position act conceitedly as though they were persons of great importance, pumping themselves up with pomp and extravagance; those who have some literacy behave as though they are learned and principled, pretending to be Confucian pedants; those merchants who know about diamonds and precious stones get involved with counterfeiting; those who have little money spend lavishly in brothels, pretending to be rich; and those fashionable prostitutes who fake their feelings and intentions, immerse themselves in lies.[67]

An ironic touch came at the end, with the speaker adding, "But, nowadays one must be an imposter, for if one is honest and upright, one will be stomped on and brushed aside by others."[68] Even Buddhist monks did not behave as they should. *Fun* reported a street fight between two monks, one of whom had accused the other of stealing his mistress's gold ring from his house. The reporter lamented: "Alas, who ever heard of a Buddhist monk owning a home and having a mistress?"[69]

In his novel *Strange Events Eyewitnessed*, which supposedly covered a span of twenty years (1884 to 1904), Wu Jianren likewise depicted more than eight hundred characters living an immoral life. These characters included officials, literati, merchants, and compradors, none of whom possessed a basic sense of moral values such as loyalty, honesty, filial piety, kindness, responsibility, or selflessness. With his typical cool irony, Wu pointed out through one character that "it is easy to identify lies in brothels, but it's not easy to realize how phony the world is."[70]

Tabloid writers noticed changes in social morality through the observance of Shanghai residents' consumption behaviour. One writer observed that ordinary folks – those who could afford only basic food and clothing – would spend up to half their annual living expenses on one meal or one dress. It was unprecedented, the writer observed, that so many folks of modest means watched theatre performances in private boxes, held banquets in brothels, dined at Western restaurants, rode in luxury horse-drawn carriages, and frequented garden teahouses on weekends. "Alas, public morals are getting more decadent day by day ... Nowadays, money contaminates the air and only the rich can serve as exemplars." The writer pleaded: "If they pay no attention to other moral values, at least they should value thrift."[71]

For tabloid writers and readers, this extravagant lifestyle came at the expense of China's future. One author, calculating the amount of money spent in a three-day horse racing event, concluded that if those people had spent their money just a bit more modestly, China's prospects for becoming a powerful and prosperous nation would not be so bleak.[72] Another essay scolded Shanghai residents for indulging in pleasures and amusements, spending too much money while neglecting their duties as citizens of the nation.[73] One reader even complained that patrons of courtesans cared only for their own pleasure, suggesting that the money wasted in brothels should instead be spent for the good of the nation.[74]

The tabloid press paid particular attention to attitudes toward money. One writer accused the Chinese of caring only about their own wealth and failing to respond to the Qing government's call for donations to ease the nation's financial problems.[75] A character in one short story condemned Chinese society as "barbaric" and lacking any sense of public good; all the Chinese cared about was money, a type of behaviour that had become habitual.[76] One writer suggested that, compared with people in other nations, the Chinese were more in love with "gold and silver" and cared less about the well-being of the nation and the public. They would do anything to make money, even if it meant disregarding honour, self-respect, and the law; they would refuse to do anything if money was not part of the deal.[77]

Tabloid writers envisioned a modern Chinese nation with citizens who adhered largely to traditional moral values. They rejected that part of Liang Qichao's vision of "new citizens" that was based on Western civic values, agreeing with Liang only when he promoted traditional Chinese values. Nevertheless, as discussed above, influenced by Liang and other intellectual elites, the writers also saw a strong Chinese nation-state as the hope for China's future and shifted their loyalties from the Emperor to the nation. Tabloid writers' traditional moral values adapted to the need to transform the people from imperial "subjects" *(chenmin)* to modern citizens.

Tabloid writers also paid close attention to the underprivileged, a stratum that Liang largely neglected. One writer observed that many young people were unable to attend school either because they were too old or because they needed to make a living.[78] Another explained: "Once sons of those families of modest means reached the age of eleven or twelve, they were sent out to earn money. If one day they did not work, then that day they would not have food to eat. As a result, many young people have little education."[79] Yet another recommended the use of educational theatrical performances to reach the illiterate.[80] Wu Jianren's stated desire was to reach those people through his magazines. Compared with Liang Qichao's publications, which attracted an elite readership, including large numbers of young students,[81] the tabloid press tried to influence an ever-widening circle of society.

The Role of the People

The idea of "new citizens" was one aspect of Liang Qichao's vision of a Chinese nation-state; popular sovereignty was the other. When Liang articulated his notion of *qun,* he linked it to popular sovereignty and popular power.[82] When he developed the concepts of guomin in 1898 and xinmin in 1902, he held not only that "a national community by its very nature had to involve the people both as rulers and ruled"[83] but also that popular sovereignty should be the moral outcome of the nation-state. For Liang, a constitutional polity was the political realization of popular sovereignty.

Tabloid literati in principle supported the idea of popular sovereignty and the polity of constitutional monarchy, but they differed from Liang Qichao in their views of the people/state relationship in such a political system. Liang cared mostly about state building and allowed for sacrificing the people for the state; the tabloid literati, acting as spokespersons for the people, put a higher priority on people's rights and refused to compromise those rights for the state.

From the very beginning, when Liang Qichao spoke of qun or "grouping" as a means of strengthening China, he saw potential conflicts between the collective and the individual. Although he had faith in democratic principles, in his meditations on citizenship he made the interests of people subservient to the interests of the nation-state. Most scholars of Liang would agree that he placed the state ahead of the people and advocated a statist approach to nation building.[84] As Xu Xiaoqing points out, Liang gave national sovereignty *(zhuquan),* not guomin, the highest priority.[85] It is likely, however, that Liang viewed public and private moralities as interdependent, with individual freedom and rights being inseparable from duty to the nation.[86]

While Liang Qichao conveniently remained silent about the repressive power of the state after 1905 as the Qing government moved toward a constitutional polity, tabloid writers unfailingly asserted people's rights and criticized the government for its treatment of them. The hero of one story published in 1908 criticized the government's educational policy:

> In former times when China had the government examination system, the so-called education [system] merely consisted of a few school officials in each prefecture, district, and county. Moreover, most now believe that such an education produces empty and useless essays; even if it were still useful, it merely would have educated a few literati for the government to use. For those whom the government had no use, it would not educate them. In the last one

or two decades, the government did establish some schools and trained some students. But it established schools merely to meet the need for certain skills, which is quite laughable. The purpose was to train skilled people for the government, not to provide education for citizens. After the government abolished the examination system, it established some elementary and middle schools. Not counting the subjects and contents of the teachings, even if the schools operate perfectly, they still merely educate a small number of people to be controlled by the government, which is no different from the times when government had its examination system. Consequently, average people have no knowledge. This wicked practice is the continuation of the Emperor of Qin's policy of making the people ignorant. The [Qing] government treated ordinary people as mere resources to tax and labour.[87]

Another piece in *Grove of Laughter* protested that ordinary people possessed no rights; officials could do whatever they wished, even at the people's expense, a condition the writer described with a traditional idiom: "Allowing officials to start a fire, but forbidding commoners to light a lamp" *(zhizhun zhouguan fanghuo, buxu baixing diandeng)*.[88] One of Wu Jianren's characters in *Touring Shanghai* said bluntly, "People of all foreign nations are protected by their governments, only we Chinese are like fat for the government that can be cut and eaten at will."[89] Sometimes writers used humour to deliver protest, as in this piece from 1907:

One former county magistrate, after being fired from his job, lived in Shanghai. He heard often from those experts of the New Learning who talked about people's rights and freedom. The magistrate responded, "You guys do not talk about the rights of officials, but only that of the people. You would know how difficult it is to be an official if you were one for just a few days. You think China does not have people's rights? I am afraid that Chinese people have more rights than people in foreign countries." When asked what rights the Chinese have, the magistrate answered, "When I was the magistrate, a bunch of vicious households resisted paying taxes; no matter how hard they were pushed, they just refused to pay. You tell me if they do not have enormous rights."[90]

Many writers also wrote and translated fiction about the historical development of foreign countries, applauding democratic practices in some countries and condemning autocratic systems in others. One novel, *The Russian Czar (Eguo huangdi)*, depicted the Russian anarchists' fight against a despotic emperor whose repression of the people was so severe that "there was not a single person in Russia who dared to demand freedom."[91] Translated fiction such as the novel *Travel Afar (Hanmanyou)* described the British parliamentary system, which was founded on the principle of people's rights.

While supporting a constitutional monarchy, tabloid writers doubted that the government would ever implement such a polity or, if it did, that it would guarantee people's rights. Liang Qichao, a crucial intellectual force behind the constitutional movement, largely ignored these concerns. In June and July 1906, he ghost-wrote reports on constitutional polity addressed to the Qing court on behalf of a committee of five high-ranking Qing officials. The previous winter, the Qing court had dispatched these officials to tour Japan, Europe, and the United States to investigate various constitutional systems. After approving the report, the Qing government, on 1 September 1906, issued its plan for preparing China for a constitutional polity.

December of that year saw public celebrations of the edict in various cities. In his short story "Celebrating Constitutional Polity" *(Qingzhu lixian)*, Wu Jianren described a large public celebration in which the protagonist jumped onto the podium, warning the audience to remember that the edict allowed only for the preparation and not the actual establishment of the polity. He then questioned the probability of establishing this polity:

> If constitutional government is actually established, the parliament will represent the people. [The parliament] will have legislative authority, and local officials will have only executive authority. If this polity is realized, the officials will have to change from being subordinates of their bosses to being servants of the people. How could they swallow such a humiliation? Wouldn't they prevent your preparation for the [constitutional] polity with all of their might?[92]

The story ended with another character in the audience deriding the protagonist: "How could [he], with equal reverence, wish for the longevity of the constitution and that of the Empress Dowager and the Emperor at the same time? There are no two of the same days in heaven, and there are no two emperors for the same people. This is truly rebellious!" In this short piece, Wu Jianren showed his readers the inherent conflict between a constitutional polity and Qing rulers and officials.[93]

Wu expressed his doubts using evocative visual images: "The people's hope for establishing a national assembly is like Zhang Guo riding his donkey backwards [toward his destination],"[94] and "the government saw the representatives who appealed for the establishment of a national assembly as vicious beggars at the gate."[95] In one of his short futuristic stories, Wu described the government as issuing the edict ordering preparation for a constitution on 13 July in the thirty-second year of Emperor Guangxu, the day of its actual issuance. As the story goes, however, it was not until the ten-thousandth year of Guangxu, an infinite time for mortals, that preparations were finally completed and the constitutional polity established.[96]

Many tabloid articles and anecdotes expressed similar skepticism and sarcasm about the prospects for constitutionalism. Articles in *Grove of Laughter* doubted that China would soon – or, in some cases, ever – adopt such a system.[97] The tabloid press also reported that some Qing officials had obstructed the constitutional process. One such report told how an official working to prepare for a constitution sent a memorial suggesting that the government postpone the inauguration of the national assembly, fearing that people would use their newly gained power only to resist paying taxes.[98]

Tabloid community members also questioned whether a constitutional polity would actually bring power to the people. One writer in *All-Story Monthly* saw that local autonomy could well lead to a concentration of power among local elites and officials, with local people still lacking the right to participate in the political process.[99] Wu Jianren insisted that the qun (collectives, groupings) ought to function on the basis of equality. In the qun, if even one individual has an elevated position, then subservience rather than equality rules. Moreover, Wu argued, there were no qun operating in China that were based on equality.[100] Expressing his frustration, he wrote a story that played with multiple meanings of the word *yifen* (one part):

> I once told others: "I am a member of China *(Zhongguo yifenzi)*." One man there regarded my words as foolish. I looked at the man, who wore a long gown with dignity, with eyeglasses on, showing that he was well educated. I asked him why. He said, "You are only a commoner in China, how can you play a part in China *(hedeyou Zhongguo yifen)*?"[101]

In his parody "Long Live the Constitutional Polity" *(Lixian wansui)*, Wu made it clear that a constitutional polity would bring little change to the people, for those in political power before would remain in power afterward. In Wu's story, the supreme god presided over the world of spirits, monsters, animals, heavenly gods, and immortals, all of whom served as officials in that world. After a long period of investigation, the supreme god finally issued an edict for the preparation of a constitutional polity. This preparation, however, merely resulted in a rearrangement of the government's organizational structures. The supreme god simply made appointments to the newly created government ministries, permitting all existing officials to keep their positions. On learning this news, the officials – including those who had previously opposed the constitutional polity – exclaimed joyfully, "Long live the constitutional polity!" All the assembled animal-officials laughed among themselves, commenting, "It turns out that the constitutional polity only means that titles of some official positions will be changed ... So there is no need for us to worry anymore about our rice bowls."[102]

Actually Liang Qichao began to see problems with the constitutional polity on returning to Japan in 1903 from a trip to America. He now doubted that the Chinese were ready to become responsible citizens endowed with political rights, and questioned the feasibility of a constitutional polity in contemporary China.[103] In February and March 1906, a few months before he ghostwrote the report on constitution polity for the Qing court, Liang published "On Enlightened Autocracy" *(Kaiming zhuanzhilun)* in *Xinmin congbao*, suggesting that a system of "enlightened autocracy" was best for China until the Chinese were ready for a constitutional polity. In his view, "it is suicide for the nation to adopt majority rule" when the people are unqualified as citizens, incapable of bearing the responsibilities required of them. "Today, Chinese can only live under an autocracy, and cannot have freedom."[104] Although Liang identified the key tasks of an enlightened autocracy as enlightening the people and promoting democracy *(xingminquan)*, in the meantime he placed trust in the ruler to govern in the interests of the people and establish a constitutional government.[105]

In contrast with Liang's enlightened autocracy, Wu Jianren developed the idea of "civilized autocracy" *(wenming zhuanzhi)*, which became his ideal model for the future. In his novel *The New Story of the Stone (Xin shitouji)*, serialized in 1907, he first articulated this idea through the voice of the character Old Youth. In Old Youth's view, a constitutional polity, under either a republican or a monarchical government, is problematic and an unsuitable model for the future. A republican government, with its unlimited number of parties, is barbaric in adhering to no single principle, always following the current winning party's policies – just like "remarried loose women" with new husbands. A constitutional monarchy, Old Youth pointed out, also has parties. Moreover:

> Although there are both upper and lower parliamentary houses, only a few have the right to vote and to be elected. Therefore, a polity dominated by royalty turns out to be one dominated by the rich; the rich then will become richer, and the poor will become poorer. The consequence of this will be the emergence of a party that stands for economic equality and hence also for socialism, and then there will be no lasting peace.[106]

Nevertheless, Old Youth conceded, until society became sufficiently civilized, a constitutional polity remained preferable to an enlightened autocracy. He reasoned that even given some evil members of parliament, others might be good, and the latter would be in a position to improve things. In an enlightened autocracy, however, the government rules from the top; even good can do nothing to improve things.

In another story, Wu elaborated on the dangers of a constitutional polity in arguing for his ideal civilized autocracy. In his opinion, a constitutional polity would lead to more local autonomy *(zizhi)*, reduce governmental control over local affairs, and expand the influence of local gentry. To support his argument, Wu pointed to a recent rise in Shanghai rice prices and the Shanghai County magistrate's inability to force rice merchants to lower prices. He argued:

> Local autonomy means some gentry now control local affairs. There are bad gentry who are also bullies, even under an autocratic polity. How much more powerful would they be if we allow them total control? Under an autocratic polity, local officials can punish them; now, as local representatives, nobody will be able to control them. In addition, in an autocratic polity, the government could remove bad local officials; the local gentry, however, would remain forever in one place.[107]

For Wu Jianren, "civilized" *(wenming)* meant "moral," and a civilized society meant a society based on traditional moral values. Once moral education expanded and penetrated every corner of society, once the ruler and the people all acted righteously, then society could abolish the constitutional polity and establish a civilized autocracy. In this autocracy, the ruler would truly govern in the people's interest. This view was encapsulated in a phrase from *Daxue:* "[Regarding public affairs,] prefer what people prefer; reject what people reject."[108]

Like Liang, tabloid writers also expressed frustration with the Chinese people's lack of national devotion and their ignorance of reform. Three months after the Empress Dowager issued the imperial edict announcing preparations for a constitutional polity, Wu Jianren wrote a short story titled "Preparing for the Constitutional Polity" *(Yubei lixian)*, venting these frustrations.[109] In this story, he depicted two characters who saw in the constitutional polity an opportunity to enrich and empower themselves. Commenting on the story, Wu spelled out the gravity of the situation: many Chinese who knew the constitutional issue held the same attitudes as the two characters; many more Chinese were not even aware of the issue at all.

Wu was furious, however, at the suggestion that the people did not deserve a constitutional polity. In his story, the protagonist gave a speech at a public assembly mocking those "self-proclaimed enlightened men" who believed that the Chinese were still unready for a constitutional polity. Likening constitutional polity to a rock, the protagonist reasoned:

> Suppose there is a big rock here and it is necessary that I lift it up. I simply try, rolling up my sleeves, crouching down, using all my strength; but having only succeeded in jerking the rock, I cannot lift it up. So, it would be correct if you had said that I did not have enough strength. If I had never seen this rock before, would it be right for you to say, without any conscience, that I do not have enough strength [to lift it up]? ... Gentlemen, have our Chinese people seen a constitutional polity before? Is it not wrong to accuse us of not being able to handle it?[110]

A sharp difference existed between Liang Qichao and Wu Jianren in their meditations on the problems of a Chinese constitutional polity. Despite his fundamental faith in this polity, Liang was willing to postpone its realization and sacrifice people's political rights in order to build the nation. Wu Jianren did not believe in a constitutional polity at all, but because he distrusted the Qing government, he argued for the immediate realization of this polity at least until Chinese society became civilized. While Liang's faith in a constitutional polity as a future ideal rested on Western-style democratic principles, Wu based his faith in a civilized autocracy on traditional understandings of people's rights. These traditional understandings, he argued, had existed even in the earliest times of Chinese history, in the Xia, Shang, and Zhou periods, and especially in the teachings of Mengzi.[111]

Wu and Liang did have one thing in common: facing late Qing political realities, they both compromised their positions and ironically ended up supporting a constitutional polity. Wu traded his long-term goal of a civilized autocracy for a constitutional polity in the present. Liang, hailed as an expert constitutionalist and ever the political pragmatist, compromised his short-term prescription of enlightened autocracy for his ideal of a constitutional polity. Liang made this compromise in ghost-writing the report to the Qing court and organizing the Political Information Institute *(Zhengwenshe)* in Japan in 1907; the institute soon joined the constitutionalists in Shanghai and became one of the major forces in the constitutional movement.[112]

Movements: The Case of Wu Jianren

Wu Jianren certainly made himself a conspicuous activist in both the Shanghai anti-Russian protests of 1901 and the nationwide anti-American boycott that began in Shanghai in 1905. On both occasions, his public speeches and writings mobilized people to act. His concerns often lay with the fate of ordinary people, and his participation signalled a strong populist attitude.

On 10 May 1905, the Shanghai Chamber of Commerce decided to boycott American goods if the US government failed to revise the Chinese Exclusion Act of 1882. This decision initiated a nationwide boycott that began on 20 July and lasted more than five months. Boycotters demanded that the US treat China as an equal and repeal the unjust law. In Shanghai, organizations of merchants, students, and professionals tried to mobilize support for the boycott by holding public meetings, sharing opinions in Shanghai presses, and sending public letters to authorities. Working in Hankou as editor of the Chinese edition of an American-owned English-language newspaper, Wu answered the boycott call, resigning his job immediately and returning to Shanghai.

On 13 July, he wrote his first letter to Zeng Shaoqing, leader of the movement at the Shanghai Chamber of Commerce, making detailed suggestions for carrying out an effective boycott. On 15 July, he again wrote to Zeng, opposing the Chamber's decision to accept the Qing government's compromise policy. Afraid of offending the US, Foreign Affairs Minister Wu Tingfang intended to negotiate a deal to remove US travel restrictions for Chinese officials, merchants, and students, while neglecting restrictions and discrimination against Chinese workers. Wu Jianren asked Zeng: "So many of these workers [are abroad], aren't all of them of our own race? In addition, officials, merchants, and students only account for a minority of those who go abroad, the majority of them are workers. Mobilizing collective forces nationwide, and only struggling for the rights of a minority, is neither moral nor does it have a heart." Wu urged the Chamber to demand that the government make public its treaty negotiations and allow the public to approve any agreement. If the Chinese government refused, he argued, the Chamber should directly demand that the American government make the negotiations public. After all, the treaty concerned the Chinese people.[113]

Wu sent yet another letter to Zeng Shaoqing, suggesting that the Chamber send activists inland from Shanghai to mobilize the people and expand the boycott nationwide. He put this suggestion into practice by travelling to Ningbo to mobilize boycott activities there.[114] On 22 July, he published an open letter to the Chamber of Commerce, calling on Shanghai merchants to maintain self-respect and carry the fight to the end, and not give up the boycott in the interest of profits.[115] From July to September, he gave numerous speeches at various public assemblies in Shanghai, including the Chamber of Commerce, the Association of Students and Teachers, the Shanghai Books and Press Guild, the Society of Public Loyalty Speech *(Gongzhong yanshuohui)*, the World Society of Chinese Students *(Huanqiu Zhongguo xueshenghui)*, and the Society of People's Mirror *(Renjing xueshe)*, an organization established solely for the movement.[116] Some of these assemblies drew large audiences ranging from several hundred to more than a thousand,[117] testifying to Wu's public reputation. Two years later, the American defence secretary enjoyed a warm welcome in Shanghai, on his way to the Philippines. Wu immediately wrote a short article, "Cries of the Ghost from the Society of People's Mirror" *(Renjing xueshe guikuzhuan)*, mocking Shanghai officials and merchants for holding a banquet for the American, playing the British national anthem in his honour, and presenting him with an honorary plaque. Wu reminded his readers of a martyr of the Society of People's Mirror who sacrificed his life protesting the Chinese Exclusion Act and chided officials and merchants attending the banquet for betraying the martyred hero and for honouring Americans who "enslave" us.[118]

Tabloid writers paid particular attention to the hardships that Chinese workers endured from racial discrimination in the US. Sun Yusheng wrote a preface to the most popular novel on the subject, *Miserable Society (Kushehui)*, published in 1905.[119] Wu Jianren's novella *Apocalyptic Ember (Jieyuhui)* also explored the difficult lives of Chinese workers in America.

Some scholars argue that the anti-American boycott demonstrates that ideas of popular sovereignty were taking root in China as merchants, students, and various professional organizations began to assert themselves and make their voices heard.[120] One of Wu Jianren's fictional characters makes a similar point, suggesting that the movement showed the Qing government the people's political power and influenced its 1906 decision to prepare for constitutional polity.[121] The tabloid press, moreover, made heroes of social underdogs by reporting how Shanghai prostitutes participated in the boycott and by shaming "respectable" Chinese who failed to do their part.

The anti-American boycott marked neither the first nor the last time tabloid writers promoted and participated in Shanghai's popular resistance to foreign aggression. In 1901, when Russia pressed the Qing government to sign a treaty ceding part of Manchuria, Wu Jianren gave many speeches at public meetings – including a rally at Zhang Garden with an audience of over a thousand – calling on the public to organize and to protest the treaty.[122] Wu had realistic expectations and set himself the modest goal of speaking out for social justice; as he pointed out, "if [the protests] achieve nothing else, at least let foreigners know that Chinese people still have their minds and heart for their country."[123]

In *The New Story of the Stone,* Wu described a demonstration against the treaty with Russia, featuring a public speech that asserted the people's right to voice opinions in national politics. The speaker was "a man about twenty years old, yellowish complexion, long hair, looking like someone in deep mourning." He said:

> The government and Russia signed a secret treaty. This is an important issue for the nation. How could a person like me be good enough to speak about this? But I think we are all Chinese; all matters of the nation are our matters.[124]

In 1907, an article in *All-Story Monthly* called all Chinese nationals to follow merchants in protesting Britain's opposition to the Qing government's attempt to monopolize opium sales. According to the article, the Qing government suspended the opium policy in response to Britain's objections. The article charged the British government with interfering in China's domestic affairs and sovereignty, and contributing to "the extermination of Chinese lives." Criticizing the Qing government's conciliatory approach while praising the efforts of the Jiangxi and Shanghai Chambers of Commerce to resist the British, it pleaded with the Chinese people and the Qing government to rally for this cause and for China's survival.[125]

Also in 1907, when the government attempted to secure a British loan to build a railway system in Jiangsu and Zhejiang, elite gentry from the two provinces initiated a series of protests against the loan and appealed to the Qing government not to proceed. Wu Jianren immediately proposed a way to stop the loan: since the Qing government planned to borrow money, people in the two provinces should raise £1.5 million (the amount of the loan) by selling railway securities, thereby eliminating the government's reason for borrowing. Wu praised ordinary people who pawned possessions, saved on food expenditures, and donated wages to a railway fund organized by local interests. He even called on one unnamed rich gentleman to donate half his wealth to the fund, apparently expecting his readers to know the man's identity.[126]

A story in *All-Story Monthly* described a beggar who donated to the railway fund one dollar that he had planned to use to buy a winter coat. The man explained that he became a beggar in Hangzhou after Russian troops took control of the Manchurian railway system, confiscating people's property and possessions and driving six thousand Chinese, including himself, out of their homes. When asked whether he would freeze to death without a winter coat, the beggar reasoned: "To live and die is one's fate. If the railway in Zhejiang is lost to foreigners, I will be pushed to death even if I have a winter coat. It is better to help the fund so that I would have a place to live through the winter." Juxtaposing the Qing foreign minister's plan to borrow the money from Britain with Hangzhou's workers and prostitutes who participated in the fundraising meetings, the author quipped: "That's why the foreign minister is a foreign minister, and workers and prostitutes are workers and prostitutes."[127] Wu openly criticized the government's inability to protect the Chinese, introducing the slogan "A useful people, a useless government."

Wu also wrote a play about the railway affair, *Wu – the Railway Martyr (Wulieshi xunlu)*. In it, he portrayed Wu Gang, an actual student at a Hangzhou railway school, who sacrificed his life to encourage people to protest the loan. A character in the play explained his perception of the crux of the issue: "If [the government] takes the foreign loan, and foreigners come to build the railway in Zhejiang, then they will get all the rights to the railway, which is like giving away all Zhejiang Province to the foreigners. By then, not to mention anything else, you would not even have a slice of land on which to put your feet."[128] Many readers of *All-Story Monthly* also wrote memorial couplets honoring Wu Gang's death.[129] Wu Jianren reprinted a biography of three Zhejiang "martyrs" in his magazine: Wu Gang, an engineer who worked for the Zhejiang railway company, and a teacher in a missionary school. All supposedly died of anger and frustration over China's potential loss of the railway.[130]

Conclusion

In the final analysis, modern Chinese nationalism was the product of foreign imperialist aggression, both real and imagined. The nationalism expressed in the tabloid press, like that expressed by Liang Qichao, was complex, multidimensional, often ambiguous, and in a constant state of flux.

Although the tabloid community showed little anti-foreign sentiment on racial grounds, they did oppose foreign imperialist domination. Barbara Mittler also notes that *Shenbao* writers expressed few anti-foreign or xenophobic attitudes,[131] but she conflates anti-imperialist with anti-foreign and xenophobic, and concludes that *Shenbao* writers were not "anti-imperialist." Mittler further downplays the role of the press in the developing modern Chinese nationalism. She acknowledges the "inherent weakness" in her argument, in which she "reduces nationalism to street nationalism [i.e., nationalist sentiments expressed in street demonstrations]," "reduces street nationalism to xenophobia and anti-imperialism," and limits her analysis to the foreign-owned presses such as *Shenbao*. She argues that Chinese newspapers could not have played a leading role in developing nationalist movements because they could not have instigated or fomented street nationalism. Mittler observes that *Shenbao* reports of the anti-American boycott of 1905 only "rekindled the boycott secondhand" and that Shanghai newspapers failed to make the city a "hotbed of Chinese nationalism." The press served essentially as "an observer rather than a leader, a critic rather than an initiator."[132]

In the case of the tabloid press, however, writers such as Wu Jianren stood at the forefront of various anti-imperialist movements. He used the tabloid press, in addition to his public speeches and organizational activities, to help keep the movements alive. It was through the press that Wu initiated appeals to the authorities, strategized ways of protesting, called for coordination among cities, informed the public of developments, and garnered public support. Moreover, the Shanghai Books and Press Guild, to which Wu belonged, actively participated in anti-imperialist movements by organizing public meetings and demonstrations. Many guild members published timely articles in their papers and magazines, facilitating such movements. Chang Tsun-wu's study of the 1905 anti-American boycott shows that Shanghai newspapers, especially *Shenbao* and *Shibao*, played an active role in keeping the movement alive by reporting news of the boycott and publishing discussions, opinions, and caricatures.[133] Thus, even in terms of Mittler's narrow definition of nationalism, the Shanghai press played a more significant role than she acknowledges.

The tabloid community assimilated much of Liang Qichao's nationalistic rhetoric and discourse on a Chinese nation-state, but they also diverged significantly from his vision of the modern state. Whereas the early Liang Qichao used Western theories of race and ethnicity to advance his political agenda of overthrowing the Qing government, tabloid writers opposed these anti-Manchu ideas and actions. They took issue especially with Liang's notions of "new citizens" and "popular sovereignty." Tabloid literati gave much more credence than Liang to the role of traditional morality in renewing the people. These literati similarly rejected Liang's statist approach to the principle of popular sovereignty, which prioritized the interests of the state over the interests of the people. These writers doubted that the new constitutional polity would benefit ordinary people, a concern that was notably absent from Liang's vision.

Tabloid writers also differed from the reform journalists depicted in Judge's study of *Shibao*. The latter supported a new citizenry similar to that envisioned by Liang and promoted a system of local self-government as part of constitutional reform.[134] Unlike the tabloid literati, these journalists adopted a more

Western-oriented approach, in which traditional values must be reformulated. Their strong faith in the constitutional polity also overrode their concern with the shortcomings of constitutional reform.

The tabloid press shaped and promoted a distinctive type of late Qing nationalism that filtered, reformulated, and rejected Liang Qichao's nationalism. Neither intellectual elites such as Liang nor staunch reformers monopolized the construction of modern Chinese nationalism in the last decades of the Qing Dynasty. In the next chapter, we turn to the tabloid community's views of nationalism's twin: Chinese modernity.

4 Confronting the "New"

Since the mid-nineteenth century, China's efforts to adopt foreign ideas and practices had stirred enormous controversy. During the Tongzhi Restoration (1862-74), the young Emperor Tongzhi and his mother, the Empress Dowager Cixi, the dominant co-regent, attempted to rejuvenate a dynasty weakened by both massive rebellions and the Opium Wars.[1] Court officials hotly debated the adoption of Western knowledge to strengthen China. The 1867 court debate over whether or not the Tongwen Guan, the first government school in the capital to train students in foreign languages, should be expanded to include scientific subjects such as mathematics and astronomy produced mixed results. On the one hand, the Emperor approved the expansion; on the other hand, because of strong opposition, only a few qualified students who wished to earn degrees through government examinations were willing to commit themselves to learning the new scientific subjects. As a result, the expansion of the curriculum occurred mostly in name only. The opposition, believing that "learning from the barbarians" would turn "Chinese into barbarians," rejected Western knowledge altogether.[2] During the entire Restoration period, every step toward adopting Western knowledge met with opposition.

By century's end, however, after thirty or forty years of self-strengthening efforts in which China adopted Western weaponry, machinery, and military technologies, perceptions began to shift. Earlier, most officials and literati opposed the adoption of any Western knowledge at all. Now, few still held that position, and the question was to what degree China should adopt such knowledge. All the political and intellectual forces wanting to strengthen China had become more pragmatic, differing only in their perception of what types of Western knowledge would be best for the country. Yet there remained enormous conflicts and struggles over the late Qing reforms, reforms that broadened China's adoption of Western ideas and practices.

Between 1895 and 1911, waves of reform initiatives swept across China, centred on the Hundred Days' Reform of 1898, Cixi's New Policy program of

1901, and the Constitutional movement of 1906. Chinese began experiencing drastic changes in the world around them, and most described these changes in terms of old and new. Thus they used the terms *xixue* (Western Learning) and *xinxue* (New Learning) to refer to the new-style knowledge, and *zhongxue* (Chinese Learning) and *jiuxue* (Old Learning) to describe traditional Chinese Learning. The term "New Learning" eventually replaced "Western Learning" altogether in the 1900s, when Chinese students went en masse to Japan to study. The contrast between old and new was also reflected in other commonly used terms. Examples include *xinxuetang*, a name for the new-style schools; *xinxuejia*, *xindang*, and *weixindang*, which refer to reformers who promoted the New Learning; and *shoujiudang* and *wangu dang*, which denote conservatives who resisted change. Another term popular at the time was *wenming*, meaning civilization; in the late Qing, it usually connoted enlightenment and modernization, as the words modern *(xiandai)*, modernity *(xiandaixing)*, and modernization *(xiandaihua)* had not yet entered the Chinese lexicon.

Along with reform and changing terminology came an array of debates and discussions in court and in public about China's adoption of Western Learning. Zhang Zhidong, an eminent official representing one of the more moderate forces of reform, coined the well-known term "Chinese Learning for fundamental principles, and Western Learning for practical application" in his 1898 meditation, *Exhortation to Study (Quanxuepian)*. Liang Qichao represented the more extreme side in promoting the New Learning. The attitudes of the tabloid community fell somewhere between Zhang and Liang. The community's views of the "New"– everything new that was then appearing in China–were complex and riddled with tension.

As *Exhortation to Study* clearly demonstrates, Confucian ethics define Zhang Zhidong's sense of China as a nation. He stated: "That sages are sages and China is China are all because of [the cardinal five human relationships]." For him, the hierarchical relationships between ruler and minister, father and son, and husband and wife are absolute principles. Thus, China must preserve the emperor's authority at all costs, the son must be filial, and equality between husband and wife is wrong.[3] Yet Zhang did not oppose adopting Western knowledge. He called for broad reforms modelled on Western practices in areas such as education, law, administration, economics, and science and technology; when the government issued its New Policy, he even supported a constitutional polity. To Zhang, reform meant a Chinese state and society that function more efficiently and competitively through new managerial practices and technologies, so long as Western ethics were not part of the package.

Liang Qichao stood at the other end of the spectrum in his willingness to adopt the New Learning. As discussed in the previous chapter, at least prior to 1902, Liang questioned the suitability of Chinese ethics to a modern world of nation-states. Throughout the last years of the Qing, he believed in the universality of Western political values and put Chinese ethical values on trial. It was not until the Republican period, and especially after the First World War, that he increasingly doubted Western values and acknowledged the importance of Chinese ethics.

Regarding their concerns with China's guiding principles, the essential difference between Zhang Zhidong and Liang Qichao lay in their attitudes toward Confucian ethics. Zhang wanted to continue following Confucian ethics; Liang questioned Confucianism's relevance in a modern Chinese nation-state, preferring to adopt various Western values.

This chapter demonstrates that, compared with Zhang and Liang, the tabloid community assumed a middle-of-the-road attitude. Its members believed in fundamental Confucian ethics but criticized certain of its aspects. The tabloids' shifting emphasis in the early 1900s, from promoting to questioning reform, clearly illustrates this moderate attitude. Initially, when the Old Learning still prevailed, the tabloid writers supported reform and promoted the New Learning. By the early 1900s, as the New Learning's prestige increased relative to the Old Learning, writers increasingly emphasized the danger of losing fundamental Confucian values. Tabloid literati revealed their adherence to the latter by participating in contemporary discussions on Chinese history, women, and marriage. In these discussions, they relied more on Confucian ethics, whereas Liang Qichao and other intellectual elites placed their faith in Western values and yardsticks.

Promoting Reform

Members of the tabloid community initially had mixed perspectives on reform. Many knew little about the newly introduced ideas and regarded reform with suspicion. When Li Boyuan began *Fun* in 1897, he had no new vocabulary to describe China's political situation. He was well aware of the weakening Chinese state: "The nation is getting poorer, people are becoming wearier, literati's morals are decaying, and commerce is becoming less orderly."[4] Words such as *weixin*, or reform, were absent from his lexicon. The short-lived Hundred Days' Reform of 1898 only increased tensions in the tabloid community's perspectives on the New. On the one hand, writers viewed positively many of Emperor Guangxu's reform measures. One writer in 1898, welcoming the Qing court's decision to shrink the government and reduce the number of officials, described Western governments as small, with simpler ranking systems for officials who were well paid and had clearly defined responsibilities. The Qing government's differences from its Western counterparts led it to become a hotbed of corruption, concluded the writer.[5]

On the other hand, community members argued over the Emperor's order to abolish the eight-legged essay style in government examinations. One anecdote mocked "a fatuous teacher" in Anhui Province for clinging to the eight-legged essay despite the Emperor's order. A few days later, the paper published a reader's response to the anecdote. The reader criticized the writer's use of the term "fatuous" and expressed dismay over those who would throw the eight-legged style into the flames. He questioned how the government could abolish eight-legged essays without also abolishing their underpinning, namely, the Four Books.[6]

The ambivalent attitude toward reform was evident in the days after 21 September 1898, the day the Empress Dowager abruptly terminated the Hundred Days' Reform and placed Emperor Guangxu under house arrest. One author, who apparently had not yet heard the news, published an essay on 26 September that supported the Emperor's decision to downsize administration and called for the government to adopt the more efficient ways of Western governments.[7] Eight days later, a two-part article unequivocally supported Cixi's decision to abort the reform and warned that Western Learning would endanger the Chinese way of life. The author listed all the foreign ways that attracted Chinese people – from clothing, food, and recreational activities to Western science and technology – and bemoaned how quickly Chinese had fallen under the sway of Western influences. He conceded that China still had to learn foreign ways in order to fight against them, but: "Reform should only be a strategy to make China strong: it is not meant to change China; it is only meant to change the way it does things, and to learn the tricks of the Western countries."[8] Many writers still supported Emperor Guangxu and his reform. One asserted that foreigners were incapable of changing the deeply rooted ethics of Chinese culture, so Chinese need not fear learning and adopting Western technology.[9]

Seemingly unaware of the rift between Empress Dowager Cixi and Emperor Guangxu, the tabloid community supported both rulers and attacked reformers instead. One reader defended the Empress Dowager's order to provincial governors that banned and punished the editors-in-chief of all newspapers supporting Kang Youwei and Liang Qichao. The reader explained that, over the previous two years, Emperor Guangxu had recognized the positive role played by newspapers in Western societies and thus promoted the publication of Chinese newspapers. He further described how the public had come to view newspapers as a source of knowledge and a vehicle of enlightenment.

Nevertheless, he criticized reform newspaper editors, especially those in Tianjin, Shanghai, and Hankou, for betraying the Emperor's trust and the public's expectations. Calling these editors "dregs of men of letters," he accused them of slander and of acting irresponsibly.[10]

Many readers vehemently attacked Kang Youwei and Liang Qichao, both of whom had fled overseas to escape the Empress Dowager's crackdown on reformers immediately after the Hundred Days' Reform. One long essay accused Kang of "hideous crimes" and questioned his ideas and knowledge about the New Learning. It called Kang a devious renegade who, in the name of Confucianism, advocated a faulty blend of Western and Eastern teachings, thus blaspheming the Chinese classics. The essay labelled Kang's *Meditations on Confucius' Reform (Kongzi gaizhikao)* a total distortion of the classical texts and teachings of the sages. Ridiculing Kang's self-promotion as a sage of the New Learning, it claimed that he based his so-called knowledge on a few books brought to China by foreign merchants and on fragmented information from newspapers published by Westerners in China. Since Kang could not read any Western language, he could not possibly understand Western society or distinguish between what was good and bad about Western Learning. The essay argued: "Kang's writings to his followers, and his petitions to the emperor for reform, were merely frivolous rhetoric and propaganda, and contained nothing original. He contributed nothing to reform but empty talk and writing." It lamented that a fraud such as Kang had gained such notoriety by simply bashing traditional teachings.

This same essay enumerated Kang's crimes against the government. Kang allegedly conspired with supporters at the imperial court, persuading the Emperor to banish Kang's opponents. He abused the trust of the Emperor, who gave him the responsibility for establishing a government newspaper. Instead, Kang took the opportunity to build his own clique, vilifying those who disagreed with him. The essay then promoted the rumour that Kang had bribed the Emperor's chamberlain to feed the Emperor a poisonous elixir that Kang had presented to the Emperor as a gift and that supposedly worsened the Emperor's health. To the writer, Kang deserved a punishment more severe than decapitation; he suggested that authorities ban, even burn, Kang's books, and concluded by demanding that Kang's followers who identified themselves with the New Learning repent their mistakes. The editor, Li Boyuan, followed the essay with a note stating that he had received the essay two days earlier and had published it faithfully in its entirety, as the writer had instructed. He added that an imperial edict had already provided information about Kang's criminal activities and had ordered the banning and destruction of Kang's books.[11]

Sun Yusheng joined in attacking Kang Youwei. He invited *Anecdotes* readers to submit ideas on how best to capture the fugitives Kang and Liang Qichao, and promised to publish the submissions. Many readers responded, displaying a knack for humour and literary playfulness, and Sun compiled the large number of high-quality responses into a booklet that he later published.[12]

The content of the tabloids in 1897 and 1898 shows clearly that writers and readers had very mixed feelings about reform. In these early years, the tabloid press was more concerned with prostitutes and flower elections than with reform. Thus, when Empress Dowager Cixi ordered the punishment of newspaper editors-in-chief, tabloid editors did not feel threatened. By 1899, however, the tide turned as anecdotes criticizing anti-reform officials began to appear. One such anecdote described an anti-reform grand official's reaction to news that Cixi had expressed interest in selected ideas of Kang Youwei and his followers. The official admitted almost losing his job when the Emperor had called for reform the previous year, and now he had no idea about his future since Cixi appeared to have changed her mind about Kang and Liang.[13] Writers became even more daring as they advertised and sold reformers' written works out of their own newspaper offices. Liang Qichao's memoir of the Hundred Days' Reform of 1898 and his new journal, *Qingyibao*, published in Japan, were sold from the office of *Anecdotes*. The office of *Fun* sold a reformer's newspaper published in Macau.[14] The writers sold the reformers' works in 1899, about the time that the Empress Dowager offered monetary rewards for the capture of Kang Youwei and Liang Qichao, and forbade anyone to buy or read Liang's *Qingyibao*.

As we saw in Chapter 2, in 1899, the tabloid community began to attack officials for their opposition to reforms and their inability to lead China to a better future. In 1900, writers displayed strong support for reform, defending Emperor Guangxu when Empress Dowager Cixi attempted to force him to abdicate. One reader expressed sympathy and support for the Emperor's reform plans, but carefully said nothing against the Empress Dowager.[15] Praising Guangxu's reform policies, another reader explained that people loved him because they believed his reforms would benefit them.[16] On the same day, another article reported that more than thirteen hundred Shanghai officials and merchants had signed a petition to the Empress Dowager to rescind her plan to remove Guangxu.

By 1901, when the Empress Dowager began endorsing reform, anti-reform voices virtually disappeared from the tabloid press, as they did nationwide. Responding to Cixi's call for reform, and in the face of increasing foreign encroachment in China, literati in general accepted the New Learning as necessary. In 1902, Yan Fu observed that many young men, especially those in their thirties with solid classical education and various levels of government degrees, wanted to go abroad to study the New Learning.[17] Many officials now actively promoted this new body of knowledge; they read books about Western political systems, helped operate new-style schools, and even went abroad to study.[18] In 1901, an estimated 274 Chinese students were enrolled in Japan; by 1904, this number had jumped almost tenfold, to 2,400. The three-year period from 1905 to 1907 saw 8,000, 12,000, and 10,000 Chinese students in Japan, respectively.[19] Topics such as how best to reform and rejuvenate China were hotly debated everywhere. A new intellectual environment took shape, in which the New was equated with the good and useful, the Old with backwardness. The tabloid press, the voice of low- and middle-ranked literati, also participated in the reform choir.

In typical manner, the tabloid writers poked fun at those who resisted change and who acted awkwardly, stupidly, or obstinately in the changing environment. One story made fun of such a person:

> A pedant was enraged, because his means of living as a teacher of Chinese Learning was threatened by the changes in the school systems. So, he wrote an antithetical couplet that is quite humorous. [The first part of the couplet is] "Big school, little school, neither too big nor too little – middle school; learn to change style of dressing, learn to cut queues, and learn to become half man and half devil." [The second part of the couplet is] "Teachers of Chinese Learning, teachers of Western Learning, neither Chinese nor Western – Chinese teachers; teach freedom, teach revolution, teach people to respect neither rulers nor fathers."[20]

Besides anecdotes, many novels were published in *Illustrated Fiction* and *All-Story Monthly*, directing scorn and sarcasm at those who were considered obstacles to reform. These novels included *A Brief History of the Evolution of China (Zhongguo jinhua xiaoshi)* by Yanshi Goutu and Li Boyuan's *A Brief History of the Enlightenment (Wenming xiaoshi)*.

In 1903, one writer expressed dissatisfaction with the pace of reform by describing the political terrain as follows:

> Some observers of the current situation regarded the politics at the imperial court, during the Reform of 1898 and during the Boxer movement, as a struggle between the reform party and the conservative party. However, neither of the two parties was unified. Among the conservatives, people divided into their own cliques and factions, while the reformers had different reform proposals,

changed them frequently, and believed they knew the correct path to reform
... After the Reform of 1898, reformers almost disappeared from the political
scene. Now, only a few had started to raise their voice for reform, but they
were cautious, slow, and content with the little that they had done.[21]

The New Learning became a source of admiration and inspiration, not only for its practical use in science and technology but also increasingly for its political, social, and cultural usefulness. One writer tried to explain China's limited success in learning from the West. In his view, China's learning was limited only to Western technology and science; the Qing government had prevented Chinese students at new-style schools from learning Western ideas about political and legal systems, and individual rights and freedoms.[22]

Li Boyuan supported the reform of the Chinese justice system, as evidenced by his novel *Living Hell (Huodiyu),* in which he exposed problems in the Chinese legal system and described the struggles between the new and the old over legal reform. In one of his stories, an old official supporting the "Old" school argued with a young member of the Imperial Academy who supported the "New" school. The old character opposed the court's intent to reform laws, warning that such reform along the lines of Western laws would lead to chaos and rebellion. The younger character rebutted the elder's argument by listing the benefits of legal reform. Li made his position clear in a third character, who found the older official's opinions ridiculous, denouncing him as a hypocrite.[23] Wu Jianren displayed frustration over a high-ranking official's complaint to the Ministry of Foreign Affairs that ideas of equality and freedom were heretical.[24] Another writer addressed the need for the government to send officials abroad to investigate how various other worthy rulers governed.[25]

Tabloid magazines regularly published translations and adaptations of Western historical fiction that described Western nations' development of political and social systems. The inaugural issues of *Illustrated Fiction* and *All-Story Monthly* published, in installments, *The Story of Western History (Taixi lishi yanyi)* and a translation of *An Abridged History of American Independence (Meiguo dulishi biecai),* respectively. Another important piece of translated fiction was *Wandering Afar (Hanmanyou),* the story of an Englishman who drifted on the sea from nation to nation, observing native political and social systems and comparing them with those of his own country. The translator described disapprovingly the political system of one unnamed nation where people had no rights, as well as England's social system, where the rich remained idle, enjoying the fruits of the labour of the poor.

Readers and writers also viewed customs such as footbinding, superstitious practices, and opium smoking as obstacles to progress, and joined the many campaigns to eradicate them. The tabloid community joined in anti-footbinding campaigns only after the nationwide campaigns had already peaked between 1895 and 1898.[26] Articles condemning the practice began to appear in 1899, as poems about the beauty of courtesans' small feet began to disappear. At first, writers criticized footbinding mainly as cruel treatment of women. One writer composed a ballad depicting the harm footbinding brought to women. He described the pain girls suffered at the age of five and six when their mothers began to bind their feet, and detailed how bound feet hampered women's daily lives, even endangering their ability to survive floods and bandit raids.[27]

When Li Boyuan became editor-in-chief of *Illustrated Fiction* in 1903, he viewed footbinding, superstition, and opium smoking in light of the Old and the New, backwardness and enlightenment. In *Awakening the Society (Xingshiyuan)*, a *tanci* piece addressed mainly to women, he revealed how footbinding handicapped women physically and how superstition handicapped them mentally:

[Chinese history] covers several thousands of years, from its beginning to the present, and the old customs have been passed down ever since. It is not surprising that foreigners laugh at us for being the Big and Old nation, incapable of reform. Such a reputation is really shameful; it is extraordinary that nobody in the empire [can do anything about it]. They say that people [in other nations] know how to reform, so that they can progress daily in attaining enlightenment and in enjoying peace. They mock us for being stubborn and for keeping to the old ways, for accepting the Old and ignoring the New. In addition, black smoke [i.e., opium] prevents men of purpose from acting, and footbinding confines women's bodies; half of the 400,000,000 people are religious. Alas, women really do not live like humans.[28]

Li's *A Brief History of Enlightenment (Wenming xiaoshi)* featured a son telling his mother that foreigners considered half the Chinese population as useless because of their bound feet.[29] In June 1905, *Fun* published a long serialized essay announcing the establishment of a society for eradicating footbinding. The author dismissed all opposing arguments, including the belief that it would weaken women, make them less attractive and eligible for marriage, and harm those who subsequently unbound their feet. Abolishing footbinding, he insisted, was good for women, for families, and for the nation.[30]

Wu Jianren, however, abhorred such popular clichés as "women are the mothers of the nation, not men's toys," "men and women have equal rights," and "women should be independent." The protagonist in one of his novels declared that these statements were not altogether wrong, but they were too high-minded and facile. For Wu, footbinding was as much a matter for men as for women. If men no longer fetishized small feet, women would no longer bind them, and this cruel custom would eventually end.[31]

Many anecdotes in the tabloids and in novels serialized in magazines criticized practices that writers deemed superstitious.[32] Chinese worshipped all kinds of deities and ghosts; they built pagodas and temples; and they sought help from Buddhist monks, fortunetellers, shamans, and Daoist "doctors." They practised *fengshui* and relied on horoscopes in matchmaking. Writers especially targeted women, in both high and low social circles, as being susceptible to superstition. Women frequented Buddhist temples and became enamoured of Buddhist monks. One anecdote described a superstitious woman who scolded her son at the dinner table simply for saying, "Mother I can't see you, and you can't see me" when he hid his eyes behind a rice bowl.[33] The writer felt no need to explain why the woman disliked her son's words. Readers apparently understood that the woman thought these words unlucky because they suggested a separation by death.

Writers tried to persuade readers to abandon superstitious practices. One outlined his purpose at the beginning of his novel:

Readers, [you] should know, the biggest obstacle to China's progress is superstition ... westerners stand on solid ground and rely on experimentation instead of illusion. [They] destroyed all belief in deities, ghosts, demons and phantoms. They can investigate the skies, navigate the seas, open up mountains, and build roads. They can measure everything; they can do everything. By so doing, they can strengthen their races and protect their nations. Therefore, to save China, we must start by reforming our customs.[34]

Wu Jianren went even further in one of his novels, explaining why it is foolish to believe in ghosts and spirits. An insightful female character recounted that ancient kings created the Way of the spirits only to better control the minds, and hence the behaviours, of uneducated people. Without this, laws were inadequate for effective rule. She then explained that nothing exists after death, and that the practice of ancestor worship merely enables people to remember their roots and encourages them to be filial and kind to deceased ancestors.[35] Li Boyuan similarly suggested that ancient kings and sages created the Way of the spirits in order to control people more easily. That is why, he explained, rulers always allowed local governments to build temples and shrines. These customs have little effect, as floods, droughts, and wars occur anyway. As Li pointed out, Taiwan and the Bay of Shandong lay in the hands of foreigners despite the Qing government's approval of the construction of several temples and shrines there.[36]

As we have seen, tabloid writers supported a broad range of reform measures. They not only embraced Western science and technology but also favoured Western-inspired reforms in constitutional polity, law, and various social and cultural practices. As late Qing reform deepened, however, and the New Learning increasingly altered fundamental Chinese ethics and ways of life, writers began to voice opposition to the blind acceptance of New Learning and Western values as good and enlightened.

Questioning Reform

The association of the New Learning with good and the Old Learning with bad came about relatively quickly. Intellectual elites such as Liang Qichao and Kang Youwei were instrumental in developing the discourse that enabled the shift in attitude. In order to legitimize and promote the New Learning, they deployed the terms "enlightened" and "barbarous" to draw a sharp contrast between the West and China. In 1898, Kang Youwei used these terms in his fifth memorial to Emperor Guangxu. He described how China lost face in the Sino-Japanese War of 1894-95 and how the "enlightened" West despised China, treated Chinese as "barbarians," and dismissed them as dimwitted and stubborn.[37] In an 1899 article, Liang Qichao outlined three stages of social evolution from barbarism to enlightenment, similar to the three stages identified by some Western scholars: barbaric, semi-civilized, and civilized. After providing detailed definitions of the three stages, Liang claimed that it was clear where China stood: China was a semi-civilized society.[38]

The elites' new vocabulary for describing China and the West seeped into the popular press around 1901. In the tabloids, frequent use of the word "enlightenment" appeared as early as 1901; the description of China as barbaric followed in 1902. Writers, in fact, regarded many aspects of Chinese life as barbaric, from its polity to its everyday practices. For example, concerning men's queues, one writer observed that students began to cut their queues once they went abroad to study, although the government forbade them to do so. The writer saw in this trend an indication that the enlightened world, symbolized by the New Learning, would soon replace the barbarous world, symbolized by queues.[39] The sharp contrast between the good West and the bad China came to be seen as increasingly self-evident and part of popular rhetoric. One 1902 piece in *Hangzhou Baihuabao* expressed this frame of mind most bluntly and succinctly: "Because the Old Learning is not good, [we] wish to build a New Learning; because the old knowledge is not good, [we] wish to build a new knowledge. To put it in one sentence, because the old China is not good, [we] wish to build a new China."[40]

This general acceptance of the New Learning was not merely an intellectual one. The Qing government sanctioned various reforms to promote the New Learning, including building new-style schools and sending Chinese students abroad to study. Most importantly, in 1902, the government formally changed the format of government examinations, requiring examinees to display knowledge of the New Learning in their essays on China's political economy. By 1905, when the Qing abolished the examination system, the Old Learning simply ceased to be the dominant means of personal advancement.[41] Thus, for ambitious individuals, acceptance of good New Learning over bad Old Learning was essential to furthering their careers.

There arose in the tabloid community an acute awareness of and uneasiness with the rapid changes taking place. One reader revealed this awareness by listing eight "oddities" in Chinese society that he deemed laughable:

1) One does not know what today's date is in the Chinese and Western calendars. 2) One speaks using a mixture of Chinese and Japanese words. 3) Today, one visiting official examines schools; tomorrow, another visiting official inspects the police. 4) In less than one year the new-style schools are everywhere in China. 5) Recent Chinese newspapers refer to Japan at the same time as they talk about America and European nations. 6) Some Japanese promote reform in customs and language. 7) One wears foreign-style clothing while greeting others with hands crossed at front of the chest.[42] 8) Chinese military officials who go to Japan for military training cannot ride a horse.[43]

Tabloid writers became increasingly alarmed by what they saw as a trend in blind and indiscriminate promotion of the New Learning. Although writers eagerly adopted anything foreign that would help make China a strong nation, they saw no need to toss out Confucian ethics in order to regenerate China. The editor of *Fun*, commenting in 1901 on a reader's letter to another newspaper, complaining that publishers translated too few books on foreign ethics, retorted: "Why do you want to throw out the sages' teachings that we already have and adopt foreign books? ... After all, foreign knowledge is only for non-essential things." For this editor, China did not lack enlightenment

– if anything, many Chinese were *too* enlightened as they valued foreign ethics over Chinese ones.[44] In 1902, one writer expressed shock at seeing how reformers, who supposedly understood current affairs, wanted to rely on translated Western and Eastern books about ethics and matters of conscience. He asked how it was even thinkable that the sages' teachings were no longer a standard. For him, the teachings of the sages ought to be the standard in these matters, and children's education ought to begin with the old Three-Word Classics and Thousand-Word Texts.[45]

From 1903 onward, voices opposing the headlong rush to reform grew louder and louder. One author saw madness in those Chinese who worshipped everything foreign. For him, those people seemed to believe that "the moon in the West is rounder" and that "the foreigners' fart is fragrant."[46] Both Li Boyuan and Wu Jianren published novels with protagonists who opposed blind adoption of the New Learning and senseless rejection of the Old Learning. Li complained of one writer who dismissed the literature of the past, such as the *Monkey King*, as old-fashioned, remarking: "Old-fashioned, old-fashioned, these words have recently become the catch phrase of the reformers. Ever since they began to use these words habitually, they also began to let down most of the sages' teachings."[47] Li's *A Brief History of Enlightenment* displayed this shift in attitude; here he initially supported constitutionalism but then attacked it harshly, pointing out its problems toward the novel's end.[48] In Wu Jianren's novel, *Touring Shanghai*, a hero warned:

> But one should know that things suitable for some people may not be suitable for others. From important topics such as national politics to children's toys, those things that are suitable in foreign countries and then introduced in China should be adopted only if they fit our customs. Not everything foreign is suitable for us.[49]

For Wu, youths tended to become enthralled by the power of Western nations, convinced that such power came from being enlightened. These youths, however, knew little about those nations and read few ancient books from their own nation.[50] Wu wrote: "I see that [Chinese] society is in crisis today; it cannot be maintained without a quick restoration of our own ethics. It is not as if improvement and reform can be achieved simply by talking about importing enlightenment."[51] Wu Jianren was well aware of the criticism that traditional ethics granted individuals, especially women, no freedom. In *Touring Shanghai*, however, he had his hero explain that the sages' teachings had been badly distorted:

> Confucians of the Song Dynasty were too hard on people. They always talked about natural principles and human desires, and said that those who conform to natural principles cannot have human desires, and those who have human desires cannot have principles. Without principles, a person becomes mean. Think about it, you, how can a person have no desires? Even if one is not fond of sex and of material wealth, one must want food and clothing. To have a full stomach and keep warm are exactly human desires. But the scholars say, "It is a small matter to die of hunger; it is a large matter to lose one's integrity." So, people, whether they turn left or right, are unable to be noblemen; they, therefore, instead tend to be mean. You think about it, does this not show the wrongs and arrogance of the Song Confucians? The sages teach us that we are moral as long as we do our best in everyday life and in dealing with relationships. Are [the sages] as severe as those [Song Confucians]?[52]

In Wu's view, "traditional ethics" referred to ancient values as they were before later Confucian scholars corrupted them. For example, the moral philosophy of medieval periods stressed the moral responsibility of officials to the ruler, Wu argued, and neglected the moral responsibility of the ruler to his subordinates. Consequently, the ruler became increasingly autocratic in Chinese history.[53]

Wu Jianren also defended the Old Learning on the grounds of the New Learning. Responding to concerns that Chinese ethics had little to say about new terms such as societal ethics *(shehui daode)*, group *(qun)*, and nation, Wu argued that the teachings of such classics as the *Daxue* actually held the same values as these new terms.[54] In one short essay, he even argued that Mencius expressed the idea of people's rights.[55] Wu confessed in 1908: "I am often in conflict with others. While they want to promote new enlightenment, I want to restore our own ethics."[56] Yet he stated repeatedly that this promotion of Chinese ethics did not mean he opposed change. Wu expressed this best: "I am frustrated with conservatives who regard the New Learning as a rebellion against the Chinese way and with those who learn superficially a little bit of Western Learning and then reject the Chinese classics at will."[57]

Tabloid writers certainly moved from their earlier reformist outlook to a more conservative one, especially after 1903. This move, however, represented more a shift in emphasis than a complete break from their early position. In the early years, drastic reforms had yet to unfold and the tabloid community did not fully understand the impact of reforms that, in its view, would threaten traditional Confucian ethics. The pro-reform forces were on the defensive in their struggles with the conservative forces that resisted change. The tabloid community thus supported reforms and attacked the conservatives. All along, however, its members embraced new ideas and practices, as long as those ideas did not infringe on fundamental Chinese ethics. In later years the community grew increasingly concerned with the erosion of Chinese ethics due to the New Learning, and began to emphasize the negative sides of reform. One fictional character explained: "I want to promote education in [Chinese] moral values, but this does not mean that I hold on to the Old Learning stubbornly. I just hope that we first become a moral society, and then adopt the enlightenment from foreign countries. By then Chinese moral values cannot be weakened and there will be only benefits and no harm."[58]

Tabloid writers cast a critical look at Confucian ethics from the perspective of the New Learning. They saw that traditional moral values did not contradict the new ideas and practices they favoured. For them, the ancient sages never advocated autocracy, and thus constitutional reform was in accord with the Confucian relationship between rulers and the ruled. While valuing Confucian family relationships, they acknowledged abuses in Chinese family life in light of the New Learning. Tabloid writers used the New Learning not to discredit Chinese ethics but to defend them. In contrast, Liang Qichao and many intellectual elites used the New Learning as a yardstick to measure Chinese wrongs. We turn now to the different yardsticks that Liang Qichao and Wu Jianren employed in their perspectives on writing history.

On Writing History

Liang Qichao was the first to bring up the idea of writing a new type of history as a way to renew China. From late 1899 to late 1902, he promoted "revolutions" in literature and history, seeing traditional poetry and fiction as unfit for a new China. Liang called for the use of new vocabularies, such as "republic, representative, freedom, equal rights," in old-style poetry to reflect a new spirit and meaning of the times. He urged poets to promote "the true European spirit and thought" and to prepare for "the coming revolution."[59] Liang proposed a similar reform in fiction, which I will discuss in Chapter 6.

Liang developed most of his ideas about writing history in his treatise "New Historiography" *(Xinshixue)*. As Tang Xiaobing points out, Liang's theory of history was based entirely on the enlightenment tradition. For Liang, the discipline of history should nurture nationalism, patriotism, and the collective welfare. He noted that Europeans have "a well-developed nationalism and have progressed daily in enlightenment" due to their approach to history.[60] Liang also argued that the study of history should assume that historical evolution was linear, as did Westerners.[61] In its two thousand years, he observed, China had accumulated a huge volume of historical writings, but they were not real histories as they demonstrated little progress over the years and failed to benefit the nation. Using a Western yardstick, Liang elaborated on the failure of Chinese history writing:

> First, [history writing] concerns itself only with dynasties, not the nation. The History of the Twenty-Four Dynasties is not history, but merely genealogies of twenty-four families ... Second, it concerns itself only with individuals, not groups. History becomes a stage for heroes ... Third, it concerns itself only with the deeds of the past, not the tasks of the present. Should history writing serve to commemorate dead and irrelevant people? [Should it] record certain past events as would a playwright? No, history should instruct and benefit the people of today ... Fourth, it only concerns itself with facts, not ideals ... The spirit of history consists of ideals.

Liang listed six problems of Chinese history writing, including its descriptive rather than analytical style. Commenting on *Comprehensive Mirror to Aid in Government (Zizhi tongjian)*, Liang called it the best analytical history written in China. "But today, using the eyes of Western readers of history, [I] feel that only 20 or 30 percent of the book is useful."[62] Liang was not alone in his views of Chinese history. Zhang Binglin also regarded Chinese historical writing as descriptive and lacking analysis; historians of the past, he argued, largely ignored psychology, society, and religion, areas important for any "history of enlightenment."[63]

When Wu Jianren advised readers on how to understand his historical novel *Change of Heart (Qingbian)*, he seemed to be directly responding to intellectual elites such as Liang and Zhang. In the preface, he told his readers:

> Use Chinese eyes, not foreign eyes, to read it; listen with Chinese, not foreign, ears ... Recently there has existed a type of people who praise everything foreign: foreigners' farts are even fragrant, but Confucius of China is foolish; foreign dogs are all good, but Chinese heroes are mean; they either admire George Washington or Napoleon, but as for Zhang Suiyang and Yue Wumu, they cannot care less; even foreigners' hypnosis belongs to psychology, but Chinese oracles are absurd. Isn't this type of person born with a pair of foreign eyes and ears?[64]

Wu also took a critical stance toward Chinese historical writing, but with an entirely different emphasis and from an entirely different perspective: unlike Liang, who dismissed Chinese historical writing as useless to national progress, Wu saw the problem as one of making history accessible to a broad public. Perhaps aware of the six problems in history writing that Liang enumerated, Wu offered his own six problems that accounted for the poor reception historical writing had experienced in the past:

> First, the content is complicated and hard to remember. Second, the writings are difficult to read, and without notes and explanations, only the learned are able to understand. Third, the massive number of history books overwhelms people. Fourth, one's energy and time is limited. Fifth, children, in their elementary education, start with brief and general histories which are no fun, which makes children from an early age regard history as boring. Sixth, before becoming educated, they turn into adults. Even if they want to study they then have no time for it.[65]

Wu's solution was to use historical fiction and narrative as a way to teach history. He wanted to improve historical writing by making it easier and more fun to read, rather than more analytical and accessible only to scholars. Yet Wu also wanted historical novels to be educational and close to historical realities. He tried out his ideas in several historical novels. In his *Painful History (Tongshi)*, he told of the loss of China to the Jin and Mongol invaders during the Song and Yuan dynasties. Through the voice of his protagonist, Wu called for patriotism, suggesting that if everyone in the country exercised their patriotic will, the nation would be indestructible. In *The History of Two Jin Dynasties (Liangjin yanyi)*, Wu claimed that he remained as faithful as possible to historical facts.[66]

Wu paid close attention to veracity in history. He repeatedly warned that one should not entirely trust the ancients. A hero in one of his novels suggested that many made-up facts and purposeful distortions and omissions existed in ancient classical histories.[67] To Wu, texts by authors of questionable integrity could not be trusted either. Ming official Qian Qianyi was such an author; Qian wrote a treatise criticizing others as traitors to the country while he himself surrendered to the Manchu Qing regime. Wu stated: "Alas, from now on I will read history with different eyes. Those ancients who talked superciliously about loyalty and righteousness, but who never suffered anything from life ... I do not believe they could act out what they believe and promote."[68] Wu's concern with veracity in history was never shared by Liang Qichao. Dissatisfied as he was with Chinese historical writing, the issue entirely escaped Liang's attention. Perhaps his Western-centred perspective shaped his focus on historical writing as furthering the nation and its enlightenment and made him less worried about its veracity.

Relying more on Western yardsticks, intellectual elites also differed from tabloid writers on issues concerning social morality, such as Confucian family relationships, especially the roles of women and marriage.

On Social Morality

As discussed in Chapter 3, Liang Qichao wanted to rely on Western civic values to transform Chinese into citizens. Tabloid writers, on the other hand, saw the social morality embedded in Confucian teachings as essential to preparing citizens for a new nation. After 1901, these writers became increasingly aware of the negative social impacts of new ideas and practices. They especially viewed the New Learning as a threat to traditional moral values relating to women, family, love, and marriage – values they considered fundamental to China's well-being.

Ever since the tabloids emerged in 1897, the tabloid community had complained about women's transgressions. Women showed up in public places where they did not belong. Concubines, often from squalid brothels, wandered freely in crowded public places, enjoying themselves at theatres and Western-style restaurants.[69] Women from good families attended obscene theatre performances wearing fancy dresses and colourful makeup. These occasions provided opportunities for women to develop illicit relations with opera actors.[70] Even in private homes, women of leisure spent time playing mahjong with male friends, potentially cheating on their husbands.[71]

Writers responded directly to the new concepts of "freedom" and "family revolution" used by some reformers to advocate the loosening of restraints on traditional family relationships. They completely rejected the concept of "family revolution," worrying that the term would destroy all moral values governing family relationships. In a story, Li Boyuan described a so-called reformer who called for a "family revolution," since in his eyes reform began with the family. This reformer chose a wife from Shanghai, believing that, of all the women in China, only those from Shanghai were enlightened. Presumably, Shanghai women knew about equality and freedom and socialized with men naturally, without shyness. Comments attached to the end of the story (presumably Li's) observed: "Alas, women are considered as enlightened because they have no sense of shyness when meeting men. There exist, then, quite a lot of enlightened women in Shanghai!" Li then derided the reformer's refusal to marry a woman chosen by his parents, along with his acceptance of foreign ideas.[72]

In typical satirical fashion, tabloid writers mocked those who followed the New Learning and tried to import Western customs and family values to China. One anecdote told of a man who greeted his sister-in-law on his return from abroad. "Intoxicated by Europeanization," and "taking after the Western custom," he attempted a kiss. The sister-in-law, shocked and frightened, scolded him. Equally appalled, the man told others, "Women in my family are quite barbaric."[73] Another of Li Boyuan's stories vividly described a confrontation between a high-ranking official and his son who had just returned from Japan on summer vacation. The son wore Western-style clothes and had a goatee, but no queue. Embarrassed, the father advised his son not to meet anyone important before changing his attire and growing back his queue. The son rebuffed his father for being "stubborn and barbaric." Strong words passed between them: "You rebel, you rebel, you treat me like this, as though you are not my son, but I have become your son." The son replied, "Based on nominal relations, you and I are father and son. Based on rights, you and I are equal. You know the custom in England, once a son is 21 years old, he is independent of his parents. I am now 24 years old; can you still repress me? ... It will be wonderful to have a family revolution."[74]

In a more straightforward manner, Wu Jianren expressed disgust with what he saw as disintegrating family values. In one story, he portrayed an official who refused to allow his grandfather, visiting from his hometown, to stay in his house in the capital. The commentator, presumably Wu, observed:

> Alas, I have seen so many strange things in families; these almost have become the rule rather than the exception! The strangest of them all is that those who have no morality and no regard for their family members are the ones who talk daily about the moral values of filial piety, loyalty, compassion *(ren)* and righteousness.[75]

In another story, Wu argued that those calling for a family revolution were actually promoting a kind of barbaric freedom, and condemned those who dismissed ancient teachings as barbaric.[76]

As for the concept of freedom, writers did not reject it per se, but they saw the notion as being widely abused and regarded many practices in its name as "excessive freedom." In one fantasy, several deities discussed problems of the human world. Some lamented that many young people wantonly practised so-called marriage freedom in the name of enlightenment, rather than adhering to traditional marriage customs. Even the Deity of Freedom disapproved this behaviour, warning: "Freedom has its boundaries. Today some naive youths behave badly in the name of freedom. Conservatives, seeing that these youths stray from Confucian principles, blame freedom for the problem ... Do [these youths] really love freedom or are they trying to destroy freedom?"

The Deity of Marriage worried that "divorce" would become a catch phrase among the youth.[77]

A great deal was written about love and marriage, perhaps in reaction to Shanghai women who increasingly rejected traditional proprieties. In *Change of Heart*, Wu Jianren painted a negative portrait of a woman who abandoned her marriage. Another writer portrayed a woman who, after marrying a man of her own choosing, became dissatisfied and found another lover. Although the author described the husband as morally despicable, he struck his strongest blow at the woman: "A woman without virtue is like a prostitute searching for a patron, who considers every man her man. Such is the result of enlightenment."[78] As for polygamy, Wu Jianren cautioned: "As to the solution to this problem [of polygamy], the most urgent and important task for China is to educate people [in proper behaviour]. A rush to promote freedom in marriage is not the solution."[79]

Tabloid writers indeed acknowledged a range of abuses in traditional family life. Much of the fiction and drama in *All-Story Monthly* criticized the mistreatment of women. The views expressed in this literature showed that writers too were influenced by new ideas concerning family relationships. One writer denounced "the barbaric and dictatorial marriage system" in which parents alone chose marriage partners for their sons and daughters.[80] Another writer attacked the traditional "three submissions and four virtues" *(sancong side)* code of behaviour for women for denying them access to knowledge, cutting them off from contacts beyond family circles, and causing them to assume the personality of slaves.[81] These opinions, published in the mid-1900s, reflected a markedly different attitude toward women from those expressed in the late 1890s.

Similarly, under the influence of the New Learning, the tabloid press promoted education for women. One author wanted to transform "200,000,000 Chinese women into full citizens." He suggested that enlightened women could in turn enlighten men: a wife could open the mind of any husband, no matter how ignorant, by telling him about constitutional polity and freedom. The author ended by criticizing the government for neglecting women's education, considering it a crucial element in China's constitutional system.[82] The protagonist in one story called for women to become economically independent and to pursue careers as professionals and scholars. He blamed women for their slave-like subordination to men, caring only about pleasing men instead of working for a living. He explained that if women stopped relying on men, those men would not dare look down on them.[83] This went a bit further than most other writers, who still defined a woman's role as helping her husband and teaching her children, a role that prioritized the family over the woman.

Yet none of the writers held traditional ethics, in its authentic form, responsible for the plight of women; instead, they blamed misunderstanding and exploitation of Confucian moral codes. According to one of Wu Jianren's female characters, one should not take the ancient teachings literally and dogmatically. Thus, the ancient teaching that "women's talk should not pass beyond the inner chambers, and men's talk should not enter into the inner chambers" does not mean that women and men should not communicate with each other – only that women should manage the family's daily life, and men should handle activities outside the family. Similarly, the ancient teaching that "women without talents are virtuous" means only that women can gain other kinds of knowledge as long as they first learn women's proper moral codes. For Wu, recent generations had interpreted ancient laws and rules as absolute, and consequently had badly mistreated women.[84] Other writers wanted to restore the simplicity of ancient practices, free of contemporary excesses and repressiveness.

Authors appeared to assume that traditional ethics were good and inalienable. Their writings clearly evinced the sense that this view existed not simply because the ethics were Chinese. Rather, the writers could not imagine the existence of a good society without Confucian ethics. For them, people must rely on those ethics as defined by *li* (compassionate human relationships) and *ren* to ensure proper behaviour as social beings.

Wu Jianren perhaps came the closest to providing a justification for the belief in Confucian ethics. For him, these ethics formed the foundation of a humane society in which people interact with *qing*, translated as love, passion, or compassion. In Wu's view, *qing* was innate and existed everywhere and always.[85] One's good relations with other people derived from this *qing*. A baby's cry and smile were a kind of *qing*; the love between men and women another. *Qing* was also manifested in one's loyalty to nation and ruler, in filial piety to parents, in kindness to children, and in friendship.[86] Thus, Wu considered Confucian ethics necessary for cultivating the proper *qing* in society. In his magazine, he divided all fiction based on *qing* into seven categories, each reflecting human relationships in a multitude of manifestations.

In several of his novels, Wu also created heroines who suffered enormous personal sacrifices but acted with love and compassion, faithfully adhering to traditional values. The female protagonist in *Sea of Regret (Henhai)* displayed unconditional compassion for her fiancé, who betrayed her repeatedly. To preserve her chastity, she became a nun after his death. Not knowing whether her fiancé was dead or alive, the heroine of *Apocalyptic Ember*

(Jieyuhui) remained chaste for twenty years, during which she overcame many near-death experiences and avoided becoming a prostitute or concubine.

Wu Jianren, in his attempt to regenerate Confucian ethics, created heroines who upheld traditional values; Liang Qichao, in his search for national salvation, sought a role model in Marie-Jeanne "Manon" Phlippon Roland (or "Madame Roland," 1754-93), a politically active supporter of the French Revolution who devoted herself to peaceful social progress.[87] These disparate choices in female role models reveal how much the two differed in envisioning solutions to China's problem, yet they shared a common male perspective. Both focused on how women could best serve either the state or the family; both created heroines who showed no concern for their own well-being. To be sure, Liang and Wu would not have opposed equal rights between men and women, but the very lack of discussion about this issue betrayed their gender bias.

Tabloid writers also differed from Liang Qichao and from revolutionary theorists in their views of family. Liang downplayed the role of family in his meditations on ethics that regulated relationships between individual, society, and nation. He sought to sever the parochial ties formed through family, occupation, and place of origin. In fact, Liang believed that abolishing traditional family-based institutions was necessary to ensuring people's devotion to the national common good.[88] Except for filial piety, Liang did not refer to any traditional family values in his concept of citizenship.

Revolutionary thinkers such as Zhang Binglin considered all social institutions to be "false," including the family. For Zhang, only the individual was "independently natured" *(zixing)*; thus, he advocated liberating the individual from the family, society, and state. Another revolutionary thinker, Liu Shipei, even declared in 1904 that all social institutions in China should be abolished – especially the repressive Chinese family and clans, the autocratic political system, and restrictive social customs.[89] Tan Sitong, a radical thinker who wrote prior to Zhang and Liu, favoured eliminating the social relationships prescribed by Confucian ethics, including that between father and son, husband and wife, elder brother and younger brother, and ruler and ruled; the only relationship that should be preserved was that between friends. For Tan, only by abolishing these four coded relationships could China become a great collective made up of "hundreds of thousands of friends."[90]

Conclusion

Members of the tabloid community regarded Chinese ethics as the essence of the Chinese way of life and identity. They believed in the values of Confucian ethics, anchored in the proprieties of the five human relationships in society.

In this sense, positioning themselves between Zhang Zhidong and Liang Qichao, the tabloid writers were closer to the former than the latter in their attitudes toward the New Learning; they went beyond what Zhang was willing to change, yet stopped far short of Liang's envisioned reforms.

On the one hand, unlike Zhang, tabloid writers acknowledged the various repressive aspects of Chinese ethical values that created inequalities in political and family systems. They supported – in principle – equality between men and women. Their belief in popular sovereignty was predicated more on the concept of people's rights than Zhang, who acted in the interest of imperial power, could ever tolerate. On the other hand, unlike Liang, the writers saw traditional ethical values as crucial to the well-being of the Chinese state and society. Although in principle they accepted Western ideas of equality, freedom, and individual rights, they saw the validity of these ideas as lying primarily in a political context that was consistent with their populist outlook. In a social and familial context, the writers deemed the application of these values as excessive. At precisely the point when the New Learning began to penetrate those social/familial realms, tabloid writers began to shift their emphasis from promoting to questioning and opposing reform.

Moreover, tabloid writers refused to accept the New Learning as universally valid, something that Liang Qichao often took for granted. While shifting over time, Liang's assessments of China's past and present, along with his blueprints for China's future, derived in part from his acceptance of the universal validity of Western evolutionary views of history. Convinced that human societies evolve in progressive stages and that the fittest survive, Liang detected failures in China's history as well as in Chinese historical texts. He saw the Chinese political and ethical system as unfit for competition in a modern world.

The tabloid literati's defence of Chinese ethics perhaps also stemmed from an emotional attachment to something so fundamentally Chinese. This attachment was clearly expressed in the fact that they were much more willing to give the benefit of the doubt to Chinese rather than Western ethical values. To be sure, China's sufferings at the hands of foreign powers contributed to these emotions. Theodore Huters closely examines two of Wu Jianren's signature novels, *Strange Events Eyewitnessed* and *The New Story of the Stone (Xin shitouji)*, and suggests that Wu's anxiety is apparent in both novels. Wu was torn between the need to reject China's past and his ideological and moral commitment to Chinese tradition.[91] He and other tabloid writers never intended to abandon Chinese ethics, as Huters notes. Thus, they displayed very little of what Joseph Levenson interpreted as Liang Qichao's predicament and emotional distress. Liang's anxiety came from both an emotional attachment to things Chinese and a rational realization that the Chinese "language" had to be altered along Western lines.[92]

Given the political and social environment, what the tabloid writers felt and thought about the New Learning was not out of the ordinary. Similar attitudes continued even in the 1920s and 1930s. In his study of "old school" Shanghai novelists of the 1920s, Perry Link finds those novelists defensive of traditional morality and critical of excessive Western influences. Their attitude toward Western ideas and values differed significantly from that of the Westernized intellectual elites of the 1919 May Fourth Movement, approximating the average and "still Chinese" urban populace.[93] This divide closely resembles the late Qing differences between the tabloid community and the intellectual elite Liang Qichao.

As indicated above, although the conflicts surrounding the New Learning centred mainly on Confucian ethics, almost all political and intellectual forces in the 1900s supported extensive reforms in the political, legal, educational, and economic arenas. Likewise, the tabloid community basically supported Empress Dowager Cixi's New Policy, even though tabloid writers never considered themselves reformers. The next chapter explores why the tabloid community had so little trust in so-called reformers and revolutionaries – the bearers of the New Learning and the reform.

5 Questioning the Appropriators

While the tabloid community continued to attack the old establishment – officialdom – it also increasingly attacked what it saw as the new establishment – the appropriators of the New Learning. As discussed in Chapter 4, the shift in legitimacy from the Old to the New Learning accelerated after 1901. Consequently, a redistribution of power took place that reflected this ideological reorientation, as those with New Learning credentials rose in status and assumed more important positions in the state and society. Implementation of the New Policy and the growing constitutional and revolutionary movements also helped redistribute power in China.

One interesting aspect of these changes, as Luo Zhitian points out, is that literati outside officialdom gained more from the New Policy than did officials. A contemporary saying expressed this phenomenon: "To be an official is not as worthy as to be a literatus."[1] In particular, local elite literati became increasingly important players in local administration and local affairs, whereas officials became relatively less influential. The former's newly found influence led to their abuse of power at the expense of the local population, who frequently rebelled violently against them, especially after 1906.[2] Yet some officials remained as powerful as ever; they subscribed to the New Learning and became part of the new establishment. Moreover, China's youth increasingly received the new-style education, obtained both at home and abroad, and became a significant force in the new establishment.

In this chapter, I analyze the tabloid community's critical views of the new establishment, particularly reformers and revolutionaries, using a concept of "capital" similar to that introduced by Pierre Bourdieu.[3] Specifically, I identify three kinds of capital. The first is economic capital, consisting of material wealth, both real (that is, physical) and financial. Economic capital defines one's material standard of living. The second is social capital, which consists of memberships in organizations and associations, links to informal social networks, connections with people in power, and other social resources. The third is symbolic capital, including prestige, status, educational attainment, rank, and reputation. The amount of economic, social, and symbolic capital a person possesses defines that person's position in society.

It is impossible, of course, to disentangle the three kinds of capital. They tend to interweave and interact; an increase in one type of capital will likely lead to an increase in another. To clarify, I use these three categories only in classifying the various critical views that the tabloid community held of the new establishment. Community members criticized reformers and revolutionaries for adhering to the New Learning only to advance their own interests – interests that took the form of economic, social, and symbolic capital. The community engaged in its struggle against reformers and revolutionaries by seeking to undermine its opponents' moral credibility. Community members invoked traditional Chinese social morality, the most powerful weapon available to them, in attempting to legitimize their own vision of and position in the world.

The New as Symbolic Capital

As discussed in Chapter 4, the tabloid community's attitudes toward reform shifted from positive to negative. Its views of reformers also shifted. Prior to 1901, it was still risky to be publicly labelled a reformer. The Qing government still wanted to prosecute Kang Youwei and Liang Qichao. At that time, the tabloid press sympathized with reformers, one author regarding them as men of conscience and advising them to play it safe in the political environment.[4] After 1901, when the government-sanctioned New Learning gained prestige and legitimacy, many sought to earn credentials as men of the New Learning. They called themselves reformers and benefited from this label. This was especially true of students who received government financial support to study abroad and who easily acquired official positions on their return to China. As the tabloid community saw it, those young reformers leveraged the prestige of the New Learning to enhance their own power and prestige. It was then, around 1903, that tabloid writers began to attack reformers mercilessly.

Various writers described how people tried to appropriate the New Learning in order to enhance their reputations; they especially criticized those who tried to gain advantage by learning foreign languages and using new vocabularies. A fictional county magistrate in one of Li Boyuan's novels informs his colleagues that knowledge of a foreign language was the number one tool for governing, potentially leading to unlimited prosperity.[5] Another writer observed how new vocabularies and terminologies became catch phrases among followers of the New Learning:

Literati of today ... constantly speak of *"fangzhen"* (policy) and *"mudi"* (purpose), frequently write about *"zuzhi"* (organization) and *"fengchao"* (trend) ... They use *"fennei zhishi"* for *"yiwu"* (obligation), and *"faren zhichu"* for *"qidian"* (point of departure). Words such as *"jieguo kaihua"* (result/outcome) and *"geren tese"* (personal character) all have equivalents [in old customary expressions]. Readers regard those who use the customary expressions as unsophisticated, and those who use the new and different terms as fresh, even if they have the same meaning and syntax.[6]

The writer observed that those who used the new terms borrowed from Japanese actually possessed little understanding of their meaning; they had not learned Japanese and could only fathom the terms' surface meanings.

Yet people seemed little bothered by how much they understood about their vocabularies. One fictional character tried to impress others by muttering words such as *qidian* and *zhongxindian* (the main point) at every opportunity. He assigned incorrect meanings to new terms and paired old words with new meanings – all to show off his grasp of the New Learning.[7] In another story, a fictional character in Zhenjiang, a small town in Jiangsu Province, joined a reading society composed of several educated people who read newspapers and translated books. After half a year of reading, the character had learned about such things as "two thousand years of history, the five continents, and the globe." Using his new vocabulary to espouse half-baked ideas, he showed off his new knowledge to other literati. The *xiucai* around him, knowing even less than he, hailed him as a reformer. Seeing this as an honour, he came to regard himself as a reformer.[8]

Besides mocking followers of the New Learning who tried out foreign phrases, tabloid writers ridiculed those who dressed in foreign clothing, ate foreign foods, and played foreign games. One author berated men who replaced Japanese-style hats with the more fashionable "Rousseau hat" or "freedom hat," a straw hat worn in the West and named after Jean-Jacques Rousseau. Still fearful of dressing inappropriately, the literati dared not wear these hats in public, but teachers, students, and youngsters donned them in the name of "enlightenment."[9] Li Boyuan described a character in a Shanghai teahouse, clad from head to toe in foreign-style attire: stylish red and yellow leather shoes, a straw hat, and Western-style cane. Li feigned surprise that the man was actually Chinese; the man's queue, rolled into a knot under his hat, gave him away.[10]

Li's subtle mockery turned bolder in another vivid story of a young student who returned home from Japan on summer vacation:

Though having learned little in his studies, he has changed his appearance a lot. Clad in foreign attire, straw hat on his head, leather shoes on his feet, when greeting his parents he took off his hat and stretched out his hands, according to the custom in foreign countries ... [His] long and thick queue was nowhere to be seen. Seeing this, his parents became sad, asking why he had cut off his queue. He answered that it is easier to carry out the future revolution without a queue ... At home, he complained about everything. The house is too small and the air is too stuffy; the food is not hygienic enough, and cannot compare with the foreign food at foreign restaurants ... The father says, "My home can only be like this, if you do not like it, you can go back to the foreign country. I am a Chinese, I do not dare to have you, a foreigner, as my son." The son then leaves home, while muttering to himself, "Now I know how bad the oppression is within a family, but I am not afraid. As for revolution, it should start with a family revolution."[11]

The commentator in Li Boyuan's *A Brief History of Enlightenment (Wenming xiaoshi)*, juxtaposed two of the novel's characters. One was a man who, having lived for a long time in Hong Kong and having acquired foreign-style attire, regarded men with queues as worthless. The other was his love object, a prostitute who hated men dressed in foreign-style clothing. Noting that even a prostitute abhorred such men, the commentator observed: "It is quite clear how valuable are those men who prefer foreign attire."[12]

Elsewhere Li described a self-proclaimed follower of the New Learning who chided a friend in a Western restaurant for his refusal to order steak. The former told the latter, "You are a person of the New Learning, but you do not even eat beef; aren't you inviting your other friends of the New Learning to laugh at you?"[13] In another piece, Li sneered at young men of Shanghai who "reformed" themselves by adopting a lifestyle modelled after Westerners in the city. These young men rode in horse-drawn carriages, wore Western-style clothing, dined at Western-style restaurants, and spoke Western languages. Li dismissed them as merely superficial; unlike Westerners, they spent extravagantly on luxuries and their Western vocabulary was limited to saying "cheers" at the dining table.[14]

Tabloid writers had nothing against Western-style clothing, food, or language per se. Rather, they targeted those who conspicuously displayed styles associated with the New Learning. Writers saw such people as merely adopting foreign affectations as props to assert their own superiority, expertly imitating Western customs of speaking, dressing, eating, and playing while bearing little if any understanding of the West. This appropriation of the New

Learning solely for the sake of enhancing prestige and social status is what I call accumulating symbolic capital.

For tabloid writers, reformers' ignorance of the New Learning went beyond mere superficial imitation of Western cultural tastes and practices. In typical satirical fashion, writers exposed those reformers who clung zealously to Western concepts as if to absolute truths. One anecdote mocked a student who, on returning from studying in Japan, flaunted his sophistication and knowledge. He mentioned "freedom" in every conversation. A friend challenged this notion of "freedom" by taking off all his clothes in public. Horrified by his friend's action, the student tried to stop the friend. The friend retorted, "You just said that a man of freedom can do anything, so can't I do something as small as taking off my pants?"[15]

Other writers ridiculed those with undeserved reputations as experts of the New Learning. One such man, a supposed expert on international politics, mistook Poland for Persia.[16] In another story, a high-ranked official with a reputation as "learned in both Chinese and Western knowledge" engaged in a new manufacturing venture. He learned from a friend, a comprador in an established foreign company, of machines that could extract kerosene from coal. The friend promised to buy these machines for the official. In the meantime, using money accumulated from selling shares in the new company, the official began buying coal in large quantities in Chongqing, inflating local coal prices there. When the official discovered the impossibility of making kerosene from coal, his company collapsed. Among the losers was a circuit official from Chongqing who bought the company shares for five thousand *liang* of silver. A commentator asserted at the story's end: "This high-ranked official is not alone among so-called learned persons who possess practical knowledge from both the West and China. Their knowledge is based merely on hearsay."[17]

Tabloid writers saw revolutionaries in the same light. For Wu Jianren, those who promoted revolution only sought fame and status. They wanted to be *mingshi*, or famed literati, a term evoking the enduring phenomenon in Chinese history in which self-styled literati strove for fame and prestige. One of Wu's protagonists explained the origin of revolutionaries:

Our China has always had the *mingshi* type, one who can write poems and classical style essays, knows a little about carving calligraphy on stone; and the best of them only are able to write commentaries about parts of a book or at most one book written by the ancients. This type of people all regard themselves as *mingshi* and as erudite, walking with their eyes cast upward, haughty and proud. Since the medieval period, those half-crazy *mingshi* kept popping up, and many unworthy fellows tried to imitate them. In recent years, encounters between the East and the West have brought a lot of new knowledge, and a group of people have begun to promote foreign practices, and to regard Chinese ancient learning as less important. So, a few mingshi realize that they can no longer rely on their old knowledge in order to show others their superiority. But they know little of the new knowledge, and after reading a couple of translated books, they become aware of the so-called theory of race and ethnicity, begin day-dreaming and acting crazily, promoting revolution and the expulsion of the Manchus, recklessly scolding others for being slaves, showing that they are superior to others.[18]

The protagonist acknowledged that those *mingshi* revolutionaries wrote well and were capable of attracting followers. Perhaps Wu Jianren had in mind Zhang Binglin, the prominent anti-Manchu revolutionary voice, when he wrote this passage.

The New as Social and Economic Capital

The tabloid community portrayed reformers as opportunists who manoeuvred to gain power and wealth by making themselves men of the New Learning. These so-called reformers came from all backgrounds: intellectuals such as Kang Youwei and Liang Qichao, officials who adopted the New Learning, students returning from abroad, and constitutionalists without official positions. In the eyes of the tabloid community, all sought to capitalize on their alleged expertise in the New Learning.

As shown in Chapter 4, the tabloid community was never fond of Kang Youwei; many articles and stories denounced him as a villain. He was portrayed as a prima donna, a charlatan, a coward, a power-seeker, and a money-grubber. Nor did writers have anything positive to say about Liang Qichao, although they treated him less harshly. One author, pretending to be a Kang sympathizer in order to remain unprovocative, spoke with a fictitious prominent guest who supposedly possessed a deep understanding of national politics. The guest asserted that Kang supported the Emperor and vilified the Empress Dowager not out of loyalty to the Emperor but, rather, because he hoped to use the Emperor in gaining political power himself.[19] Another article expressed indignation about the pitiful fate of Kang and Liang, who were forced to flee abroad to escape the Qing government's persecution. The article sneered at them for not being able to visit their ancestral tombs while in exile, something dear to any Confucian son.[20]

In *A Brief History of Enlightenment,* Li Boyuan cast Kang Youwei and Liang Qichao as two despicable characters. In this novel, Kang called a meeting without revealing its purpose. He then recorded the names of attendees and submitted the list to a newspaper, claiming that the attendees signed on as members of his reform association. Li's novel described a Liang-like character as a braggart good at making money, a hypocrite who took the government examination while criticizing it, a worthless friend, and a plagiarizer. Although he did not use real names, readers familiar with Kang and Liang would have had no difficulty identifying them, and Li knew this as well.[21] Another anecdote poked fun at Liang Qichao's pen name, Yinbingshi Zhuren, which literally means the master of "ice-drinker's studio." The story described Liang gorging on expensive ice cream every day while in exile in Japan, implying that he was living a luxurious life there.[22]

The few tabloid pieces that gave Kang Youwei some credit included a drama about the 1898 Hundred Days' Reform published in *Fun*. In one scene, Kang was shown promoting his reform ideas with nationalistic fervour to his students. When the students asked about the consequences of introducing Western social and political practices to China, Kang described the power and glory accumulated by nations such as the United States, Britain, and France and noted that Japan, too, became a strong nation after the Meiji reform. The students expressed frustration that those foreign powers looked down on China after its repeated military defeats, war indemnities, and territorial concessions. Kang Youwei replied emotionally, calling for strong and wise leadership and for reform, to avoid the enslavement of the Chinese people by foreign nations.[23] Although this piece is unusual in being relatively sympathetic toward Kang Youwei, it is not entirely surprising, as tabloid writers tended to distinguish between reformers and the reforms they promoted.

While Kang Youwei and Liang Qichao were two obvious targets, other reformers did not escape the tabloids' attention. Writers believed that the reformers' real goal was to secure lucrative appointments to government-sponsored reform projects. Li Boyuan concluded *A Brief History of Enlightenment* – a novel replete with provocative and brutal portrayals of reformers – with a dramatic scene. More than a hundred reformers gathered over a two-day period at the guest hall of the vice censor-in-chief, hoping to be chosen to join his retinue on a trip abroad to examine foreign constitutional polities. The vice censor-in-chief informed his guests:

> You all have specialties, some are teachers (at new-style schools), some are translators, some have toured abroad, some have received recommendations, some have managed schools (new-style ones), some have managed mines, some are private assistants to officials, and some are benevolent officials. So

many talents and it's hard to choose. All of you are smart and talented, and want to have this opportunity as a step toward advancement ... All of your daily behaviours are being collected as material for *A Brief History of Enlightenment*; the sixty chapters of the book portray [you] more accurately than can any Western camera, and more revealingly than any Western oil painting.[24]

As Wu Jianren observed about this sort of people, "reformers wanting to become officials resemble maidens desiring a young man."[25] In traditional Chinese morality, a woman's desire for a man was taboo and an embarrassment.

Fictional accounts also took notice of the Qing government's new policy of recruiting officials among students returning from abroad with a formal education in the New Learning. Li Boyuan spoke bitterly about returning students who passed the government examinations and received the *jinshi* degree, becoming members of the Imperial Academy.[26] Wu Jianren, too, looked askance at students who capitalized on their spurious credentials to climb to the top. He told a story of a man who returned to China after only three months of study at a foreign university. On learning that the government planned an examination for returning students, the man sent the university a telegram to buy a degree certificate for three thousand pieces of silver; he then became a member of the Imperial Academy. Indeed, many students hoped to climb the governmental ranks by purchasing degrees. Expressing frustration, Wu Jianren lamented in the same story: "How can I not loathe this society, seeing students abroad acting like this?"[27] Attacking from another angle, Zhou Guisheng discredited students' learning experiences in Japan. According to him, when government-sponsored students felt even a little unwell, they hurried for treatment to Japanese hospitals, where they could find young, beautiful Japanese nurses, fine food, and a clean environment – all paid for by the government. Zhou wrote scornfully: "Alas, there are a lot of sick people from the sick nation."[28]

The many stories about students studying abroad to get ahead in society reflected the realities of late Qing society. At first, those travelling to Japan to study favoured subjects relating to government administration and teaching. Yang Shu, the Qing ambassador to Japan at the time, reported in 1903 that among 1,300 students studying in Japan, over 1,100 majored in humanities and were mostly interested in politics and law, the military, and teaching.[29] In his memoir, Bao Tianxiao recalled several friends who went to Japan and studied politics and law, while others attended normal schools; few cared about other disciplines. These students believed that studying these disciplines would lead to careers as officials or teachers in new-style schools on their return to China.[30] Even in childhood, many youths planned to study abroad, believing it the surest way to succeed.

For most tabloid writers, the reformers' aim of gaining positions of power was inseparable from their goal of accumulating wealth. Countless stories and reports described reformers scrambling to enrich themselves financially. Many reformers exploited the commercial opportunities that the New Learning provided. Ouyang Juyuan described them in the following portrait:

> At that time, Shanghai almost became a hideout for reformers. Those who had money and talent published newspapers; those who had talent but no money translated books; those who had neither money nor talent relied totally on their pretense as reformers to incite and swindle. Those who were able to make profit from these activities were bold and presumptuous; those who failed to do so were dirt poor and ragged.[31]

This image of Shanghai as a battleground for reformers fighting to secure a piece of the New Learning pie was also evoked by Li Boyuan, who observed that many business-minded people had recognized the potential profits in selling books and translations about the New Learning. Book merchants who used to sell books preparing people for the government examinations now sold newspapers and books about the New Learning. Bookstores began to specialize in such books, advertising them with large signs on their storefronts. To profit from the boom, many merchants tried to publish textbooks for new-style schools. Authors supplying such texts often claimed them as their own work, although they were often little more than hastily assembled pieces from other texts.

The content of these New Learning books was questionable, not only because of the haste with which they were put together but also because they were produced merely to maximize their market value. One story described how book publishers – themselves self-proclaimed reformers – hired individuals who had studied in Japan to translate popular Japanese New Learning books. Many of these translations were self-help books on improving one's sex life. Some dealt with problems of pregnancy while others offered compendia about semen, all intended as instructions for producing sons. In another story, a disloyal bookstore employee revealed the actual purpose of one reformer-turned-book merchant: "It doesn't matter if the books are for enlightenment or not; what matters is that they make profit."[32]

Writers also poked fun at the new fundraising phenomenon in which reformers collected public donations and used the money for private consumption. Young reformers would raise money during New Year campaigns and then head straight to brothels; any remaining money was spent at gambling tables.[33] One short story featured a literatus who hated everything about reform yet became a reformer himself after reading a newspaper article that inspired a get-rich-quick scheme. Taking advantage of the wave of protests opposing government indebtedness to foreign nations, he made speeches inciting protesters and collected donations from them; he figured he could make a profit of ten thousand *yuan*.[34] In one novel, Li Boyuan vividly portrayed a group of reformers who gave patriotic speeches in order to raise money that they secretly divided among themselves. A speech by the group's chief organizer, Wei Bangxian, underscored both his skill in stirring up audiences and his demeanour as a quack:

> Wei Bangxian walked to the podium. Placing his hands on the table, he positioned himself right in the middle, raising his loud voice that sounded like sawing wood, and said, "Gentlemen, gentlemen. Disaster is right in front of us, don't you gentlemen know?" On hearing this, the audience became alert. Wei Bangxian spoke again, "Today's China is like me, a human being; its 18 provinces are like my head, two hands and two feet. Now the Japanese occupy my head, the Germans occupy my left arm, the French my right arm, the Russians have my back, the English my belly, the Italians ride on my left leg, and Americans on my right leg, Alas, can you see how I have been divided and possessed by those foreigners? How could one allow this? Can you imagine what a short life I will have?" The audience began to applaud. Wei Bangxian closed his eyes, taking a short break with a couple of breaths, and spoke again. "Gentlemen, gentlemen, reaching this point, are you still not willing to organize yourselves? If you organize, the Japanese will not dare to have my head, the Germans and the French would not snatch my arms, the Americans and Italians would not take my legs, the Russians would not dare to cut my back, and neither would the English score my belly. If you organize, [the nation] will not be divided, if you cannot organize, [the nation] will be immediately divided. You gentlemen must think, which is better – to organize or not to organize?" Again, the audience applauded, understanding that Wei Bangxian had not yet finished his speech, and expecting more sophisticated talk to follow ... Wei Bangxian, holding onto the table with his two hands, coughing a bit, uttered these words: "Gentlemen, gentlemen." Who would have thought that after this he could utter no more.[35]

Clarifying the monetary goal of this sham performance, Wei finished the speech and then blocked the assembly hall doors, holding his outstretched hands palm up in a plea for money.

Besides commercializing the New Learning, reformers also exploited new opportunities created by the government's reform policies. Stories abounded showing how new-style schools enabled reformers to enrich themselves. In one piece, a school superintendent revealed how he once made a profit of as much as one thousand foreign dollars *(yangqian)* per year after taxes. His income decreased with the establishment of more schools, and he wanted the government to prohibit other schools from opening. The story's commentator explained: "[They] talk about making money through exclusive licensing of a school. So, you know what their purpose is."[36] Also appearing in the tabloids were many reports of officials and local elites who embezzled government funds that were earmarked for establishing new-style schools. One county magistrate allegedly embezzled five hundred yuan from a school.[37] These reports reflected contemporary reality. One leading cause of the local population's violent attack on local gentry was the latter's imposition of a local tax to fund new-style schools, which everyone knew wound up mainly in the gentry's pockets.[38] The state education bureau had to issue an order forbidding the use of temple and monastery property for schools in order to prevent local gentry from profiting.[39]

One of Li Boyuan's fictional characters described the type of people involved with new-style schools. The best might know nothing about education but genuinely wanted to train students to help build China. The next best wished to establish a school only because their superiors supported education. They could kill two birds with one stone: satisfying their superiors and making money themselves from tuition. The worst were jinshi degree holders and members of the Imperial Academy without official posts; they establish schools merely in search of fame and money.[40] To Li Boyuan, most school officials cared only for themselves and their material well-being. Many other anecdotes depicted self-proclaimed reformers employing various strategies aimed at personal gain and fame while they ran new-style schools (Figure 11).

Tabloid writers described how political, commercial, and industrial power combined to create a gentry-capitalist class, a new type of late Qing elite resulting directly from various reform measures. One writer condemned officials who ran government-sponsored new-style schools while at the same time engaging in commercial and industrial ventures. Only such officials, he claimed, could afford to spend lavishly on courtesans in the city.[41] This writer later reported that one such official, a general administration circuit official in charge of both school and business bureaus, had been fired from his position.[42] Another writer showed that many power brokers in the provinces were actually members of the Imperial Academy. Supposedly, these grand

Figure 11 Opening a new-style school as a fast track to officialdom.
Source: Illustrated Fiction [*Xiuxiang xiaoshuo*] 3, 21 (March 1904) (Shanghai: Shanghai shudian, 1980, reprint) (volume reference is to reprint edition, issue reference is to original).

literati found little success in the capital and thus went to the provinces seeking money-making opportunities. Many indeed used their prestige and connections to raise funds for new commercial and industrial ventures; knowing nothing about business, they wound up squandering the money on themselves.[43] *Fun* published a ballad, contributed by a reader, that depicted these new elites lining their pockets through inept management of schools and businesses, wearing silk clothing, gorging on rich foods, and escorting their concubines to expensive stores selling imported goods.[44]

Wu Jianren ended his fantasy novel, *The New Story of the Stone (Xin shitouji)*, with a poem, curiously written in English, mocking those who made a living through adherence to the New Learning:

> All foreigners thou shalt worship;
> Be always in sincere friendship.
> This the way to get bread to eat and money to spend.
> And upon this thy family's living will depend;
> There's one thing nobody can guess:
> Thy countrymen thou can't oppress.[45]

As for revolutionaries, they were as bad as, if not worse than, reformers. For the tabloid writers, some revolutionaries saw destruction of the dynasty as a means to social advancement; others strove to destroy for the sake of destruction. In Li Boyuan's fiction, revolutionary leaders came from families of either officials or merchants. Some even held jinshi or *juren* degrees and were Imperial Academy members. Many wanted to revolutionize both the dynasty and/or the family system. They appealed to China's youth, who in general tended to be hot-blooded and rebellious – especially those studying in Japan. These youths gravitated toward revolutionary messages, thinking that a revolution would free them from the restrictions of "fundamental principles, laws of the state, and proprieties of human relations." Li described these youths as "wanting to become either revolutionary militants or China's rulers."[46]

Two readers commented on a well-known event that occurred in 1907, in which the Qing government killed a small group of revolutionaries; among the dead was Qiu Jin, a woman who had plotted to overthrow a local Qing administration in Zhejiang. One reader said that these revolutionaries were merely young people who were under the spell of a European brand of nationalism and who fantasized that they too could become emperors and rulers. The reader warned others not to follow them.[47] A second reader, a woman, wrote a long verse commemorating Qiu Jin. She expressed admiration for Qiu's talent and courage, but thought it useless to sacrifice one's life for revolutionary ideas. She too asked others, especially talented women, not to follow Qiu's example.[48]

While showing how disingenuously reformers and revolutionaries pursued power and wealth in the name of reform, tabloid writers also voiced concern for the underprivileged, paying particular attention to educational opportunities. Their concerns were not unwarranted. Beginning in 1902, when the Qing government initiated its new education policies, authorities repeatedly ordered provinces to establish new-style schools; the provinces had complied by 1904. In 1909, about 5,700 new-style schools of various levels had opened, with an enrollment of approximately 1.6 million. One thousand were at the middle and high school level, with an enrollment of 190,000.[49] The new-style schools were still limited in number, however, and could neither satisfy educational needs nor yet replace the traditional tutorial system. In addition, unlike the traditional tutorial system, new-style schools had strict admission requirements. In the beginning, students around twenty years of age often studied at middle and elementary schools; only later did students become progressively younger.[50] Because the supply of new-style schools was relatively small and the demand large, tuition was much higher than for traditional schools.

In his memoir, novelist Zhang Ziping recalled that in 1906 he wanted to attend a government new-style middle school in Guangdong; the school offered the highest level of education in the province. Tuition cost twenty yuan per year, excluding expenses for food, lodging, and school uniform. Zhang's father, a tutor, at best earned close to seventy yuan for teaching twenty-five or twenty-six students, and could not afford the forty-yuan tuition to send both his son and a nephew under his care to attend the new-style school.[51] High tuitions similarly turned away the sons of many families.

In the past, because of the traditional tutorial system's local roots, the families and clans of poor students were probably still able to provide financial support for education. This time, however, authorities built most new-style schools far away, and students could receive little assistance to attend them. Thus, only well-to-do families could afford the new education that enabled their sons to earn graduation certificates, an important credential in the job market.[52] The problems of high tuition and age discrimination in new-style schools prompted a long debate in *Shenbao* between 1901 and 1904. Some even proposed that the government refrain from completely abolishing the examination system because of these problems.

Li Boyuan described how even a well-off literatus had difficulty sending his son to a new-style school because of high tuition.[53] As for students who studied abroad, Li explained that they could afford the five hundred-yuan annual tuition to study in Japan because their wealthy families had the financial resources to support them.[54] Wu Jianren expressed frustration at having no opportunity to study abroad due to his need to make a living.[55] Tabloid writers saw the new type of education as developing into an elite institution, shutting off educational opportunities for less well-to-do families and for older adults. Reformers and revolutionaries, however, were able to claim New Learning credentials and climb the social and economic ladders.

The Immoralities

To undermine the claims of reformers and revolutionaries to symbolic, social, and economic capital derived from the New Learning, tabloid writers and readers attacked them on moral grounds. As in their critiques of Qing officials, the tabloid community portrayed reformers and revolutionaries as frauds and hypocrites. Li Boyuan's *A Brief History of Enlightenment* had three characters who were devotees of the New Learning: Jia Ziyou, Jia Pingquan, and Jia Geming, which in Chinese mean "fake freedom," "fake equal rights," and "fake revolution," respectively. No reformer in the novel amounted to anything; all were dishonest, self-interested, opportunistic, and harmful to China and its people.

In countless stories, tabloid writers exposed the contradictions between the public rhetoric and private lives of reformers and revolutionaries. Some reformers were simultaneously enamoured with the smallness of women's bound feet and passionately promoting women's equality; they idealized a foot that they could hold in one hand. One humorous story in *Fun* featured a man named Jiang, a long-time supporter of reform. When discussing China's current situation, he displayed an air of "regarding all things under heaven as his responsibility" *(yi tianxiashi wei jiren)* – an old expression indicating devotion to the well-being of the country and its people. But Jiang fell in love with a courtesan named Hua Xiaobao on his arrival in Shanghai. Forsaking his original plan to remain in the city for only a short while, he extended his stay indefinitely. To his friends' repeated inquiries as to why he was still in Shanghai, he always responded that he planned to leave the following week. One friend laughed, "You came when the willows just turned light green, and now the loquats have already turned yellow. If one month has four weeks, how many weeks still remain in this month?" To this teasing, Jiang had no response.[56] The story invokes an irony readily recognizable in Chinese tradition: for beauties, "great men" forget their duties.

Writers criticized revolutionaries with equal zeal. In his novel *Touring Shanghai (Shanghai youcanlu)*, Wu Jianren showed many revolutionaries, usually militant and angry, without exception turning "soft-boned and limp-bodied" in the presence of prostitutes, their rage disappearing without a trace. The novel's hero claimed that "the prostitutes of Fourth Street in Shanghai have rendered a great service to the Qing emperor."[57] One of Wu's poems read: "An army of ladies defeats an army of revolutionaries"; it described revolutionaries coming to Shanghai with large sums of money to promote their political agendas but instead squandering it in brothels, forgetting their missions entirely.[58] Although exaggerated, Wu's portrayal of Shanghai's revolutionaries was not unfounded. In fact, Chen Yingshi, the commander-in-chief of the revolutionary forces in Shanghai, often carried out business in brothels.[59] Wu had no intention of excusing revolutionaries even if, according to Bao Tianxiao, they frequented brothels only to hide their activities from the Qing government.[60]

To tabloid writers, reformers and revolutionaries supposedly adopted the New Learning only to free themselves from traditional moral constraints and to justify their depravity (Figure 12). One such reformer justified his opium smoking thus:

> In principle, persons of the New Learning should not smoke opium, since it is harmful to Chinese. Initially I also wanted to quit smoking, but then I thought that one should have the happiness of freedom to live in this world. My smoking is my freedom; even my parents could not interfere with it ... What a person of the New Learning detests the most is to give up one's freedom.[61]

Similarly, in *Touring Shanghai*, a revolutionary justifies his opium smoking as an act of resistance against the government's policy forbidding it. Anecdotes abounded about sons using Western values to justify demanding equality with their fathers, or failing to accept responsibility for their widowed mothers.

To the tabloid community, reformers and revolutionaries were devoid of principles and did whatever was necessary to acquire power. In the futuristic parody *Touring Utopia (Wutuobang youji)*, the protagonist offered an old Buddhist priest an earful about contemporary reformers:

> We have had people of great purpose in our country before, whose mouths incessantly uttered reform and constitution. In truth, they had no guiding principles and were no match for those people of purpose in Western European countries who were hot-blooded men, who kept struggling and risking their

Figure 12 Smoking opium while talking excitedly about reform.
Source: Illustrated Fiction [*Xiuxiang xiaoshuo*] 2, 18 (December 1903) (Shanghai: Shanghai shudian, 1980, reprint) (volume reference is to reprint edition, issue reference is to original).

lives in order to reform the government and gain the right of freedom for people. Those people of great purpose in my country, when they were outside of the government, kept on criticizing the decay of the government and the corruption of officials; they also kept on pushing to reform the government and to rectify officialdom. Until one day, when the emperor made them officials, they totally forgot what they had said before. They became very different people, and what they did was ten times worse than the decay of the government and of officialdom which they had scorned before.[62]

Readers and writers mocked those who cut their queues when studying abroad then scrambled to replace the queues when they returned. One reader remarked that men's queues were precious in China, for without them men could acquire neither fame nor fortune, especially since candidates needed to have queues in order to qualify for the government examinations. He laughed: "Talented examinees crowd around the academic department waiting to take the examinations; buyers stream into the hair department to buy wigs." Beside the word "hair," the reader wrote the word "France" in parenthesis – a play on words since "hair" and "France" are homophones in Chinese. The reader derided students who had their queues cut in France: "It is quite a pity that those students threw away their useful queues in a land where 'queues' are useless."[63] In another of Li Boyuan's stories, a student who was determined to go to America to study cut his queue for the trip. When he could not go and returned to the capital to attend the advanced government school, he found a way to get his queue back quickly: "There are barbershops now that sell queues." These people dared to cut their queues, Li Boyuan pointed out, only because they could buy a wig that no one could detect as fake.[64]

Just like reformers, revolutionaries could quickly reverse themselves and embrace the government. A revolutionary character in one of Wu Jianren's short stories confessed how he chose political causes:

If today [I] have a chance to make money as a revolutionary, I'll promote a revolution. If tomorrow [I] can become an official as a constitutionalist, I'll support constitutional polity. Don't you see that quite a few people who once supported the revolution are now among those who dance vigorously and sing loudly for the Empress Dowagers and Emperor?[65]

Writers also saw that reformers failed to live up to their roles in strengthening China and working for the well-being of ordinary people. Wu Jianren described one reformer who placed such faith in everything foreign that he wished he had foreigners as his parents. Instead of nurturing patriotism among the Chinese, he became an obstacle to it. Wu remarked bitingly: "I am afraid that those patriotic foreigners would not want to have such an unworthy son."[66] Reformers acted recklessly when imposing taxes and "contributions" to fund reform ventures such as toll roads and the construction of city gates and bridges. As one commentator remarked: "Listen, all you who have invented the bureau of 'contributions'! [Now] even sons and grandsons have all contributed their rice bowls."[67]

In sum, tabloid writers and readers rarely acknowledged the existence of authentic reformers and revolutionaries. They focused instead on the moral corruption of adherents to the New Learning. In fact, the tabloid community's criticisms of reformers and revolutionaries – with their mad scramble for symbolic, social, and economic capital and shameful behaviour in the private and public arenas – all had roots in the community's concern for moral integrity.

Conclusion

It seems paradoxical that the tabloid community, while essentially supporting reform, ruthlessly tarnished reformers. Writers questioned the authenticity of these presumed agents of change, challenged the legitimacy and the power they acquired, and attacked them on moral grounds. Yet if we examine the consistently populist outlook the community displayed, this apparent contradiction is easy to explain. The bottom line is that, while upholding reform, tabloid writers deeply distrusted anyone in a position of political power and privilege. They assumed that everyone who held or wished for a position of power and privilege was morally handicapped, motivated primarily by self-interest. Even those who genuinely cared for the well-being of China considered their own power and prestige to be their highest priority. This behaviour directly contradicted Chinese moral teaching. To be sure, the tabloid community attacked reformers and revolutionaries for their views on the New Learning and their solutions to China's problems; however, it is the community's contempt for reformers' and revolutionaries' claims to power in the name of the New Learning that explains why the tabloid press struck its heaviest blows against its opponents' moral integrity. The community saw itself and the larger public as underdogs, possessing none of the advantages available to those who benefited from the New Learning; thus, its writers made themselves the spokespersons of the disadvantaged and discontented.

How, exactly, were tabloid writers able to turn their perceptions into public discourses? The next chapter explores the role of the late Qing literary marketplace in influencing what, how, and for whom the writers wrote.

6 The Market, Populism, and Aesthetics

The late Qing periodical press created an unprecedented literary market. With newspapers and magazines appearing at regular intervals, the production and consumption of literature became routine activities, and reading and writing were transformed into activities regulated by the calendar and the clock. The tabloid press, a star of the rapidly expanding commercial literary market, helped shape the new relationship between this market's producers and consumers. As producers, literati no longer wrote only for themselves and their peers as in earlier times, nor did they write solely to prove their literary worth. They wrote instead for money. To be sure, throughout Chinese history, many authors have written to entertain and reach a large readership, but most did not write to entertain and to earn profit. The tabloid writers departed from the previous norm in their drive to make their works profitable commodities. As consumers, readers were no longer passive, reading only what elites and authorities fed them. Acting through the market, they now directed literary production, and producers had to satisfy their tastes and preferences in order to survive. The rise of fiction, a late Qing literary phenomenon, exemplified the impact of this new reader/writer relationship. On the one hand, the late Qing tabloid press helped spearhead the development of an entirely new kind of market, one that met the demands of an extended readership that increasingly included non-literati. On the other hand, late Qing tabloid production could never have enjoyed such success if the reading market had not responded enthusiastically.

This interdependent relationship between the tabloid press and its reading market – with writers actively guiding and satisfying readers' interests and tastes, and readers shaping the content and style of tabloid literary commodities – gave rise to a tabloid populism that opposed the political and intellectual establishment, and a tabloid aesthetic that reinforced and potentiated this populism.

The Literary Market

The new interdependent relationship between writers and readers in the marketplace helps to explain the so-called rise of fiction in the late Qing literary market. This rise was manifested in a drastic increase in both the production of fiction and the status of fiction in Chinese literature. Intellectual elites observed the popularity of fiction and promoted it as a tool for reform and public education. In doing so, they helped change the traditional reputation of fiction as an inferior literary form. Intellectuals had little control over the type of fiction produced, however. In contrast, tabloid writers, highly conscious of readers' need for entertainment, saw the value of fiction in serving this need. The tabloid press played an instrumental role in the rise of fiction by providing a space for novelists to publish and by creating a demand for serialized fiction. It also played an important role in developing a diverse reading public that included people of various educational and social backgrounds. The press produced fiction both to entertain the public and to condemn the political and intellectual establishment. Tabloid writers thus appropriated – and in turn subverted – the intellectual elites' prescribed role for fiction.

The Rise of Fiction and the Tabloid Press

A number of scholars have estimated the increase in new works of fiction in China, including short stories, novellas, and novels. Ouyang Jian compares the number of fiction pieces published in China from 1840 to 1900 with the number published from 1901 to 1911. One hundred thirty-three works were published in the former period, for an average of 2.2 per year, and 529 in the latter period, for an average of 48 per year.[1] Chen Pingyuan estimates that 1,145 works of fiction were published in China between 1898 and 1911, compared with only 834 in the previous 250 years of the Qing Dynasty.[2] Lin Mingde considers the years from 1902 to 1911 as "the most productive period of fiction publication in Chinese history" and estimates that the "four major late Qing literary journals" alone published 461 works of fiction and 608 translations of such works.[3] These four journals were *Illustrated Fiction (Xiuxiang xiaoshuo)*, *All-Story Monthly (Yueyue xiaoshuo)*, and *Grove of Fiction (Xiaoshuolin)*, all published in Shanghai, as well as Liang Qichao's *New Fiction*, published first in Yokohama in 1902 and in Shanghai a year later. Yuan Jin pinpoints the late Qing increase in fiction production as occurring around 1902 and 1903, and notes that 70 percent of this new fiction was published in Shanghai.[4] Teruo Tarumoto counts 1,531 fictional works and 1,101 translated works produced in late Qing China. These figures are low, as he has since uncovered previously unknown works.[5] Advertisements for fiction also pervaded late Qing newspapers and magazines.[6]

Late Qing fiction achieved an unprecedented level of respect in Chinese literature. The traditional cultural and literary establishment had regarded fiction as a low form of literature with little educational or literary value, and thus with no place in serious literature. The name *xiaoshuo,* or small talk, given to fiction reflects this attitude. For centuries, authors of serious literature such as political essays and histories wrote in classical Chinese and hence reserved their work for highbrow readers. Fiction, often written in vernacular Chinese, was frivolous writing fit only for lowbrow readers. The orthodox tradition discouraged literati from reading this type of literature. The complete reversal in the status of fiction was made possible by late Qing campaigns on behalf of fiction, together with the growth of the tabloid press.

While promoting the publication of newspapers to enlighten readers, intellectual elites such as Liang Qichao and Kang Youwei noticed fiction's growth in popularity as a literary form. As early as 1897, Kang, while visiting Shanghai, observed that classics and history did not sell as well as the "eight-legged" works, and that these in turn were outperformed by fiction. In Kang's estimation, readers with lower or average levels of literacy were unlikely to read classical texts and much more likely to read fiction.[7]

Chinese scholars have generally attributed the rise of fiction to Liang Qichao, whose promotion of fiction helped elevate its literary status. Two of Liang's essays provide evidence of this.[8] In "Preface to Translating and Publishing Political Fiction," a short article published in the 1898 inaugural issue of his *Qingyibao,* Liang stressed the importance of political fiction in influencing public opinion in Western nations and Japan. Echoing Kang Youwei, Liang promoted fiction as an effective tool for political education. In his 1902 article "On the Relationship between Fiction and Popular Sovereignty," published in the inaugural issue of his *New Fiction,* Liang further elaborated on the role of fiction as an important tool for social transformation. He argued that political fiction played an important part in developing democratic political systems in the West and in Japan. He criticized traditional Chinese fiction for its exclusive focus on the past and its preoccupation with motifs such as ghosts and spirits, bandits and villains, and love between talented scholars and beautiful maidens. In this article, he proposed a "new type of fiction" to portray contemporary society and enlighten people about popular sovereignty. *New Fiction,* he stated, was established to realize these goals.[9]

Theodore Huters traces the post-1895 call to use fiction for public education to foreign missionaries and Chinese reformers. The earliest advocates include John Fryer (Fu Lanya), Timothy Richard (Li Timotai), Yan Fu, Xia Zengyou, and Kang Youwei. Huters also discusses commentators and critics, including Liu Shipei and Huang Ren, who wrote about the social role of fiction. Chinese intellectuals generally saw fiction as an elixir for regenerating China. Liang Qichao led the charge in popularizing the term "revolutionizing fiction" and promoting the new type of fiction.[10]

Campaigns by intellectual elites certainly influenced tabloid writers who also saw fiction as an effective educational tool. This proved especially true when Li Boyuan and Wu Jianren became editors of *Illustrated Fiction* and *All-Story Monthly*, respectively; many articles published in these magazines shared this view.[11] Li Boyuan, echoing Liang Qichao's suggestions, stated unequivocally in 1903 that he refused to publish any work featuring traditional subjects such as ghosts and spirits or romances between talented scholars and beautiful maidens. A major contributor to Liang Qichao's *New Fiction*, Wu Jianren began serializing his novel *Strange Events Eyewitnessed* in the journal's inaugural issue, which categorized the serial as "social fiction" instead of "political fiction."[12] As Xia Xiaohong points out, the two met twice in 1903 and 1904 when Wu began to publish in Liang's journal. Wu also maintained a close relationship with Liang's Guangzhi Publishing House in Shanghai, which published Wu's works.[13]

If tabloid writers listened to the intellectuals' ideas on fiction, it was because they saw those ideas as advantageous. Fiction represented an opportunity to make profit and to influence people. Kang Youwei and Liang Qichao did not "invent" the market for fiction; it already existed. Neither did the two cause tabloid writers to move to fiction; writing and selling fiction was already on the minds of many Shanghai writers before the elites began to promote it. In fact, some writers had already published fiction when Kang and Liang emerged as important voices. As Des Forges points out in his study of installment fiction of the late Qing and early Republican periods, the 1890s witnessed a boom of novels about Shanghai by Shanghai writers.[14] As early as 1892, Han Bangqing published China's first literary journal, *Shanghai Wonders (Haishang qishu)*, which was printed and distributed by *Shenbao*, where Han worked. This journal lasted for less than a year but featured most of Han's literary works, including installments of his novel *Biographies of Shanghai Flowers (Haishang hualiezhuan)*. By 1899, tabloid writers such as Zou Tao, Wu Jianren, and Li Boyuan had already serialized their novels about life in Shanghai.

From the very beginning, tabloid writers used fiction as bait to entice readers and establish a stable market for their newspapers. Before they began including novels directly as text, the daily newspapers would "give away" one page of serialized fiction as an insert. *Fun* began with a new novel by a female author, *Paired Flying Phoenixes (Fengshuangfei)*, in November 1897. Accompanied by illustrations, the daily series was not completed until March

1903.[15] Zou Tao gave away one page per day of the novel *The Heartbroken Stone Tablet (Duanchangbei)* when he began publishing *Qubao* in 1898.[16]

Sun Yusheng was supposedly frustrated that he could not persuade *Xinwenbao*, a mainstream newspaper where he worked as editor-in-chief, to serialize his fiction, and he decided to publish *Anecdotes* in July 1898. In the first few issues, he announced that, with each issue, the paper would give away one page of the illustrated new novel *Dream of Shanghai Splendor* – without mentioning that he himself was the author.[17] To enhance its appeal, Sun printed the insert on red, yellow, green, blue, and white paper. It took him over two years to complete the series; later, he expanded and published the novel as a three-volume book.

Tabloid writers produced fiction principally to sell papers and magazines. Their main strategy for attracting readers was to serialize their new novels in their own tabloids and journals, usually before publishing them as books. In 1899, Li Boyuan expressed his desire to write novels about contemporary society to complement *Fun*.[18] He serialized his first novel, *The National Incident of 1900 (Gengzi guobian tanci)*, in his new tabloid, *Splendid World (Shijie fanhuabao)*, in 1901, before Liang Qichao's call for a new type of fiction in 1902. After publishing twenty-five chapters, Li advertised *Splendid World* in *Dagongbao*, Tianjin's most reputable newspaper, using his novel to attract potential subscribers to his tabloid.[19] Once the series was complete, he wrote and serialized a drama adapted from the translated Japanese novel *Heroic Nation (Jingguo meitan)*, first published in Liang's *Qingyibao*.[20] Li also serialized his signature novels in his papers and magazine, including *Officialdom Unmasked (Guanchang xianxingji)* in *Splendid World*, and *A Brief History of Enlightenment (Wenming xiaoshi)* and *Living Hell (Huodiyu)* in *Illustrated Fiction*. Wu Jianren employed the same strategy. In 1898, he wrote and serialized his first novel, *The Wonder Book of Shanghai's Famous Courtesans: The Buddha's Four Warrior Attendants (Haishang mingji sida jingang qishu)* in *Pastime*, where he worked as an editor. *Splendid World* serialized part of Wu's *The Muddled World (Hutu shijie)*, and *All-Story Monthly* published his novellas *Apocalyptic Ember (Jieyuhui)*, *Touring Shanghai*, and *The History of Two Jin Dynasties (Liangjin yanyi)*.

When Sun started *Grove of Laughter* after selling off *Anecdotes*, he immediately serialized *Martial Art Heroes with the Flowered Sword (Xianxia wuhuajian)*, a novel he probably wrote himself.[21] He assured his readers that regardless of the enormous cost, he would commission a well-known artist to illustrate the installments.[22] The paper sold very well at the time; the illustrations were especially popular, and Sun often could not meet the demand for them. Likewise, the editor of *Allegories* serialized a sequence of novels after its inauguration in 1901, including *Strange Things in Peaceful Garden (Danyuan shuyi)* that same year and *Historical Anecdotes about Imperial Dynasties (Huangchao zhanggu congtan)* in 1902.

From the beginning, fiction appeared in every issue of the tabloids, and it became a permanent feature. In fact, serialized fiction became a major form of late Qing popular literature. In his memoir, Bao Tianxiao recalls the popularity of fiction in Shanghai; readers were choosy, and tabloid newspaper sales depended greatly on fiction installments.[23] One can imagine the allure of these daily installments for eager readers anxious to discover each new plot twist in a favourite story. The one-page inserts in the early tabloids made it easy to collect individual pages into volumes. In this way, frugal readers could compile their own copies of the novels.[24]

The tabloid installments had special appeal because of their treatment of contemporary social and political events, celebrities, and entertainment. Around 1903, many of Li Boyuan's and Wu Jianren's bestsellers created a new literary genre called the "fiction of censure." These novels built on and extended a range of piecemeal articles and anecdotes published in the tabloids. It was in the tabloids that writers first developed their particular ways of addressing social and political problems using humour, sarcasm, and profanity. The tabloids' fictional exposés of officials, reformers, and revolutionaries complemented their exposés of courtesans.

The tabloid press created an entirely new venue for publishing fiction. Perry Link suggests that the development of both journalism and modern printing in China provided the "material base" for China's modern popular fiction. He supports this statement by examining literary columns in the mainstream papers *Shibao*, *Shenbao*, and *Xinwenbao;* which serialized fiction after 1904.[25] It was the tabloid press, however, that first began to systematically serialize fiction. Link further suggests that *Shenbao*'s famous "unfettered talk" column, initiated in 1911, marked the establishment of fiction as a permanent fixture in the modern Chinese press.[26] In fact, however, it was the Shanghai tabloids that played the pivotal role in establishing serialized fiction as an integral part of Chinese newspapers.[27] Moreover, Li Boyuan and Wu Jianren served as editors-in-chief of two of the four major late Qing literary journals, *All-Story Monthly* and *Illustrated Fiction*. Each of these tabloid journals serialized more previously unpublished novels than the other two major literary journals – *New Fiction* and *Grove of Fiction* – combined.[28] The tabloid press thus played a major role in influencing the form and content of late Qing fiction.

Tabloid writers mimicked the elite's rhetoric about fiction as an educational tool, but they did not conform to the elite vision of education. In the inaugural issue of *All-Story Monthly*, Wu Jianren mocked novelists who "follow the lead voice," referring specifically to Liang's proposal in 1902 to make fiction a tool of his political agenda.[29] Wu stressed the importance of fiction in educating people in Chinese history and ethics. In particular, he wrote historical novels such as *Painful History (Tongshi)* to promote patriotism, and novels such as *The Sea of Regret (Henhai)* to promote traditional ethical values in love and marriage.

While Liang Qichao understood well the popularity of fiction as a literary form, he paid less attention to the artistic and entertainment aspects of fiction than to its political and educational roles. In the *Future of New China (Xinzhongguo weilaiji)*, the only fictional piece he ever wrote, political discussions among the characters drive the narrative, making the novel more about political indoctrination than about art and entertainment. Liang admitted his purpose in the novel's preface: expressing political opinion. A contemporary critic later wrote to Liang, observing frankly that the work was neither entertaining, clearly written, nor well thought out.[30]

Tabloid writers, in contrast, viewed entertainment as a necessary feature of fiction and stressed that the form's popularity stemmed directly from its entertainment value. As one writer put it, excessive discussion in narratives is a poor way to write fiction.[31] Wu Jianren wrote to entertain, and had no qualms about addressing subjects that Liang Qichao might have regarded as frivolous and trivial. Whereas Liang wrote a biography of Li Hongzhang, a leading late Qing statesman, Wu wrote a biography of Hu Baoyu, a famous courtesan. Wu modelled his biography – its genre, narrative style, and structure – after Liang's,[32] intending to demonstrate through this deliberate parody that the history of courtesans was just as important as the history of top officials.

Toward a Broad Readership

In order to maximize profits, tabloid writers from the beginning catered to diverse audiences with various levels of literacy. In his 1897 statement of purpose for *Fun*, Li Boyuan proclaimed that his paper would publish articles written in vernacular Chinese and local dialects for ease of comprehension. Li especially had in mind female readers, who usually had a low level of literacy.[33] In the inaugural issue of *Illustrated Fiction*, he repeated his intention to appeal to both the well educated and those with only basic literacy.[34] Similarly, *All-Story Monthly* enumerated the types of people who ought to read the magazine, from officials to reformers, historians, merchants, writers/poets, and women, and explained the magazine's benefits to each group.[35]

Like Li Boyuan, all tabloid writers saw language usage as crucial for broadening general readership. To accommodate both the literate and the semiliterate, the tabloids used the vernacular universally, which set them apart from mainstream papers such as *Shenbao* that were written exclusively in classical Chinese.[36] Over the years, the tabloid press also employed fewer and fewer classical and literary references. As early as 1898, *Fun* began publishing fictional news stories entirely in vernacular Chinese, among the earliest efforts in the late Qing campaign for vernacular writing.[37] Writers also paid attention to the use of dialect. Generally speaking, national news stories used the colloquial Beijing dialect, whereas local news about courtesans was often reported in local dialects. Tabloids often used local slang phrases and homespun expressions to evoke a sense of familiarity and intimacy in local readers. At the same time, they ran articles in Beijing dialect in an attempt to reach wider audiences.

Tabloid writers also made sure that their novels appealed to readers of diverse social and cultural backgrounds. They deliberately chose to write and publish so-called vernacular novels, novels written in a vernacular Chinese that closely resembled the spoken vernacular. Writers meticulously applied this practice to all the novels they published – their own as well as translations. They even rewrote novels written by others, using the vernacular. Wu Jianren rewrote into the vernacular several classical Chinese works, including the drama *The Western Chamber (Xixiangji)* and the translated novel *Wonders of Electricity (Dianshu qitan)*, adding humour and changing foreign names and places to Chinese ones to make the works more accessible to a wider reading public.[38]

The choice of vernacular came from writers' knowledge of the market for fiction. They recognized its new popularity and understood the general reading tastes of different groups. One article in an early issue of *Illustrated Fiction* ranked the popularity of various types of literature: pictorials were the most popular, followed by fiction and then by books on history, science, and the classics. The author identified two kinds of fiction, one for scholars and literati written in classical Chinese, and another for women and the "unsophisticated" written in vernacular Chinese.[39] This division of fiction into two types was common at the time.[40] Hu Shi recalled that vernacular literature in the late Qing was suited to unsophisticated readers in the lower social strata, while classical Chinese literature was aimed at the well educated.[41]

Tabloid writers knew that fiction written in classical Chinese sold very well. The traditional view that fiction was unsuitable for literati began to dissolve in the late Qing, as literati increasingly made fiction part of their reading repertoire.[42] According to one author writing for a Shanghai literary journal in 1908, 90 percent of the readership had a traditional education; the rest were "ordinary people" or people with a new-style education.[43] Most foreign novels translated into classical Chinese were aimed at literati with a new interest in foreign literature;[44] Lin Qinnan was well known as a prolific translator of foreign novels into classical Chinese, mainly for literati readers. Tabloid writers, however, sought a readership beyond the literati. They calculated that traditionally trained literati could and would read novels in both classical and vernacular Chinese, but that novels in classical Chinese would pose a challenge for readers with rudimentary literacy. They also knew that a large proportion of potential readers belonged to the latter group. The choice of vernacular can therefore be seen as a strategy to capture the largest possible market.

Besides language, writers used many popular literary tactics and genres to expand their readership. Knowing the popularity of pictorials, authors tried to enhance the popularity of their texts with visual effects. Although no cost-effective way to print images on paper existed, writers often provided printed illustrations for the novels – hence the name of the magazine *Illustrated Fiction*.

The tabloid press mainly published fiction by Chinese authors. This was because many readers had trouble understanding the unfamiliar subject matter often found in translations of foreign authors. *All-Story Monthly* published almost exclusively Chinese fiction. *Illustrated Fiction* did serialize a few translated works, usually written in vernacular Chinese and adapted to Chinese contexts. Writers also persisted in writing novels in the traditional popular narrative mode featuring separate chapters; they avoided the new experimental style that eliminated chapters and posed more difficulties for readers.

Tabloid writers also produced forms of writing with easy-to-read rhyme and rhythm, which were very popular among people of various literacy levels. They told stories in verse constructed in four-word, five-word, or seven-word rhymes, or in rhythmic texts using traditional rhyme schemes.[45] They also published a significant number of folk ballads, some written in the style of "bamboo twigs" that was popular among literati.[46] Ballads about current events appeared in almost every issue of *Illustrated Fiction*. Similarly, many news stories were composed as rhythmic narratives in the storytelling genres of *qu* and *chuanqi*, rooted in traditional dramatic performances that combined singing and speaking. Such a musical style of storytelling was easy to read and had wide appeal.

Recognizing that half the population consisted of women, the tabloid literati assumed from the outset that women would comprise an important segment of their readership. Indeed, many of those ballads and rhythmic narratives, genres especially popular among women, targeted female readers. Li Boyuan wrote many novels in *tanci*, a Qing-era genre combining easily read texts and rhymed verses. *Tanci* performance, a popular form of oral storytelling in the Jiangnan region, attracted in particular both literate and illiterate female audiences. The performances combined speech and singing, and were accompanied by string instruments such as the *sanxuan* and *pipa*. Many *tanci* storytellers were illiterate and had to memorize the scripted storylines. These stories, told in either regional dialect or mandarin Chinese, were customarily very long and the telling often took days to complete.[47] Li Boyuan wrote his first novel, *The National Incident of 1900*, in the *tanci* style, becoming the first writer to deal with political issues in *tanci*, which departed from the traditional subjects of love, ghosts, and retribution.[48] In addition, the first serialized novel that Li inserted in *Fun* as a "free gift" was in *tanci*. When *Illustrated Fiction* first began publication, Li immediately serialized his *Awakening the Society (Xingshiyuan)* in *tanci*. In the introduction to this novel, he explained that he wrote it because both women and children loved reading *tanci* about the trivialities of everyday life.[49] In an article in Liang Qichao's *New Fiction*, Wu Jianren likewise contemplated popular forms of reading for women, observing that *tanci* was favoured in the Jiangnan region while *muyu*, a counterpart of *tanci*, prevailed in the Guangdong region.

Tabloid writers tried to educate women about reform using simple verses and texts. These texts informed women of national problems and the domination of foreign powers, and scolded them for their ignorance on such matters. They called for the elimination of practices that particularly afflicted women, including footbinding and superstition. These writers never acquired a significant female readership, however. As time passed, *Illustrated Fiction* published less and less content for women, indicating that the number of female readers did not justify the expense and effort. Tabloid writers could not connect with female readers, partly because most discussions of women were aimed at male readers and reflected male interests. Barbara Mittler observes that *Shenbao* published materials for female readers, along with a variety of views on women ranging from conservative to radical. She suggests that newspapers and magazines made women their implied readers, but that Shanghai women largely ignored these publications.[50]

During the 1910s, the mass readership that the tabloid press tried to create was largely realized. In his analysis of popular fiction readership in early-twentieth-century China, Link suggests that both the upper and middle classes read popular fiction during this decade. The upper class included "wealthy bankers, merchants, and industrialists," and "politicians, some writers, intellectuals and students." The middle class, known as *xiaoshimin*, included "small merchants, clerks, high-school students, housewives and other modestly educated marginally well off urbanites."[51] The tabloid press actually helped pave the way for the market success of the popular "mandarin duck and butterfly" fiction of the 1910s. Not only had its writers developed strategies for capturing those middle and upper class groups in the 1910s but they also helped create the genre itself. Emerging in Shanghai, this genre focused on love between men and women, perhaps taking its name from the romantic image of paired ducks and butterflies cohabiting in their natural environments.[52] As Link points out, the late Qing "novels of sentiment" by Wu Jianren and others were precursors of the butterfly fiction of the 1910s.[53]

Tabloid Populism

The symbiotic relationship between readers and writers points to the commercial nature of tabloid populism. Tabloid writers and readers communicated to shape the anti-establishment content of the papers and magazines. Writers spoke to readers through editorials, editor's notices, book prefaces, and book commentaries. They worked by trial and error, always gauging their readers' tastes by scrutinizing sales and making adjustments accordingly. Readers commented on what they read, expressing likes and dislikes through letters to the editor and private channels. The ultimate power of readers over tabloid writers should not be underestimated. Sun Yusheng originally planned to write only thirty chapters of *Dreams in Splendid Shanghai*. Twice he was forced to continue the popular novel after his readers, in their letters to the editor, demanded more. Sun wrote thirty more chapters the first time, forty more the second time. The finished novel came to about 700,000 words; it took over two years for *Grove of Laughter* to serialize just the first thirty chapters.[54] Likewise, Wu Jianren was unable to end his popular *Strange Events Eyewitnessed*. Liang Qichao's *New Fiction* (Xinxiaoshuo) serialized forty-five chapters of that novel between 1903 and 1906, the year the journal ceased publication. Wu continued writing until 1910, when *Strange Events Eyewitnessed* was published as a book, with 108 chapters in eight volumes. These were enormously long novels by Chinese literary standards. Tabloid populism was thus a product of the commercial reading market.

At first, as we saw in Chapter 1, tabloid literati focused overwhelmingly on life in Shanghai's pleasure quarters and on literary games. By early 1898, however, readers had begun to develop an appetite for political and national news – a response, no doubt, to controversial incidents such as the German occupation of Shandong and the eventful years at the turn of the twentieth century. National and foreign news became important to more and more readers, and the tabloids had to satisfy this growing demand to remain profitable. Thus, in early 1898, *Fun* began publishing news from wire services, although it later discontinued this practice, possibly due to its high costs.

Immediately after the Boxer Uprising in 1900, several other tabloids, including *Anecdotes,* began using wire services for national and foreign news, along with news translated from English newspapers such as the Shanghai-based *North China Daily News.* The papers continued this practice off and on, depending on affordability and readers' interests.

After 1898, the press increasingly published literature that opposed political and intellectual elites, as discussed in previous chapters. This literature dealt almost exclusively with contemporary issues and problems; tabloid magazines published novels about current topics only. *All-Story Monthly* even had an editorial policy not to publish historical novels unless they were relevant to contemporary issues.[55] The press's emphasis on the present both influenced and reflected the general trend in the late Qing production of fiction. Prior to the turn of the century, popular novels dealt almost exclusively with traditional subjects. In contrast, most novels from that point onward concerned contemporary Chinese and Western societies.[56] Hu Shi and Lu Xun, two cultural icons in early Republican China, made several observations about the present-centred literary marketplace. Hu noted three hot topics in late Qing novels: officialdom, prostitutes, and the middle stratum of society, such as students studying abroad and female students.[57] As discussed in Chapter 5, around 1903, the tabloid writers, while continuing to attack officials, began targeting persons of New Learning, including reformers and students abroad. They used these new targets as a gimmick to engage readers. Lu Xun, asking why exposés of the dark side of late Qing life were so popular, suggested with his typical penetrating insight that they served as textbooks for those seeking shortcuts to social advancement.[58]

Readers welcomed the tabloid anti-establishment literature and turned many novels into bestsellers; they must have felt that such works helped them connect with contemporary society. The popularity of this literature enables us to gauge "the popular mind," as suggested by Link. Link found, by studying butterfly fiction of the 1910s and 1920s, that "the reading of popular fiction had a place within the life patterns of readers, where it filled psychological needs its readers regularly felt."[59] The very popularity of tabloid literature suggests that in some ways it spoke to readers personally and intellectually.

How readers felt about the tabloid literature depended on their position in the political, social, and economic power structures.[60] In the tabloid community, most readers, as low- to middle-ranked literati and urbanites of various social and economic backgrounds, were on the margins of these power structures and were keenly aware of that fact. To varying degrees, they experienced the uncertainties and anxieties caused by the rapid changes taking place around them. Although an individual's position in society does not determine precisely his or her views about state and society, it does play a role in shaping his or her perceptions and consciousness. Thus, tabloid readers in general tended to interpret tabloid literature from their position as underdogs. Interpretation, of course, involves both analytical and psychological faculties. The literature certainly satisfied readers who bore real grudges against officials, reformers, and revolutionaries, but even an average reader in search of literary entertainment could delight in discovering moral degeneration in the establishment. As underdogs who sought ready answers to contemporary problems, readers probably found the tabloid populism appealing. The literature that made the establishment and privileged classes into scapegoats for everything wrong in contemporary China thus struck just the right chord in their ears, echoing and articulating what they already felt. Of course, however, many other factors also contributed to the development of this populism, as discussed in previous chapters and in the Conclusion.

Tabloid Aesthetics

Just as tabloid readers and writers jointly gave rise to tabloid populism, they also fostered a distinctive mode of literary representation in the press. For tabloid literati, style was as important as content in a modern newsprint medium that aimed at an ever-expanding readership. For these writers, pleasing readers – and hence maximizing readership – required a new aesthetic, different from the orthodox literary aesthetics that valued seriousness, correctness, accuracy, and indoctrination. Aesthetics in general is about taste: what is pleasing and desirable. Taste in reading is by nature personal and depends on an array of factors: emotion, intellectual and educational orientation, social position, gender, economic and cultural background, and so on. Yet, diverse though reading tastes may have been, there existed common threads of aesthetic values in the market for popular literature. Readers exhibited these values when they spent money on such literature. Market-savvy tabloid writers, observing and anticipating their readers' aesthetic preferences, developed certain practices in their writing.

Despite their great diversity in style and panache, writers consistently employed certain representational strategies that became distinctive to tabloids. The essence of these strategies included a focus on entertainment and an ingenious, daring breach of conventional representation. This was especially true in treatments of political and social reality, which blurred traditional boundaries between truth and fiction, reality and fantasy. Tabloid writers dragged politics from its exalted position down to the mundane level of public entertainment.

Merry Laughter and Angry Curses

Nothing was more important for tabloid writers than entertaining their readers. What style of writing would best serve this purpose? Li Boyuan ruminated on this question in listing the six dos and four don'ts in "playful writings" *(youxi wenzhang)*. To Li, the deadliest enemy of "playful writings" was serious and straightforward didactics. He stressed the importance of oblique or implied expressions, as readers would find them intriguing, enchanting, and imaginative. In order to write implicitly and to avoid a monotonous, straightforward style, Li suggested humour, sarcasm, allegory, and analogy as literary devices. He also advised writers on writing about obscene subjects, urging them to employ neither explicit lewdness nor blunt disparagement, but rather sarcasm and inference.[61] Wu Jianren spoke on various occasions about the entertainment value of literature. He wrote: "Talking about literature, direct and pointed words are not as appealing as humorous words. That is why humour and fiction are good."[62] Commenting on a chapter in a novel "translated" from French, in which the translator inserted his own humour, Wu explained that humour and jokes were necessary, otherwise the chapters' slow development would bore readers.[63]

Tabloid writers evaluated each other largely on how well they wrote "playful writings," and many of them built their literary reputations on this standard. They characterized their writing style as "merry laughter and angry curses." Li Boyuan used this very phrase to describe his writing style in early issues of *Fun*.[64] Qiu Shuyuan praised Li as a rare talent and master of a diverse array of genres, possessing a writing style full of emotional "merry laughter and angry curses." Li succeeded, said Qiu, in capturing the very essence of literary "playfulness." Qiu praised other writers, including Gao Taichi, Zhou Bingyuan, and Wu Jianren, for excellence in writing playful poems.[65] Sun Yusheng described Li Boyuan as "particularly good at playful writing, such as humorous conversations and doggerels."[66] He praised Wu Jianren for unrestrained and fine poetry and prose, especially in his excellent short humorous pieces.[67] Sun also commissioned Zhou Bingyuan specifically to write humour for his *Grove of Laughter*. Reviewers complimented Wu Jianren for his exceptional ability to transform the absurdities of everyday life into humour. One contemporary noted Wu's talent for humour and added that "when he speaks, everyone listens in admiration."[68]

As a literary style, "merry laughter and angry curses" belongs basically to satire. According to Alvin Kernan, one important attribute of satire is the combination of two opposing sentiments. On the one hand, the satirist writes with emotions such as hate, scorn, ridicule, and contempt. Satire is thus driven by fury and outrage; it uses "language like a fist." On the other hand, the satirist imbues the work with amusement and laughter: "Wit has been the principal means by which satire has made itself respectable."[69] The tabloid writers recognized this juxtaposition of opposing elements, aptly characterizing their work as "merry laughter and angry curses," "humour and sarcasm," and "playful." Words such as "laughter," "humour," and "sarcasm" often appeared in titles of tabloid columns.

Writers used a range of literary devices, including lighthearted banter, slapstick comedy, witticism, sarcasm, humour, irony, parody, profanity, facetiousness, and dramatic shock and surprise. The previous chapters have offered many examples of those strategies at work. The following piece, "Down to the Sea, the Steamboats," combines many of those strategies:

A young man from a rich family in Anhui came to Shanghai, bringing with him a huge sum of money. He planned to purchase four or five small steamboats to use on Anhui's inland rivers. His friend in Shanghai took him to a brothel for some fun; thereupon, he was enchanted and ensnared by a prostitute, and he indulged himself with her day and night, forgetting his mission altogether. Even when his huge sum of money was about to be depleted, he still could not think of going back home. One day, he said to his friend, pointing at the prostitute's crotch, "A sea is there." His friend replied with a laugh, "Calling it a river is already enough, don't you think it is an exaggeration to call it a sea?" "No," the young man replied, "If a small steamboat cruises around on an inland river, one would feel that the boat is imposing and lonely for having no sizable boats as companions; now, four or five of my steamboats have already ventured there, and not a single trace of them could be found; so, what else could we call it besides a sea?"[70]

To give readers an easy laugh and quick gratification, writers often favoured the "low" style by including vulgarities. Street slang insinuating male and female genitalia and copulation appeared casually in the tabloids, and writers had no qualms about applying them to officials, revolutionaries, and the like.

Humour from one era very often falls flat in another. The particular humour in tabloid literature worked because readers found that it revealed much about contemporary conflicts and elucidated an often perplexing reality. The rapidly changing times mingled the old with the new, creating ample material for ridicule. Readers laughed at Qing rulers and officials, for though they were dying out, they were still powerful. Readers laughed at women and conservative literati for they were changing in social statuses, the former ascending and the latter descending. Readers laughed at the appropriators of "the new" because they had gained prestige and power that others could only have dreamed about. Ultimately, readers welcomed humour because they felt no sympathy for the objects of ridicule. Skeptical laughter gave them the sense of belonging to the laughing community and the pleasure of seeing through a society in which nothing could be taken for granted.

In his study of the sixteenth-century writer Rabelais, Mikhail Bakhtin shows the writer using a literary mode that he calls "carnivalesque" – the use of humour and chaos to subvert dominant modes of literary expression.[71] Rabelais's carnivalesque writing reflected his source materials: the folk culture of humour in Medieval Europe. To Bakhtin, this culture took the form of "carnival festivities," "comic spectacles," and various ritual practices in which laughter was the foundation. Analyzing the subversive nature of laughter, Bakhtin suggests that this folk culture created a world outside the authority of Church and State; he further argues that this carnival world of laughter opposed the official world of Church and State. Bakhtin's study reveals that form (laughter) is inseparable from content (anti-establishment), and that, indeed, form is message.

In a similar way, the late Qing "merry laughter and angry curses" *form* was also a *message*; yet this message was perhaps even more potent than Bahktin's carnivals in the unequivocal way in which it attacked the establishment. As "merry laughter and angry curses" predominantly and directly targeted the political realm, we see clearly how tabloid aesthetics (form) and tabloid populism (message) worked together effectively to shape the defiant tabloid community.

Politics and Entertainment

Examining the massive late Qing tabloid literature, one can see that from the very beginnings of their careers, writers perceived and conceived politics as inseparable from entertainment. Their work clearly reflected this attitude, especially as the political environment became more permissive after 1900. Like Liang Qichao and others who promoted the educational use of literature, they realized that fiction, as a form of entertainment, was an effective means of communicating their own political messages to readers.

Writers therefore coupled politics with entertainment and made politicians, political activists, and political issues an integral part of fun making. Tabloid literati turned policy making at the imperial court and intellectual debates of the day into colourful subjects of everyday amusement; they portrayed rulers and officials, reformers, and revolutionaries as actors, clowns, and game players, all sharing a common trait: moral degradation. One could find amusement in discovering how politicians lied, cheated, and repressed others for their own benefit. Those exposed by the writers' pens became so comical, so humourless, pretentious, self-righteous, fastidious, and lustful, that the only possible reaction from readers was laughter and curses. Beginning in 1898, the tabloids published hardly an issue without making fun of politicians and political issues. Making sensationalism work hand in hand with sentimentality, writers transformed serious political events and issues into anecdotes, poetry, novel chapters, and dramatic scenes. As Chen Pingyuan points out, it was the work of Wu Jianren and Li Boyuan that turned the "fiction of jokes" into a literary genre.[72]

Laughing and cursing at the establishment had become the spirit of the time. Never before in Chinese history had political issues and political figures become objects of public scrutiny in such a pervasive and systematic way. Never before in Chinese history had entertainment been cemented so firmly to representations of politics and politicians. This engagement between literature and society had been previously unthinkable. In the past, contemporary politics rarely entered into the public domain, and literati could only write about politics from either a historical distance or a safe private corner. As we saw in previous chapters, in the late Qing, the dark side of society became public knowledge with "journalistic immediacy."[73] It was through entertainment that countless readers met political figures and experienced political events and issues. The imperative of entertainment had become the norm for how people imagined politics and politicians.

Along with this laughter came doubt and the realization that dignified officials, high-minded reformers, and revolutionaries really wore no clothes, their presumed power and righteousness little but counterfeit. Nothing erodes authority and claims to righteousness more than satirical and skeptical laughter. Tabloid writers shaped their lenses with irony and ridicule and led readers to peer through these lenses at the established and the high-minded. The more wicked, pretentious, and self-righteous the exalted ones appeared, the heartier the laughter became. The more powerless one felt, the louder the laughter, and hence the more damaging to the power and prestige of authority figures. Laughing at the powerful, the powerless in turn became empowered. "Laughing and cursing together," collectively, helped fashion a consciousness of "us" as the politically powerless yet righteous, and "them" – officials and the privileged – as the politically powerful and immoral.

News and Fiction
Another anti-establishment aesthetic arose from the tabloid writers' deliberate blurring of boundaries between news and fiction. The two became virtually

interchangeable and indistinguishable: news was fictionalized and fiction read like news. As Des Forges put it, "news items mimicked the installment fiction," and installment fiction constantly shifted from "fictional" narrative to "journalist" narrative.[74] Writers competed with one another in exaggerating what they perceived as political and social evils. Humour, their major literary device, worked precisely through gross exaggeration. Yet this exaggeration grew out of some fundamental truth. Tabloid writers were neither entirely factual nor completely fanciful; rather, they seamlessly interwove fact and imagination to create a new "reality." They made every attempt to convince readers that this new reality was the true reality of the Chinese state and society.

This intersection of reality and fiction was readily apparent in novels, which writers tried to make "real" and news-like. Usually set in the present, these novels foregrounded major national events and situated protagonists in real social, political, and cultural environs. Wu Jianren had characters reading actual newspapers, including Liang Qichao's *Qingyibao* and *Shiwubao*.[75] The novel *Strange Events Eyewitnessed* includes an account of its own publication history: it was sent by a character to Liang Qichao's *New Fiction*, then to the Shanghai Guangzhi Publishing House to publish. While the character was fictitious, the novel and its place of publication were factual. Writers also turned real people into fictional characters. Studies of late Qing fiction have identified dozens of such characters – including top-ranking officials and members of the Imperial Academy in Li's *Officialdom Unmasked* and *A Brief History of Enlightenment* and Wu's *Strange Events Eyewitnessed*.[76] Yeh also notes that novels about courtesans took a "realistic approach" in portraying courtesan life, and that although the novels were not "raw sociological data," neither were they "pure fiction."[77]

Thus, the writers consistently retained a kernel of truth in both news reports and fiction. When they mocked the poor quality of new-style schools, deriding the poorly qualified superintendents and teachers and the inferior textbooks and equipment, they were not fictionalizing these problems. Contemporary reports showed that new-style schools in the Jiangnan area in fact performed poorly, suffering from all the problems the writers identified. When writers ridiculed students of the New Learning for behaving as though they had "no father and mother," they effectively captured the real sense of the youth's rebellion against the traditional family system. Writer and translator Yang Jiang recalled in 1993 a scandal when her father returned home to Wuxi in 1902 after graduating from Tokyo's Waseda University. When her father refused to bow his head to his ancestors at the clan's temple, a relative wanted to expel him from the clan.[78]

Writers repeatedly insisted on the factual nature of their work. They claimed that news reports about people and events were factual, and that even their novels and plays rested on "historical facts," "eyewitness reports," real experiences of acquaintances, and information from major Chinese and foreign newspapers. Wu Jianren maintained that he based *Cutting the Heart Open (Pouxinji)* on historical documents and that he did not fabricate a single event.[79] Defending *Strange Events Eyewitnessed*, which took him over seven years to write, Wu claimed that he had directly seen and heard everything reported in the novel.[80] Li Boyuan often reminded readers of the credibility and impartiality of his paper, attesting to his own fairness in judgment and care in verifying information.[81] Yeh affirms the reliability of early tabloids as factual sources.[82] Of course, early modern Chinese journalism did not as a whole subscribe to a strict standard for factual news reports. Mittler finds that *Shenbao*'s news intertwined elements of fiction and fact.[83] Tabloid writers, however, felt compelled to assert their innocence since they knew that they intentionally blurred the line between news and fiction.

To establish credibility, writers often listed source materials for their fiction, including confidential conversations with "insider" friends and acquaintances, reports from major foreign and Chinese newspapers and journals, and historical documents. In describing his sources in the foreword to *The National Incident of 1900*, Li claimed that 40 to 50 percent came from Chinese and foreign newspapers, 30 to 40 percent from friends knowledgeable about the incident, and only 10 to 20 percent from his own head. Wu Jianren listed six sources that he used for *Gallivanting in Yunnan (Yunnan yecheng)*, including Ming-era books on Yunnan and a diary from the Yuan Dynasty.[84]

Writers kept persuading readers to accept their fiction as factual portrayals of contemporary China. Wu Jianren wanted his readers to believe what they read as true and real, although they were fully aware of its fictitious nature.[85] In the middle of his novel *Touring Shanghai*, Wu reminded readers: "Readers, don't think fiction is mere fabrication, this passage tells the truth."[86] Li Boyuan also warned readers not to treat *The National Incident of 1900* as fiction. Through one of his characters, he defended his portrayal of reality as more accurate than photographs and more revealing than oil paintings. Writers displayed no qualms about presenting their hyped-up reality as factual, their fiction as actual reality. For them, this was how contemporary Chinese should be represented. Li Boyuan expressed frustration with his reading public when he marvelled at Western readers of "yellow newspapers" who were tolerant of factually inaccurate accounts.[87] David Wang suggests that late Qing exposé writers no longer felt obligated to obey established ways of thinking and representing reality, or to comply with conventional literary moral restraints.[88]

Indeed, the tabloid literati were at their best in creating the impression of a degenerating state and society when they conflated fiction and reality in their narratives.

To a large extent, the reading public appeared to find the writers' versions of reality credible. Sun Baoxuan, a literatus from a family of prominent officials, recorded in his diary a conversation with a friend about *Officialdom Unmasked:* "The novel is good at depicting society. The novel leaves nothing unrevealed about how people treat each other – their every move and action, their every word and sentence – in the real world. The author of the book is truly malicious."[89] Hu Shi also regards *Officialdom Unmasked* as "materials of social history" and "reflecting the actual officialdom of the time."[90] A contemporary writer observed: "Every time an installment came out, people read it with cheer. Those who knew about society all said, 'The author must have had experiences in officialdom, otherwise he would not have been able to write like this.' Those social climbers would say, 'All the officials [in the novel] are our teachers.'"[91] Yet another contemporary praised Wu Jianren's *Strange Events Eyewitnessed* as a superb piece of work, noting that careful readers should have no difficulty identifying many personalities in the novel.[92] If the well-educated trusted the writers' veracity, average readers perhaps simply preferred to believe what they read since they were sympathetic toward the views expressed, especially when writers spoke in moralist tones and in the name of the people.

Moreover, writers successfully tapped into the powerful credibility that literature traditionally enjoyed with Chinese readers. Even as late as the 1890s, Shanghai residents performed ritual ceremonies to show reverence for written words, and local governments enforced regulations concerning the respectful treatment and disposal of written materials.[93] Readers tacitly trusted writers' authority in providing truth. As Andrew Nathan points out, "the sense that what is recorded is ultimately true, either true to fact or true to life – remains a fundamental underpinning in both the historical and fictional branches of the Chinese narrative tradition."[94]

Conclusion

This chapter shows how the interactive relationship between tabloid writers and readers functioned as market forces, and explores how those forces shaped the populism and aesthetics of the tabloid press. Tabloid populism and aesthetic practices focused ultimately on one goal: to make literature engaging and popular. Des Forges's study of serialized fiction of the period elucidates this market-driven literary phenomenon. He identifies four narrative aesthetics, all geared to some extent at maximizing readership.[95]

As tabloid populism and aesthetics worked together to ensure the commercial success of the tabloid press, they intertwined and reinforced each other. While tabloid aesthetics made populism fun, easy to digest, and thus more popular, these aesthetics were also anti-establishment. The three couplings – merry laughter and angry curses, politics and entertainment, news and fiction – challenged orthodox literary values that bolstered the authority of the political establishment.

The traditional orthodoxy saw literature as a means of teaching the Way. Respectable literature had to be "serious" in form and content; the exalted subject of politics should never be combined with frivolous matters of entertainment. For the tabloid literati, however, politics and politicians were not at all sacred. It was precisely through entertainment that they could best destroy politicians' claims to power and undermine their legitimacy. These writers showed not only that "serious matters" could be fused with entertainment but also how powerful this fusion could be. The popularity of tabloid literature is evidence of how far the late Qing literary public had deviated from the literary austerity and political correctness of orthodox ideology.

The orthodox view of literature denounced fiction as insignificant and frivolous, not only because it was mere entertainment but also because it was potentially dangerous. The political establishment understood that fiction could be confused with fact, and hence undermine their interpretation of reality. After all, the authorities' power rested on their versions of truth and reality. By blurring news and fiction, tabloid writers raised two vital questions: the nature of reality, and whose reality literature represents. Writers challenged the political and intellectual establishments' monopoly on defining reality and representing truth. They saw themselves as providing the "true reality." For these writers, it was precisely the "aesthetic gap" between news and fiction, between the represented and representation, that enabled them to subvert politics and politicians.

While tabloid aesthetics strengthened anti-establishment tabloid populism, the latter enabled the former to develop fully as a fashionable way to represent politics, society, and elites. To be sure, past writers had also displayed a satirical flair in criticizing the government. For example, Wu Jingzi's satirical novel *The Scholar (Rulin waishi)*, completed around 1750, targeted the government examination system. However, never before in Chinese literature had such aesthetic practices been so collectively, persistently, and grotesquely employed. Tabloid populism, developed collectively in the name of the "people" and from the perspectives of political and intellectual underdogs, helped create defiant tabloid aesthetics as its most fitting mode of representation.

This chapter has identified the driving force behind the development of tabloid aesthetic populism: namely, the literary marketplace. The concluding chapter will summarize the entire late Qing tabloid phenomenon and its historical significance.

Conclusion

The tabloid press and its community were hallmarks of *fin de siècle* China and the late Qing revolution in print journalism. They constituted the active core and the voice of the low- and middle-ranked literati. They also were the source of an aesthetic populism that spread its subversive and anti-establishment sentiments and discourses to an even broader public. Relying on the agency of the tabloid community, the once powerless low- and middle-ranked literati pushed themselves to the centre of the political stage.

Aesthetic populism developed in the late 1890s and came into full bloom in the last years of the Qing Dynasty. Two forces came together to create this aesthetic populism. First was a tremendous demand for print entertainment in Shanghai and elsewhere that arose in conjunction with the newly developed modern media. The tabloid press met this demand by catering to low- and middle-ranked literati, who comprised a large part of the literate population and provided a market for this print medium. The entrepreneurial producers of the tabloid press – the writers, publishers, and editors – came from this same social stratum.

Second, the political, social, and intellectual storms enveloping China heightened the concerns and anxieties of the low- and middle-ranked literati. As traditionally educated men on the lowest rungs of the political ladder, they felt threatened by the changes taking place. They were concerned not only with their own futures but also with the future of their nation. The tabloid press gathered this otherwise diverse group into a coalition of the aggrieved, giving vent to their fears and frustrations. The press provided a forum for this community to simultaneously enjoy literary entertainment and express their political views. Although the press focused on literary games and tantalizing stories about Shanghai's pleasure quarters in the early years, in the years after 1901, when the Empress Dowager Cixi began supporting reform, the tabloids became intensely political, seamlessly intertwining political criticism with entertainment. This book has told the story of how this transition occurred.

The tabloid community formed as professional writers sought to earn a living with their pens and readers made the press a part of their everyday entertainment. Readers shared news, stories, and rumours about courtesans and Shanghai's leisure activities. They patronized the city's establishments, using information and reviews provided in the tabloids. They expressed opinions, participated in riddle games, and used the press to organize literary societies. By using courtesans as muses in a decadent literary-erotic carnival, writers and readers became bound together into one community.

On the surface, tabloid writers wanted only to make a fast buck and readers were interested only in having fun. Underneath, however, lay a range of other interests and concerns. After all, China was at the brink: foreign imperial powers stood ready to strike and dominate anytime they wished, and domestic conflicts challenged the foundations of both state and society. Readers wanted to know and comprehend what was happening around them. They wanted to express their opinions and determine how best to survive and advance in an uncertain environment. Writers listened closely to their readers, adapting to the demand for politically relevant content; thus, political issues and opinions became increasingly central to the tabloid press. At the same time, tabloid readership expanded nationwide, as did the audience for literature published by tabloid writers in other presses and formats.

The urgent question for the tabloid community was how to account for China's decline. Who was responsible for China's deplorable state of affairs? The Qing government and officials were obvious culprits. The community witnessed firsthand the crisis in the Chinese state and the government's diplomatic and military ineptness in dealing with foreigners. Especially damaging to the Qing government was the Boxer Uprising in 1900, when the imperial family had to flee foreign troops and ended up having to pay a huge indemnity to foreign governments. It became clear to everyone that the Emperor wore no clothes. Some who aspired to official positions saw their hopes dashed with the termination of the government examination system and the rising legitimacy of the New Learning, while others saw a career in officialdom as unworthy. As outsiders, they all resented the insiders – the officials – whom they accused of failing in their responsibilities.

Writers and readers launched an unprecedented attack on officialdom in the press. Denouncing officials became a sport and the basis of a new genre of fiction – the fiction of censure. Tabloid writers in this genre produced many bestselling novels that became emblematic of this official-bashing fad. Using humour and satire, the press portrayed officialdom as a swamp of immorality and incompetence. Immorality was the press's primary concern, and its pages were filled with stories of officials' iniquitous behaviour, including debauchery, greed, arrogance, maliciousness, deceptiveness, and nepotism. Underlying these attacks was a combination of traditional Chinese ethics and new foreign values. This moral mixture turned into a potent weapon that disenfranchised outsiders deployed against politically powerful insiders. The press successfully conveyed the message that officials had only their own wealth and status in mind, not the welfare of the public, and that the Qing state had failed miserably in governing the nation.

This critical posture was connected directly to another urgent question: why had China fallen so low in the hierarchy of international powers, and what should the government do about it? This was not merely a theoretical question. Associated with it was a range of real emotions: shame, frustration, anger, despair, and hope. As foreign political philosophies of race and ethnicity, Social Darwinism, the nation-state, and popular sovereignty made their way into China, its citizens applied this new knowledge in evaluating their own country, rethinking political and ethnic foundations and seeking ways for China to become a strong competitor in the new world order.

Modern Chinese nationalism, in all its forms, developed in this changing environment. The tabloid community conceived its own brand of nationalism, which resembled ideas held by the intellectual and political elites in some ways but differed markedly in others. The community fretted about China's fate as the nation confronted the imperialist powers, which tabloid writers and readers held in contempt, but it was not anti-foreign per se, at least not in any racial sense. In a similar vein, it condemned the Qing government but was not anti-Manchu per se. In fact, the tabloid community adamantly opposed a revolution to overthrow the Qing regime. For it, the Qing rulers offered a better alternative than the revolutionaries because the former more closely adhered to Chinese ethical values, to which the community still subscribed both intellectually and emotionally.

The community appropriated the intellectual elite's discourses on popular sovereignty and constitutional government, but later turned these ideas against them. Writers criticized the elites' disingenuousness for professing belief in these new political ideas while in actuality still placing the interests of the state ahead of the people. Unlike the elites, the tabloid community doubted that the political establishment would ever actually implement a constitutional government. Nor did they believe that such a government would ever faithfully act on behalf of the people – especially not if China's elites came to occupy elected posts.

The influx of new foreign ideas and practices posed a great challenge to traditional Chinese values. Were the old Chinese ways no longer suitable in the new international order? Had China been doing it all wrong, employing the wrong political institutions and mistaken ethics? Was this the cause of China's dire situation? A wide spectrum of answers arose to these questions. On one end stood Liang Qichao, who essentially accepted the universality of Western ideas and practices, using them as a yardstick in evaluating China. At the other end stood Gu Hongming (1857-1928), well-versed in both Western and Chinese culture, who rejected outright the validity of Western ideas and practices and who used only a traditional Chinese yardstick to appraise China. The tabloid community stood somewhere in between. To be sure, they supported in principle almost all reform measures proposed by reformers and the government – campaigning, for example, for the eradication of footbinding, a cultural practice that Gu wanted to preserve. Like Gu, however, they believed strongly in Chinese ethics and saw Western values as threatening the Confucian morality that regulated family and society. They called for a regeneration of Confucianism as the ethical foundation of the Chinese state and society, promoted only a selective adoption of Western ideas and practices, and warned against blind admiration of the West.

Nevertheless, Western ideas gained increasing legitimacy and respectability, and the rules governing social advancement shifted in favour of the so-called reformers. Some benefited directly from new government opportunities created by reform; others improved their chances for advancement by obtaining credentials through a new-style education. Unable to benefit from these new opportunities and lacking appropriate credentials, members of the tabloid community resented the privileged few who were able to capitalize on the New. They began to attack reformers in the same way they attacked officials, mainly by targeting their alleged moral depravity. They accused reformers of appropriating the New Learning to gain symbolic, political, and economic power, and of caring little about the nation and its people. They targeted local gentry for exploiting people through the New Policy reform, and attacked revolutionaries on the same moral grounds.

Tabloid writers developed two distinctive aesthetic styles. First, they made politics entertaining, dubbing their narrative style "merry laughter and angry curses." They accomplished this by using parody, satire, and humour to depict and discuss vital political issues of the day. They applied this style to a variety of genres, including fiction, *tanci*, drama, plays, ballads, and poetry. Second, the writers deliberately blurred divisions between news and fiction, and between fact and rumour. News reports and fictional accounts thus became indistinguishable.

These aesthetic styles enabled the tabloid community to perceive, interpret, and represent contemporary society from a populist perspective. Laughter and mockery became powerful weapons in the underdogs' fight against the powerful and privileged. Nothing cast doubt on the legitimacy of the elites more cynically or more effectively. Conflating news and fiction served the community's anti-establishment agenda. By purposely simplifying reality, the press could easily stereotype and demonize officials, reformers, and revolutionaries; fictionalizing reality also challenged the establishment's claims to truth.

Driven by the pursuit of fame and profit, tabloid writers played a leading role in developing aesthetic populism, but it was the readers who enabled this development that articulated their sentiments and opinions. Thus, writers and readers, representatives of the low- and middle-ranked literati, formed their own political identities and participated in the late Qing transformation.

Historians have not given the late Qing tabloid phenomenon the attention it deserves, particularly its role in political, social, and intellectual developments of the period. The rise of the tabloid community signalled the late Qing disintegration of the state/literati relationship. For a thousand years, literati and the state were interdependent, each relying upon the other for survival. The state provided legitimacy and privileges that sustained the literati as a ruling class; the literati, in turn, provided services that enabled the state to function. The tabloid community's actions and sentiments at the turn of the century demonstrate the severing of this traditional cooperative relationship, especially for the urban and lower echelons of the literati. The community displayed a profound and pervasive alienation from the state. Frustrated with the Qing state's inability to ensure the well-being of the nation, many community members also saw the state as directly responsible for the difficulties in their own lives. They complained about their marginal political voice, the decline of their social status as literati, and their poverty, all of which resulted largely from the rapid political, social, and intellectual changes taking place. By pursuing fame and fortune in the marketplace, tabloid literati demonstrated their increasing independence and decreasing reliance upon the state for their social and economic well-being. All of these indicate that the rank-and-file literati, like many elite literati, contributed to the weakened state/literati nexus, thereby undermining the source of their status as a ruling class. The disintegration of the literati class as the servant of the state conditioned – but did not necessitate – the 1911 Revolution.

Roger Chartier's work on the cultural origins of the French Revolution sheds some light on the relationship between "alienated intellectuals" and revolution. Chartier identifies a broad range of cultural developments centred on the world of print in prerevolutionary France. He examines the emergence of professionalism among ambitious and disenfranchised authors attempting to live by the pen in commercial literary markets and traces the close connection between those "alienated intellectuals" as authors and the rise of an ideology critical of the state and the church. The written word enabled private citizens to discuss ideas and engage in critical thinking. This realm of public discourse contributed to a decline in both political and religious authority in the decades leading up to the French Revolution. Chartier further argues that this transformation perhaps constituted a necessary condition in the making of the Revolution.[1]

In similar fashion, China's alienated literati helped bring about the end of the Qing state. In the last decade of the Qing, literati endeavoured to bring about a political and ideological transformation in the Chinese state and society. High- and middle-ranked literati, including even some top-level government officials, changed their minds fundamentally in favour of reform, as Douglas Reynolds notes in his study of the New Policy reform *(xinzheng)*.[2] In the final years of the Qing, literati in many Chinese provinces directly challenged the state's authority, as when they protested the state's plan to control Chinese railway lines. Although literati at all levels participated in the late Qing revolution in print journalism and fashioned critical discourses opposing the state, it was the tabloid literati who most closely resembled Chartier's "alienated intellectuals" and their role in influencing the general public. The tabloid community in particular emerged as a distinctive and powerful voice that represented the low- and middle-ranked literati and fostered a popular anti-government culture that was hostile towards the state. It did so by a massive decade-long official-bashing campaign that helped to destroy the legitimacy and symbolic power of Qing rule. Wanting only to reform, not topple, the Qing government, they unwittingly helped prepare the cultural ground for the 1911 Revolution.

Moreover, in the name of the people, the tabloid community distrusted and opposed anyone they regarded as powerful and privileged; they relied primarily on Chinese ethics as a weapon of choice in attacking their opponents' discourses and behaviours. The community's fundamental belief in Chinese ethical values only strengthened with the rising tides of the New Learning. The community differed notably from the intellectual elites in its views on politics, ethics, and ethnicity. It opposed conservatives, reformers, and revolutionaries, along with their political and intellectual prescriptions for China's future. It deliberately cultivated a consciousness of "Us" as the politically and socially powerless, versus "Them" as the powerful and privileged. This tabloid populism gained persuasiveness and appeal precisely because community members saw themselves as outsiders and underdogs, taking on the mighty political and intellectual "insiders." They created a subversive culture of doubt, distrust, and defiance that empowered the literate public. This culture reflected public opinion and sentiment; it is one of the first outgrowths of China's media-driven "mass culture."

The late Qing tabloid phenomenon formed one important link in China's long history of subversive print media. As early as the Song Dynasty, Zhou Linzhi, an official living around 1160 CE, reported to the emperor about the circulation of a tabloid newsletter. The following excerpt from his report puts the late Qing tabloid experience in historical perspective:

> At times when Your Majesty promulgated drastic measures through your edicts, there were always rumourmongers who spread sensational news misleading the public. For instance, when Your Majesty summoned some of your old ministers back to power the other day, there was a great deal of talk around town emanating from an unknown source. On close examination, I found that these rumours always began with the tabloid news, which leaked out from the Bureau of Official Reports and were the work of the official agents of the residences. In recent years, whenever there is news in the air and the public is held in suspense, these agents would snatch at the chance to write the news on little scripts and circulate them around. This is the so-called *xiaobao*. For instance, they often say, "So-and-so was summoned to an imperial audience today," or "So-and-so was dismissed," or "So-and-so got an appointment." This news is often inaccurate or even [based on] groundless fabrications, but scholars at the capital would say, on hearing such news, "We have already read it in the *xiaobao*," and magistrates in the country would say on hearing the news, "We have received the *xiaobao* already." Sometimes it turned out to be true and sometimes it turned out to be false. If it was true, the news should not have been permitted to leak out, and if it was false, it was misleading. I rather think that as trivial as the subject seems to be, the spreading of news through such channels is injurious to the administration and demands our attention. I humbly petition that Your Majesty issue an edict prohibiting their circulation with definite forms of punishment attached to it. In this way, people will learn about government orders without conjecturing about them, and whatever is issued will be correct and reliable. In this way, the dignity of the government is upheld and the source of publicity will be unified.[3]

Here, Zhou vividly described a tabloid newsletter's usurpation of the government's monopoly on information control, thereby sabotaging the imperial reputation and authority.

Seven centuries later, the Qing state knew well the dangers of the unauthorized release of sensitive information. From its very beginning, the state had maintained strict control over the circulation of literature and the release of information. It ruthlessly punished anyone who dared to write, read, or collect seditious and subversive literature.[4] Only in the last decade of the Qing, when the government was forced to relinquish this control, did the tabloid press come into existence as an opposition force.

The late Qing tabloid press also set a precedent for the tabloids that flourished during the Republican era. Multiple political authorities and various intellectual forces dominated that era, and the tabloids challenged them all – the left, the middle, and the right. Republican Shanghai tabloids competed for media dominance, successfully capturing Shanghai's "petty urbanites," who comprised most of its reading public. The success of Republican tabloids, like that of their predecessors, relied on making politics the subject of entertainment.

Today, as the post-Mao political environment becomes more permissive, tabloid publications are once again flourishing, performing their historical role of challenging the authorities and the privileged in the guise of entertainment. Moreover, in today's digital age, which increasingly threatens the state's ability to control public communication, ordinary Chinese have taken advantage of the Internet, blogosphere, and social media to raise their political voices. As though history were repeating itself, Chinese bloggers have produced a vast literature criticizing government injustice and exposing officials' corruption. This literature distinguishes itself with black humour and outright rage. Thus, the late Qing tabloid phenomenon left an enduring legacy: tabloid literature remains a powerful weapon for the public to wield in censuring anyone who betrays the public interest.

Notes

Introduction
1. Yao Gonghe, *Shanghai xianhua* (Shanghai: Shangwu yinshuguan, 1933), 176-77. Also see Chen Boxi, *Shanghai yishi daguan* (Shanghai: Shanghai shudian chubanshe, 2000), 269.
2. Chen Boxi, ibid., 269-70.
3. Joan Judge, *Print and Politics: "Shibao" and the Culture of Reform in Late Qing China* (Palo Alto, CA: Stanford University Press, 1996), 41.
4. Leo Ou-fan Lee and Andrew J. Nathan, "The Beginnings of Mass Culture," in *Popular Culture in Late Imperial China*, ed. David Johnson, Andrew J. Nathan, and Evelyn S. Rawski (Berkeley: University of California Press, 1985), 370-73; Perry Link, *Mandarin Ducks and Butterflies: Popular Fiction in Early Twentieth-Century Chinese Cities* (Berkeley: University of California Press, 1981), 151.
5. Peter G. Zarrow, "Introduction: Citizenship in China and the West," in *Imagining the People: Chinese Intellectuals and the Concept of Citizenship, 1890-1920*, ed. Joshua A. Fogel and Peter G. Zarrow (Armonk, NY: M.E. Sharpe, 1997), 4.
6. Yao Gonghe, *Shanghai xianhua*, 184.
7. See Judge, *Print and Politics*, and Barbara Mittler, *A Newspaper for China? Power, Identity and Change in Shanghai's News Media, 1872-1912* (Cambridge, MA: Harvard University Asia Center, 2004).
8. As "little papers," tabloids were small in terms of the number of pages. In the early years, most Shanghai tabloids and mainstream newspapers printed their issues on one side of an identically sized sheet of standard Chinese-made rough paper. For tabloids, each sheet had three horizontally arranged pages, or sections. Chinese readers read text from right to left and from top to bottom. By the end of the first decade of the 1900s, the tabloids and mainstream papers used different sheet sizes, with the former half the size of the latter. See Ma Guangren, ed., *Shanghai xinwenshi* (Shanghai: Fudan daxue chubanshe, 1996), 145. See also Wei Shaochang, ed., *Shiliao suoyin ji*, vol. 30 of *Zhongguo jindai wenxue daxi* (Shanghai: Shanghai shudian, 1996), 177-208.
9. *Fun*, 4 October 1897.
10. S.A. Smith, *Like Cattle and Horses: Nationalism and Labor in Shanghai, 1895-1927* (Durham, NC: Duke University Press, 2002), 15.
11. Zhou Wu and Wu Guilong, "Wanqin shehui," in vol. 5 of *Shanghai tongshi*, ed. Xiong Yuezhi (Shanghai: Shanghai renmin chubanshe, 1999), 362; Xiong Yuezhi, "Lüelun wanqing Shanghai xinxing wenhuaren di chansheng yu huiju," *Lishi yanjiu* 4 (1997): 257-73.
12. Yuan Jin, *Yuanyang hutianpai* (Shanghai: Shanghai shudian chubanshe, 1994), 34.
13. Smith, *Like Cattle and Horses*, 3.
14. Catherine Vance Yeh, *Shanghai Love: Courtesans, Intellectuals, and Entertainment Culture, 1850-1910* (Seattle: University of Washington Press, 2005), 179.
15. Gail Hershatter cites a 1908 guide that lists 1,219 high- and middle-ranked courtesans. Gail Hershatter, *Dangerous Pleasures: Prostitution and Modernity in Twentieth Century Shanghai* (Berkeley: University of California Press, 1997), 39.

16   Li Boyuan, "Jinxian baochen," in vol. 5 of *Li Boyuan quanji*, ed. Xue Zhengxing (Nanjing: Jiangsu guji chubanshe, 1997), 25-27.
17   *Fun*, 25 August 1897. See also *Fun*, 8 June 1899.
18   Christopher A. Reed, *Gutenberg in Shanghai: Chinese Print Capitalism, 1876-1937* (Vancouver: UBC Press, 2005), 104-14.
19   Hong Yu, *Jindai Shanghai xiaobao yu shimin wenhua yanjiu* (Shanghai: Shanghai shudian chubanshe, 2007), 99.
20   The monetary unit *yuan* refers to the Chinese silver dollar. The yuan, in turn, was subdivided into 1,000 wen. Introduced in 1889, the yuan was equivalent to about 0.70 silver taels *(liang)*. Based on estimates by Allen and colleagues, the average daily wage in late Qing Beijing was 0.079 taels. Assuming that an average Shanghai worker received the same wage as a Beijing worker, and assuming that he worked six days a week and fifty weeks per year, this translates into an annual wage of approximately 24 taels, or roughly 34 yuan. Robert C. Allen, Jean-Pascal Bassino, Debin Ma, Christine Moll-Murata, and Jan Luiten van Zanden, "Wages, Prices, and Living Standards in China, 1738-1925, in Comparison with Europe, Japan, and India," *Economic History Review* 64 (2011): 8-38. More specifically, in the early 1900s, the monthly wage was eight yuan for rank-and-file police officers and workers at large factories in Shanghai.
21   Yao Gonghe, *Shanghai xianhua*, 213.
22   Link, *Mandarin Ducks and Butterflies*, 143.
23   Li Boyuan, *Wenming xiaoshi*, in vol. 1 of *Li Boyuan quanji*, ed. Xue Zhengxing (Nanjing: Jiangsu guji chubanshe, 1997), 309.
24   Hong counts forty-six tabloids in late Qing and Republican Shanghai: *Jindai Shanghai xiaobao yu shimin wenhua yanjiu*, 388-91. Also, Meng Zhaochen asserts that there were forty-one tabloids and Qin Shaode suggests forty. Meng Zhaochen, *Zhongguo jindai xiaobao shi* (Beijing: Shehui kexue chubanshe, 2005), 13; and Qin Shaode, *Shanghai jindai baokan shilun* (Shanghai: Fudan daoxue chubanshe, 1994), 141.
25   "Eight-legged essays" were written according to very strict rules. The essay topic was limited to the standard *Four Books* and *Five Classics*. The format and literary form was fixed, as were the use of language and the number of words. The voice must be that of the ancient sages, and there could be no reference to contemporary social issues. "Eight-legged" means that the essay had a fixed format consisting of eight parts, the first of which was the introduction to the topic while the last part was the conclusion. Some parts were limited to a certain number of sentences. Other parts consisted of paragraphs paired according to content and literary style. Writing an essay became a game of words. At times, authors deviated from the strict format, for example, by eliminating a few parts.
26   *Tanci* is both a literary and a performing art. The text of tanci includes easily read prose and rhymed verse. When performing tanci, a storyteller typically narrates the text in a local dialect and sings the verse while playing a stringed instrument.
27   Wang Xuejun, *Li Boyuan nianpu*, in vol. 5 of *Li Boyuan quanji*, ed. Xue Zhengxing (Nanjing: Jiangsu guji chubanshe, 1997), 20-23.
28   Bao Tianxiao, *Chuanyinglou huiyilu* (Taiyuan: Shanxi guji chubanshe, 1999), 571.
29   Ma Guangren, *Shanghai xinwenshi*, 149.
30   Chen Wuwo, *Lao Shanghai sanshinian jianwenlu* (Shanghai: Shanghai shudian chubanshe, 1997), 250; and *Fun*, 8 June 1899.
31   In his study of Shanghai prostitution, Christian Henriot suggests that only nine out of twenty-five courtesans could read and write: *Prostitution and Sexuality in Shanghai: A Social History, 1849-1949*, trans. Noel Castelino (New York: Cambridge University Press, 2001), 30.
32   Yeh, *Shanghai Love*, 16.
33   Bao Tianxiao, *Chuanyinglou huiyilu* (Hong Kong: Dahua chubanshe, 1971, 1973), 318.

34 Sun Baoxuan, *Wangshanlu riji*, vol. 1 of *Zhonghua wenshi luancong zhongkan* (Shanghai: Shanghai guji chubanshe, 1983), 364.
35 *Grove of Laughter*, 4 February 1903.
36 Quoted in Alexander Des Forges, *Mediasphere Shanghai: The Aesthetics of Cultural Production* (Honolulu: University of Hawai'i Press, 2007), 108.
37 Teruo Tarumoto, "Yūgi shujin sentei 'kōshi zuikyū kasen,'" *Shinmatsu shōsetsu kenkyū* 5 (1981): 18.
38 Ma Guangren reports that *Fun*'s circulation was between 7,000 and 8,000 per day, although he does not provide the exact dates of this estimate: *Shanghai xinwenshi*, 149. One contributor mentioned that *Fun* sold 10,000 copies: *Fun*, 26 November 1897. Also, Li Boyuan claimed that he could sell 10,000 copies of *Fun* when he attached to each issue a photograph of a courtesan who won the "flower election." *Fun*, 30 September 1898.
39 Zeng Xubai, ed., *Zhongguo xinwenshi* [The journalistic history of China] (Taipei: Sanmin Shuju, 1984), 270.
40 Judge, *Print and Politics*, 41.
41 The Jiangnan area had more distribution points, which included bookstores, teahouses, private establishments, etc. It is not known how many copies actually sold at these venues.
42 *All-Story Monthly [Yueyue xiaoshuo]* 4, 13 (1908): 9-18 (Shanghai: Shanghai shudian, 1980, reprint) (here and below, volume reference is to reprint edition, issue number reference is to original).
43 *All-Story Monthly* 3, 12 (1908): 227.
44 Denise Gimpel, *Lost Voices of Modernity: A Chinese Popular Fiction Magazine in Context* (Honolulu: University of Hawai'i Press, 2001), 179.
45 Gu Jiegang, *Gu Jiegang zishu* (Zhengzhou: Henan renmin chubanshe, 2005), 23.
46 Xu Zhenyan, "Shixi xiuxiang xiaoshuo di duzhe dingwei," *Mingqing xiaoshuo yanjiu* 62, 4 (2001): 158.
47 Quoted in Xu, ibid., and in Yuan Jin, "Shilun wanqing xiaoshuo dizhe di bianhua," *Mingqing xiaoshuo yanjiu* 59, 1 (2001): 20.
48 Link, *Mandarin Ducks and Butterflies*, 11-12.
49 Su Tiege, "'Xinhainian' (Beijing) aiguobaosuozai wanqing xiaoshuo sanzhong shulüè," *Mingqing xiaoshuo yanjiu* 61, 3 (2001): 90-97.
50 Huang Biao, *Haishang xinjuchao: Zhongguo huaju di xunli qidian* (Shanghai: Shanghai renmin chubanshe, 2003), 107; Jiao Runming and Su Xiaoxuan, *Wanqing shenghuo lueying* (Shenyang: Shenyang chubanshe, 2002), 216.
51 Link, *Mandarin Ducks and Butterflies*, 118.
52 One exception is Harrison's excellent study of a rural literatus. Henrietta Harrison, *The Man Awakened from Dreams: One Man's Life in a North China Village, 1897-1942* (Palo Alto, CA: Stanford University Press, 2005).
53 See, for example, Daniele Albertazzi and Duncan McDonnell, *Twenty-First Century Populism: The Spectre of Western European Democracy* (New York: Palgrave Macmillan, 2008); Harry Chatten Boyte and Frank Riessman, *The New Populism: the Politics of Empowerment* (Philadelphia: Temple University Press, 1986); Ernesto Laclau, "Populism: What's in a Name?" in *Populism and the Mirror of Democracy*, ed. Francisco Panizza (London: Verso, 2005); Ernesto Laclau, *On Populist Reason* (London: Verso, 2005); Jim McGuigan, *Cultural Populism* (New York: Routledge, 1992); Yves Mény and Yves Surel, eds., *Democracies and the Populist Challenge* (New York: Palgrave Macmillan, 2002); Francisco Panizza, "Introduction: Populism and the Mirror of Democracy," in *Populism and the Mirror of Democracy*, ibid.; Paul A. Taggart, *Populism* (Buckingham, UK: Open University Press, 2000); and Kurt Weyland, "Clarifying a Contested Concept: Populism in the Study of Latin American Politics," *Comparative Politics* 34, 1 (2001): 1-22.
54 Albertazzi and McDonnell, *Twenty-First Century Populism*, 3.

Notes to pages 21-31   189

55 Laclau, "Populism: What's in a Name?" 38.
56 Panizza, "Introduction," 10.
57 Wolfgang Iser, *The Implied Reader: Patterns of Communication in Prose Fiction from Bunyan to Becket* (Baltimore: John Hopkins University Press, 1978), 294.

Chapter 1: Community of Fun

1   *Fun*, 25 August 1897.
2   Ibid., 19 November 1897.
3   Wang Xuejun, *Li Boyuan nianpu*, in vol. 5 of *Li Boyuan quanji*, ed. Xue Zhengxing (Nanjing: Jiangsu guji chubanshe, 1997), 37.
4   Sun Yusheng, *Tuixinglu biji*, vol. 80 of *Jindai Zhongguo shiliao congkan*, ed. Shen Yunlong (Taipei: Wenhai chubanshe youxian gongsi, 1972), 154.
5   *Fun*, 28 August 1899.
6   Ibid., 22 November 1900.
7   Qin Shaode, *Shanghai jindai baokan shilun* (Shanghai: Fudan daxue chubanshe, 1993), 135.
8   Wang Xuejun, *Li Boyuan nianpu*, 39.
9   Ye Xiaoqing, *The Dianshizhai Pictorial: Shanghai Urban Life, 1884-1898* (Ann Arbor: University of Michigan Center for Chinese Studies, 2003), 15; see also Catherine Vance Yeh, *Shanghai Love: Courtesans, Intellectuals, and Entertainment Culture, 1850-1910* (Seattle: University of Washington Press, 2005), 230.
10 Wang Xuejun, *Li Boyuan nianpu*, 38.
11 Chen Wuwo, *Lao Shanghai sanshinian jianwenlu* (Shanghai: Shanghai shudian chubanshe, 1997), 196-97.
12 Ibid., 47-48.
13 Ibid., 195-96.
14 Ibid., 203.
15 *Fun*, 17 August 1897.
16 Wang Xuejun, *Li Boyuan nianpu*, 49-50.
17 Chen Wuwo, *Lao Shanghai sanshinian jianwenlu*, 218-21.
18 *Fun*, 5 August 1897.
19 Ibid., 28 October 1897.
20 Ibid., 22 November 1897.
21 Ibid., 23 August 1897.
22 Ibid., 11 August 1897.
23 Ibid., 27 August 1897.
24 Ibid., 17 August 1897.
25 Ibid., 18 August 1897.
26 Ibid., 27 September 1897.
27 Ibid., 5 August 1897.
28 Ibid., 11 August 1897.
29 *Allegories*, 11 March 1901.
30 Ibid., 10 July 1901.
31 Ibid., 29 September 1901.
32 *Fun*, 9 April 1901.
33 *Anecdotes*, 27 October, 28 November, and 23 December 1899.
34 Ibid., 25 January and 8 February 1900.
35 Wang Xuejun, *Li Boyuan nianpu*, 147.
36 *Splendid World*, 6 October 1901.
37 *Allegories*, 20 May 1902.
38 *Fun*, 17 October 1900.
39 Zheng Yimei, *Yimei zazha* (Jinan: Qilu shushe, 1985), 148-51.

40 *Fun*, 21 June and 8 July 1899.
41 Ibid., 19 June 1899.
42 Ibid., 12 May 1899.
43 *Anecdotes*, 9 February 1899.
44 *Fun*, 31 August 1897.
45 Ibid., 17 October 1900.
46 Wang Xuejun, *Li Boyuan nianpu*, 124.
47 Ibid., 123-24.
48 Li Boyuan had a close relationship with Li Pingxiang in the early 1900s: Yeh, *Shanghai Love*, 211.
49 *Splendid World*, 27 September 1901.
50 Wang Xuejun, *Li Boyuan nianpu*, 165.
51 Sun Yusheng, *Tuixinglu biji*, 145-46.
52 Ibid., 181-82.
53 *Fun*, 28 May 1899.
54 Ibid., 15 July 1899.
55 At the time, in 1898, the technology of printing photographs in newspapers was not yet available to tabloids.
56 *Fun*, 30 September 1898.
57 Ibid., 12 March 1899.
58 *Anecdotes*, 21 August 1898.
59 *Fun*, 20 September, 4 November, and 14 November 1898.
60 Ibid., 26 November 1897; Wang Xuejun, *Li Boyuan nianpu*, 97-98.
61 *Fun*, 17 May, 20 May, and 3 September 1899.
62 *Fun*, 16 May and 19 May 1899.
63 Zhu Junzhou and Huang Peiwei, *Zhongguo jindai wenyi baokan gailan (II)*, in *Shiliao suoyinji*, vol. 30 of *Zhongguo jindai wenxue daxi*, ed. Wei Shaochang (Shanghai: Shanghai shudian, 1996), 197.
64 *Fun*, 23 August 1897.
65 Wang Xuejun, *Li Boyuan nianpu*, 162.
66 *Fun*, 15 July 1899.
67 *Yusheng* literally means "born out of jade."
68 *Grove of Laughter*, 2 April 1901; *Anecdotes*, 27 October 1899.
69 *Fun*, 8 March 1899.
70 *Grove of Laughter*, 4 February 1903.
71 *Anecdotes*, 28 November 1899.
72 *Fun*, 22 September and 8-9 November 1897.
73 Wang Yan, "'Xiuxiang xiaoshuo' gaikuang," in vol. 1 of *Illustrated Fiction [Xiuxiang xiaoshuo]* (Beijing: Beijing tushuguan chubanshe, 2006, reprint), 25 (reference is to the Beijing reprint edition unless otherwise noted).
74 *Fun*, 22 September 1898.
75 Chen Wuwo, *Lao Shanghai sanshinian jianwenlu*, 353.
76 *Fun*, 28 August 1897.
77 Ye Zhongqiang, "Youzou yu chengshi kongjian: wanqing minchu shanghai wenren de gonggong jiaowang," *Shiliin* 4 (2006): 131. See also Teruo Tarumoto, *Qingmo xiaoshuo yanjiu jigao*, tr. Wei Chen (Jinan: Qilu shushe, 2006), 182-86.
78 According to Chinese custom, a night consists of five two-hour periods. The fifth period of night is between 3:00 and 5:00 AM.
79 Chen Wuwo, *Lao Shanghai sanshinian jianwenlu*, 339-44.
80 Ibid., 350.
81 Ibid., 352-53.

Notes to pages 40-46   191

82 *Fun*, 21 January 1904.
83 Sun Yusheng, *Tuixinglu biji*, 223-24.
84 *Fun*, 27-30 January and 16-17 April 1902.
85 *Grove of Laughter*, 10-19 December 1902.
86 Ibid., 231.
87 *Fun*, 15 July 1902.
88 *All-Story Monthly [Yueyue xiaoshuo]* 4, 14 (1908): 209-10 and 211-14 (Shanghai: Shanghai shudian, 1980, reprint) (volume reference is to reprint edition, issue number reference is to original).
89 *Grove of Laughter*, 15 July 1902.
90 Ibid., 2 April 1901 and 15 July 1902.
91 *Fun*, 30 September 1898.
92 Ibid., 22 August 1897.
93 Chen Wuwo, *Lao Shanghai sanshinian jianwenlu*, 367.
94 *Fun*, 2 October 1897.
95 Chen Boxi, *Shanghai yishi daguan* (Shanghai: Shanghai shudian chubanshe, 2000), 156.
96 *Fun*, 2 September 1897.
97 Ibid., 2 October 1897 and 12 March 1899.
98 Today the street *Damalu* is named *Nanjing Donglu*.
99 Chen Boxi, *Shanghai yishi daguan*, 270.
100 Chen Wuwo, *Lao Shanghai sanshinian jianwenlu*, 380.
101 Ibid., 91.
102 *Fun*, 9 July and 23 August 1899.
103 Ibid., 21 March and 22 August 1899.
104 Ibid., 27 August 1899.
105 Ibid., 21 May 1902.
106 Chen Wuwo, *Lao Shanghai sanshinian jianwenlu*, 370-71.
107 *Fun*, 21 May and 11 June 1902.
108 Chen Wuwo, *Lao Shanghai sanshinian jianwenlu*, 381; *Fun*, 17 July 1897.
109 *Fun*, 14 August 1897 and 6 August 1899.
110 Chen Wuwo, *Lao Shanghai sanshinian jianwenlu*, 379; *Fun*, 16 October 1897; *Anecdotes*, 31 July 1898.
111 *Fun*, 20 February and 24 February 1899.
112 Ibid., 23 August and 25 August 1897.
113 Ibid., 29 August and 24 April 1899, 24 September 1898.
114 *Anecdotes*, 28 December 1899.
115 Like *tanci*, *pinghua* is a genre of performative storytelling. A performer narrates a story by speaking and singing in *wu* dialect and playing a stringed instrument. People often refer to pinghua and tanci together as *pingtan*.
116 This joke was predicated on the four-character set phrase *zoutou wulu*. In this phrase, the character *tou* means "go to, join" and has the same pronunciation as the character for "head." Switching the word *tou* in this set phrase for the character for head, and then using this set phrase literally, nicely describes Jin's way of entering the storytelling house.
117 Chen Wuwo, *Lao Shanghai sanshinian jianwenlu*, 47.
118 Sun Yusheng, *Tuixinglu biji*, 175-76.
119 *Fun*, 10 November 1897.
120 Wang Xuejun, *Li Boyuan nianpu*, 144.
121 Ibid., 85, 153-54. See also Yeh, *Shanghai Love*, 210, and Wang Yan, "'Xiuxiang xiaoshuo' gaikuang," 25.
122 Wei Shaochang, ed., *Shiliao suoyin ji*, vol. 30 of *Zhongguo jindai wenxue daxi* (Shanghai: Shanghai shudian, 1996), 193.

123 Ibid., 167.
124 Ibid., 155-56.
125 Ibid., 171.
126 Wang Xuejun, *Li Boyuan nianpu*, 96.
127 Sun Yusheng (under pen name Haishang Lanshisheng), "Baohai qianchenlu – xiaolin baoguan zhi huiyi," *Xinyebao*, 24 June 1934.
128 *Anecdotes*, 11 August 1898.
129 Ibid., 9 August 1898.
130 *Grove of Laughter*, 4 August 1902.
131 Wu Jianren, "Li Boyuan zhuan," in *Li Boyuan yanjiu ziliao*, ed. Wei Shaochang (Shanghai: Shanghai guji chubanshe, 1980), 10.
132 Wang Xuejun, *Li Boyuan nianpu*, 71.
133 Chen Boxi, *Shanghai yishi daguan*, 55.
134 Pei Xiaowei, "Wu Jianren yenjiu ziliao huibian," in vol. 10 of *Wu Jianren quanji*, ed. Haifeng (Harbin: Beifang wenyi chubanshe, 1998), 39.
135 Ibid., 19.
136 Sun Yusheng, *Tuixinglu biji*, 132.
137 Wang Xuejun, *Li Boyuan nianpu*, 130.
138 Ibid., 217-20.
139 Pei Xiaowei, "Wu Jianren yenjiu ziliao huibian," 58-59.
140 *Splendid World*, 5 December 1901.
141 Wang Xuejun, *Li Boyuan nianpu*, 200-1.
142 *Allegories*, 9 March 1901.
143 *Grove of Laughter*, 5 August 1902.
144 Zhang Chun, "Youxibao: Wanqing xiaoshuo yanjiu ziliao de dafaxian," *Mingqing xiaoshuo* 4 (2000): 217.
145 *Fun*, 10 November 1897.
146 *Allegories*, 9 March 1901.
147 Wang Xuejun, *Li Boyuan nianpu*, 195.
148 Ibid., 39.
149 Zuo Songtao, "Shilun qingdai seqingye fazhan yu zhengfu yingdui," *Fujian luntan (Renwen shehui kexueban)* 4 (2003): 50-51.
150 *Fun*, 7 January 1899.
151 Yeh, *Shanghai Love*, 16.
152 Meng Yue, *Shanghai and the Edges of Empire* (Minneapolis: University of Minnesota Press, 2006), 88-105.

Chapter 2: Officialdom Unmasked

1 Scholars have described the violent contest for power among local political and military elites during the revolution and the slaughter of the Manchu banner populations in the regions where they were concentrated. For a description of the bloodshed of Manchus at the hands of Han revolutionary forces, see Edward J.M. Rhoads, *Manchus and Han: Ethnic Relations and Political Power in Late Qing and Early Republican China, 1861-1928* (Seattle: University of Washington Press, 2001).

2 Zhang Ming, "Minyi yu tianyi: xinhai geming de minzhong huiying sanlun," in *Xinhai geming yu ershi shiji de Zhongguo*, ed. Association of the Chinese Society of History (Beijing: Zhongyang wenxian chubanshe, 2002), 1645. Similar observations were made by Chen Sanjing, "Xinhai geming qianhou di Shanghai," in *Xinhai geming yantaohui lunwenji* (Taipei: Zhongyang yanjiuyuan jindaishi yanjiusuo, 1983), 72, and Xiong Yuezhi, "Zhengju biandong yu minxin xiangbei" *Shilin* (February 2000): 17-19.

3 Bao Tianxiao, *Chuanyinglou huiyilu xubian* (Taiyuan: Shanxi guji chubanshe, 1999), 2.
4 Chen Pingyuan notes that nineteen novels published between 1903 and 1917 contained the word "officialdom" in their titles and that most other fiction said something negative about officials. Chen Pingyuan, *Ershi shiji Zhongguo xiaoshuoshi (1897-1916)*, vol. 1 (Beijing: Beijing daxue chubanshe, 1989), 231-32.
5 *Fun*, 21 November 1897.
6 Its editors categorized these as historical, nihilistic, idealistic love *(xieqing)*, bitter love *(kuqing)*, unusual love *(qiqing)*, chivalrous love *(xiaqing)*, detective, social, citizen, humour, short story, science, family, philosophy, educational, utopian, adventure, tanci, constitutional *(lixian)*, and miscellaneous notes *(zhaji)*.
7 Wu Jianren, *Huaji tan*, vol. 7 of *Wu Jianren quanji*, ed. Haifeng (Harbin: Beifang Wenyi Chubanshe, 1998), 451.
8 Ibid., 452.
9 *Fun*, 29 December 1901.
10 *Splendid World*, 5 August 1905.
11 *Fun*, 12 July 1899.
12 Ibid., 21 July 1899.
13 *Allegories*, 20 May 1902.
14 One *liang* equalled approximately 0.06875 pounds.
15 *Fun*, 20 July 1899.
16 *Splendid World*, 11 September 1903.
17 Ibid., 16 December 1904.
18 *All-Story Monthly [Yueyue xiaoshuo]* 5, 18 (1908): 197-98 (Shanghai: Shanghai shudian, 1980, reprint) (here and below, volume reference is to reprint edition, issue number reference is to original).
19 *Splendid World*, 24 June 1901. Li Lianying was the head eunuch of the Qing inner court.
20 *Grove of Laughter*, 22 February 1903.
21 Wu Jianren, *Huaji tan*, 450.
22 *Grove of Laughter*, 31 December 1906.
23 *All-Story Monthly* 6, 23 (1909): 126.
24 *Splendid World*, 24 February 1905.
25 It was amusing because the two terms – "morally pure officials" and "virgin sing-song girls" – have the same pronunciation and use similar Chinese characters.
26 *Fun*, 15 October 1897.
27 *Splendid World*, 18 December 1904.
28 *Fun*, 14 August 1899.
29 *Splendid World*, 14 July 1905.
30 Ibid., 27 September and 1 October 1901.
31 For example, *Splendid World* had special columns in every issue devoted to prostitutes, including a column titled "Records of Brothels."
32 *Splendid World*, 24 June 1901. *Jin* is a measure of weight and equals 1.2 pounds.
33 Ibid., 10 December 1904.
34 Ibid., 16 July 1905.
35 Ibid., 9 March 1906.
36 Ibid., 6 May 1905.
37 Ibid., 9 March 1905.
38 Ibid., 15 December 1904.
39 Ibid., 8 May 1905.
40 Ibid., 22 June 1905.
41 *Fun*, 17 February 1903.

42 *Splendid World*, 1 July 1905.
43 Ibid., 10 August 1905.
44 *Fun*, 12 and 20 March 1899.
45 Ibid., 14 July 1899.
46 Ouyang Juyuan, "Guanchang xianxingji xu," in vol. 1 of *Ershi shiji Zhongguo xiaoshuo lilun ziliao (1897-1916)*, ed. Chen Pingyuan and Xia Xiaohong (Beijing: Beijing daxue chubanshe, 1997), 71.
47 *Allegories*, 8 January 1903.
48 See, e.g., *Splendid World*, 13 March and 2 April 1905.
49 Ibid., 26-27 May 1905.
50 Ibid., 11 August 1905.
51 Ibid., 24 July 1908.
52 Ibid., 11 January 1905.
53 *Fun*, 25 and 27 November and 6 and 22 December 1901.
54 *Splendid World*, 23 June 1905.
55 *Fun*, 24 December 1901.
56 Ibid., 8 March 1902.
57 *Splendid World*, 11 January 1905.
58 *Allegories*, 24 June 1905.
59 *Splendid World*, 20 July 1905.
60 *Allegories*, 26 December 1901.
61 *Fun*, 9 April 1901.
62 *Splendid World*, 1 January 1902.
63 Ibid., 15 December 1901.
64 Ibid., 7 July 1905.
65 Ibid., 28 July 1905.
66 MacFarquhar and Schoenhals make a similar observation about officialdom in Chinese history. Roderick MacFarquhar and Michael Schoenhals, *Mao's Last Revolution* (Cambridge, MA: Belknap Press, 2006), 452.
67 *Fun*, 3 October 1898.
68 *Anecdotes*, 21 March 1900.
69 Wang Wenshao was a member of the Grand Secretariat of the government.
70 The area around Dongting Lake in Hunan Province is known for producing delicious tangerines.
71 *Splendid World*, 15 December 1901.
72 *Fun*, 20 June 1899.
73 *Splendid World*, 13 May 1907.
74 *Fun*, 18 February 1899.
75 Ibid., 14 March 1899.
76 Li Boyuan, *Wenming xiaoshi*, in vol. 1 of *Li Boyuan quanqi*, ed. Xue Zhengxing (Nanjing: Jiangsu guji chubanshe, 1997), 204 and 210.
77 Ibid., 236.
78 *Splendid World*, 31 March 1905.
79 *Fun*, 28 August 1899 and 2 January 1902.
80 *Splendid World*, 10 April 1905.
81 Ibid., 25 January 1905.
82 Wu Jianren, "Wu Jianren ku," in vol. 8 of *Wu Jianren quanji*, ed. Haifeng (Harbin: Beifang wenyi chubanshe, 1998), 232.
83 *Grove of Laughter*, 6 December 1906.
84 Wu Jianren, *Ershinian mudu zhi guaixianzhuang*, vol. 1 of *Wu Jianren quanji*, ed. Haifeng (Harbin: Beifang wenyi chubanshe, 1998), 98-99.

85 *Splendid World,* 9 March 1905.
86 *Fun,* 28 July 1899.
87 *Splendid World,* 5 December 1901.
88 Ibid., 2 April 1905.
89 *Fun,* 1 and 4 September 1899.
90 Ibid., 8 January 1904.
91 *Anecdotes,* 3 June 1900.
92 *Allegories,* 24 January 1902.
93 *Grove of Laughter,* 5 and 7 June 1907.
94 *Fun,* 2 August 1904.
95 Ibid., 29 November 1897.
96 Li Boyuan, *Wenming xiaoshi,* 420-21.
97 *Fun,* 19 November 1897.
98 Sun Yusheng, *Tuixinglu biji,* vol. 80 of *Jindai Zhongguo shiliao congkan,* ed. Shen Yunlong (Taipei: Wenhai chubanshe youxian gongsi, 1972), 133.
99 Fan Boqun, "Teyuan shishi yaoqiu yihe shiren shihao: yipingyi Lu Xun, Hu Shi de youguan youguan 'qianze xiaoshuo' lundian weishongxin," *Suzhou keji daxue xuebao (shehui kexue)* 22, 1 (2005): 79.
100 Lu Xun, *Zhongguo xiaoshuoshi lüè* (Beijing: Renmin wenxue chubanshe, 1956), 341.
101 Bao Tianxiao, *Chuanyinglou huiyilu* (Taiyuan: Shanxi guji chubanshe, 1999), 572. See also Sun Yusheng, *Tuixinglu biji,* 546.
102 *Fun,* 18 September 1898.
103 Wu Jianren, *Ershinian mudu zhi guaixianzhuang,* 706.
104 *Splendid World,* 25 August 1905.
105 *Allegories,* 24 January 1902.
106 Ordinary people could only appeal in writing to their local magistrates and officials. They did not have the legal right to appeal to government officials above the lowest local administrative level. Occasionally, some would risk their lives by prostrating themselves before high officials passing through their local area, demanding attention and appealing for justice.
107 *Splendid World,* 24 and 25 April 1905.
108 Ibid., 21 April 1905.
109 *Grove of Laughter,* 18 November 1902.
110 This form of poetry evolved from folksongs. It was colloquial and easy to understand, and contained no rigid tonal patterns. It was commonly written in four lines with seven characters per line.
111 *Fun,* 20 July 1899.
112 Ibid., 28 July 1899.
113 Ibid., 30 July 1899.
114 Zheng Yimei, *Shubao hua jiu* (Shanghai: Xuelin chubanshe, 1983), 115.
115 Bao Tianxiao, *Chuanyinglou huiyilu xubian,* 322.
116 In fact, because government papers in Shanghai could not compete with local commercial newspapers, officials would subsidize commercial papers to speak on their behalf. Chen Yushen, *Wanqing baoyeshi* (Jinan: Shangdong hubao chubanshe, 2003), 296.
117 Li Boyuan, *Wenming xiaoshi,* 309-12.
118 Chen Yushen, *Wanqing baoyeshi,* 296.
119 Wu Jianren, *Yiwang Hankou Ribao zhi zhubi Wu Woyao zhi Wuchang zhifu Liang Dingfen shu,* vol. 10 of *Wu Jianren quanji,* ed. Haifeng (Harbin: Beifang wenyi chubanshe, 1998), 120-22.
120 *All-Story Monthly* 3, 9 (1907): 209.
121 Ibid., 213.

122 Youhuan Yusheng, "Guanchang xianxingji xu," in vol. 1 of *Ershi shiji Zhingguo xioashuo lilun ziliao (1897-1916)*, ed. Chen Pingyuan and Xia Xiaohong (Beijing: Beijing daxue chubanshe, 1997), 72.
123 Robert Darnton, *The Forbidden Best-Sellers of Pre-Revolutionary France* (New York: Norton, 1996).

Chapter 3: Imagining the Nation

1 This definition synthesizes various others provided by Lowell Dittmer and Samuel S. Kim, "In Search of a Theory of National Identity," in *China's Quest for National Identity*, ed. Lowell Dittmer and Samuel S. Kim (Ithaca, NY: Cornell University Press, 1993), 1-31; Lucian W. Pye, "How China's Nationalism Was Shanghaied," in *Chinese Nationalism*, ed. Jonathan Unger (Armonk, NY: M.E. Sharpe, 1996), 86-112; S.A. Smith, *Like Cattle and Horses: Nationalism and Labor in Shanghai, 1895-1927* (Durham, NC: Duke University Press, 2002); and James Townsend, "Chinese Nationalism," in *Chinese Nationalism*, ed. Jonathan Unger (Armonk, NY: M.E. Sharpe, 1996), 1-30.
2 For example, see Hong-Yuan Chu and Peter Zarrow, "Modern Chinese Nationalism: The Formative Stage," in *Exploring Nationalisms of China: Themes and Conflicts*, ed. C.X. George Wei and Xiaoyuan Liu (Westport, CT: Greenwood Press, 2002), 3-26; and Frank Dikötter, *The Discourse of Race in Modern China* (London: Hurst, 1992), 61-125.
3 Bao Tianxiao, *Chuanyinglou huiyilu* (Hong Kong: Dahua chubanshe, 1971), 135-45.
4 *Fun*, 25 August 1897.
5 Ibid., 4 September 1898.
6 Ibid., 1 April 1899.
7 Ibid., 9 April 1899.
8 Ibid., 1 January 1898.
9 Chen Wuwo, *Lao Shanghai sanshinian jianwenlu* (Shanghai: Shanghai shudian chubanshe, 1997), 15.
10 *Illustrated Fiction [Xiuxiang xiaoshuo]* 3, 26 (1904): 1-2 (Shanghai: Shanghai shudian, 1980, reprint) (volume reference is to reprint edition, issue number reference is to original).
11 *Grove of Laughter*, 10 July 1902.
12 Ibid., 5-7 June 1907.
13 Wu Jianren, *Xin shitouji*, in vol. 6 of *Wu Jianren quanji*, ed. Haifeng (Harbin: Beifang wenyi chubanshe, 1998), 42-43.
14 Wu Jianren, *Ershinian mudu zhi guaixianzhuang*, vol. 1 of *Wu Jianren quanji*, ed. Haifeng (Harbin: Beifang wenyi chubanshe, 1998), 169-70.
15 Li, Boyuan, *Wenming xiaoshi*, in vol. 1 of *Li Boyuan quanqi*, ed. Xue Zhengxing (Nanjing: Jiangsu guji chubanshe, 1997), 212.
16 Ibid., 207.
17 *Fun*, 25 December 1901.
18 *Grove of Laughter*, 20 May 1906.
19 *Fun*, 18 February 1899.
20 *Splendid World*, 17 December 1904.
21 *Fun*, 18 July 1899.
22 Stefan Tanaka, *Japan's Orient: Rendering Pasts into History* (Berkeley: University of California Press, 1995), 1-9.
23 *Fun*, 21-26 June 1902.
24 Ibid., 21 and 22 June 1902.
25 *All-Story Monthly* 6, 24 (1909): 47-59 (Shanghai: Shanghai shudian, 1980, reprint) (here and below, volume reference is to reprint edition, issue number reference is to original).
26 In 1896, Liang Qichao envisioned that in the next century a worldwide war between the white and yellow races would take place. Liang argued that because 70 to 80 percent of the

yellow race was Chinese, a strong Qing state was needed. Liang Qichao, *Yinbin shi wen ji* (Taipei: Taiwan zhonghua shuju, 1983), 77-83.
27. *Fun*, 22-24 January 1904.
28. In fictional pieces, writers sometimes used the word *yi* (barbarian). For example, Wu Jianren used the term in his short story *Lixian wansui*, published in *All-Story Monthly* 2, 5 (1907): 167-80. Indeed, the Chinese government had already abandoned use of the word *huayi* (Chinese and barbarian) on formal occasions in the 1870s and 1880s.
29. *Fun*, 18 February 1899.
30. Murata Yūjirō, "Dynasty, State, and Society: The Case of Modern China," in *Imagining the People: Chinese Intellectuals and the Concept of Citizenship, 1890-1920*, ed. Joshua A. Fogel and Peter G. Zarrow (Armonk, NY: M.E. Sharpe, 1997), 113-41.
31. *Fun*, 20 November 1901.
32. *Grove of Laughter*, 2 April 1901.
33. *Fun*, 8 March 1899.
34. *Splendid World*, 16 July 1905.
35. *Fun*, 23 November 1901.
36. Liang insists that "reform must start with erasing the gap between Han and Manchus" in general discussions of reform. Liang Qichao, "Lun bianfa bizi pingmanhan zhijie shi," in vol. 1 of *Yinbin shi wen ji dianjiao*, ed. Wu Song et al. (Kunming: Yunnan jiaoyu chubanshe, 2001), 68.
37. Ma Guangren, ed., *Shanghai xinwenshi* (Shanghai: Fudan daxue chubanshe, 1996), 39, 201.
38. *Shijie fanhuabao*, 28 July 1905.
39. *Grove of Laughter*, 10 and 14 July 1907.
40. Wu Jianren, *Shanghai youcanlu*, in vol. 3 of *Wu Jianren quanji*, ed. Haifeng (Harbin: Beifang wenyi chubanshe, 1998), 466.
41. *All-Story Monthly* 6, 23 (1909): 146.
42. It seems that the press in general only rarely used the term *zuguo* in the late Qing.
43. Kauko Laitinen, *Chinese Nationalism in the Late Qing Dynasty: Zhang Binglin as an Anti-Manchu Propagandist* (Surrey, UK: Curzon Press, 1990), 67.
44. In late Qing Chinese, the term *guo* meant both nation and state.
45. Peter Zarrow, "Introduction: Citizenship in China and the West," in *Imagining the People: Chinese Intellectuals and the Concept of Citizenship, 1890-1920*, ed. Joshua A. Fogel and Peter G. Zarrow (Armonk, NY: M.E. Sharpe, 1997), 14.
46. *Fun*, 14 October 1898.
47. Ibid., 22-24 January 1904.
48. *Anecdotes*, 6 February 1900.
49. Examples of discussions about of the survival of the Chinese race and the nation-state appear in *Fun*, 16 March 1899 and 21-26 June 1902, and *Grove of Laughter*, 21 November 1902 and 25 July 1907.
50. *Anecdotes*, 22 October 1903.
51. The term "constitutional polity" here implies a constitutional monarchy combined with a parliamentary system.
52. Zhang Yufa, "Cong gaizao dao dongyuan," in *Liang Qichao yu jindai Zhongguo shehui wenhua*, ed. Li Xisuo (Tianjin: Tianjin guji chubanshe, 2005), 1-6.
53. Ibid., 6.
54. Wang Fanshen, "Evolving Prescriptions for Social Life in the Late Qing and Early Republic: From *Qunxue* to Society," in *Imagining the People: Chinese Intellectuals and the Concept of Citizenship, 1890-1920*, ed. Joshua A. Fogel and Peter G. Zarrow (Armonk, NY: M.E. Sharpe, 1997), 258-78.
55. Benedict Anderson, *Imagined Communities: Reflections on the Origin and Spread of Nationalism* (London: Verso, 2006).

56 Zhang Pengyuan, *Liang Qichao yu qingji geming*, 2nd ed. (Taipei: Zhongyang yanjiuyuan jindaishi yanjiusuo zhuankan, 1999), 23 and 77-78.
57 Huang Ko-wu, *Yige bei fangqi di xuanze: Liang Qichao tiaoshi sixiang zhi yanjiu* (Taipei: Zhongyang yanjiuyuan jindaishi yanjiusuo zhuankan, 1994), 70-71.
58 Huang Ko-wu, "Liang Qichao yu rujia chuantong: yiqingmo wangxue wei zhongxin zhi kaocha," *Lishi jiaoxue* 3 (2004): 21.
59 Huang Ko-wu, *Yige bei fangqi di xuanze*, 72.
60 Wang Fanshen, "Congxinmin daoxinren: jindai sixiangzhong di 'ziwou' yu 'Zhengzhi'" in *Zhongguo jin dai sixiangshi de zhuanxing shidai*, ed. Wang Fanshen. (Taipei: Liangjing chuban shiye gufen youxian gongsi, 2007), 176 and 199.
61 Zarrow, "Introduction: Citizenship in China and the West," 18.
62 Zhang Yufa, "Cong gaizao dao dongyuan," 6.
63 *Fun*, 8 March 1902.
64 Huang Ko-wu, *Yige bei fangqi di xuanze*, 74. See also Li Xisuo and Qing Yuan, *Liang Qichao zhuan* (Beijing: Renmin chubanshe, 1993), 202.
65 Wu Jianren, *Shanghai youcanlu*, 479.
66 *Zaju* is a form of poetic drama intertwining performances and songs throughout the play. The format of zaju underwent constant change throughout China's history. Li Boyuan may have commissioned the play.
67 Chen Wuwo, *Lao Shanghai sanshinian jianwenlu*, 319-21.
68 Ibid.
69 *Fun*, 2 September 1897.
70 Wu Jianren, *Ershinian mudu zhi guaixianzhuang*, 722-23.
71 *Grove of Laughter*, 2 October 1902.
72 *Fun*, 25 March 1899.
73 *Grove of Laughter*, 24 July 1907.
74 Ibid., 20 June 1906.
75 *Fun*, 23 December 1901.
76 *All-Story Monthly* 6, 23 (1909): 23-38.
77 *Grove of Laughter*, 9 June 1907.
78 *All-Story Monthly* 6, 21 (1908): 26.
79 Ibid., 6, 23 (1909): 72.
80 Ibid., 4, 13 (1908): 6.
81 Huang Ko-wu, *Yige bei fangqi di xuanze*, 51-56.
82 Wang Fanshen, "Evolving Prescriptions for Social Life in the Late Qing and Early Republic: From *Qunxue* to Society," 262-64.
83 Zarrow, "Introduction: Citizenship in China and the West," 18-19.
84 Many scholars agree that Liang Qichao placed the interests of the nation before those of the individual. These scholars include Henrietta Harrison, *China: Inventing the Nation* (Oxford: Hodder Arnold, 2001), 104; Wang Fanshen, "Evolving Prescriptions for Social Life in the Late Qing and Early Republic: From *Qunxue* to Society," 262-64; Zhang Yufa, "Cong gaizao dao dongyuan," 6; and others cited by Huang Ko-wu, *Yige bei fangqi di xuanze*, 51-56.
85 Xu Xiaoqing, "Shuangchong zhengzhi wenhua rentong de kunjing: jiedu Liang Qichao minzu guojia sixiang," *Journal of Xiangfan University* 21, 1 (2000): 81-83.
86 Huang Ko-wu believes that Liang also recognized individual interests as important and regarded the relationship between individuals and the public as interdependent.
87 *All-Story Monthly* 6, 21 (1908): 25.
88 *Grove of Laughter*, 20 December 1902.
89 Wu Jianren, *Shanghai youcanlu*, 490.

Notes to pages 100-7 199

90 *All-Story Monthly* 2, 7 (1907): 227.
91 Ibid., 5, 19 (1908): 17.
92 Ibid., 1, 1 (1906): 242.
93 Ibid., 244.
94 Wu Jianren, "Baixiangtu," in vol. 8 of *Wu Jianren Quanji*, ed. Haifeng (Harbin: Beifang wenyi chubanshe, 1998), 451. According to Chinese legend, Zhang Guo was an immortal who travelled around on a donkey at the speed of the wind, sitting backwards while reading books. The donkey had no need to eat and drink, and could be folded like a piece of paper while Zhang Guo rested.
95 Wu Jianren, *Baixiangtu*.
96 *All-Story Monthly* 4, 13 (1908): 115-22.
97 *Grove of Laughter*, 4 June 1907.
98 *Splendid World*, 24 July 1908.
99 *All-Story Monthly* 1, 4 (1907): 218.
100 Wu Jianren, "Wu Jianren ku," in vol. 8 of *Wu Jianren quanji*, ed. Haifeng (Harbin: Beifang wenyi chubanshe, 1998), 233.
101 Ibid., 227-28.
102 *All-Story Monthly* 2, 5 (1907): 188.
103 Even in 1901, Liang expressed a similar idea. Zhang Qiang, "Wu Jianren 'wenming zhuanzhi' sixiang tanwei," *Zhengzhou daxue xuebao* 4 (1996): 102.
104 Huang Ko-wu, *Yige bei fangqi di xuanze*, 145. See also Zhang Pengyuan, *Liang Qichao yu qingji geming*, 136 and 170-72.
105 After 1911, and by 1915 and 1916, Liang further developed his "statist" nationalism, locating sovereignty *(zhuquan)* in the state *(guojia)* rather than with the people or the ruler, while at the same time trying to make the republic ultimately work on democratic principles. See Zarrow, "Introduction: Citizenship in China and the West," 23.
106 *All-Story Monthly* 2, 6 (1907): 229.
107 Wu Jianren, *Shanghai youcanlu*, 487-88.
108 Wu Jianren, *Xin shitouji*, 207-9.
109 *All-Story Monthly* 1, 2 (1906): 181-90.
110 Ibid., 1, 1 (1906): 240-41.
111 Wu Jianren, "Wu Jianren ku," 234-35.
112 Zhang Pengyuan, *Liang Qichao yu qingji geming*, 138.
113 Chang Tsun-wu, *China's Boycott against American Goods (1905-1906)* (Taipei: Academia Sinica, 1972), 59-60.
114 Ibid., 102-3.
115 Wu Jianren, "Wu Jianren zhi shanghuihan," *Shenbao*, July 22, 1905, 2; reprinted in *Shenbao yinyingben*, vol. 80 (Shanghai: Shanghai shudian, 1985), 697.
116 Pei Xiaowei, "Wu Jianren yenjiu ziliao huibian," in vol. 10 of *Wu Jianren quanji*, ed. Haifeng (Harbin: Beifang wenyi chubanshe, 1998), 213; Li Yuzhong, "Wu Jianren shengping jiqi zhuzuo," in vol. 10 of *Wu Jianren quanji*, ed. Haifeng (Harbin: Beifang wenyi chubanshe, 1998), 98-99; and Chang Tsun-wu, *China's Boycott against American Goods*, 101.
117 Chang Tsun-wu, ibid., 102.
118 "Renjing xueshe guikuzhuan," *All-Story Monthly* 3, 10 (1907): 232.
119 Chang Tsun-wu, *China's Boycott against American Goods*, 103.
120 Zarrow, "Introduction: Citizenship in China and the West," 26.
121 Wu Jianren, *Xin shitouji*, 319-20.
122 Ren Fangqiu, *Zhongguo jindai wenxueshi* (Kaifeng: Henan daxue chubanshe, 2005), 309.
123 Wu Jianren, "Wu Jianren jun yanshuo," in vol. 8 of *Wu Jianren quanji*, ed. Haifeng (Harbin: Beifang wenyi chubanshe, 1998), 237-38.

124 Wu Jianren, *Xin shitouji,* 137.
125 *All-Story Monthly* 3, 9 (1907): 215-22.
126 Ibid., 3, 11 (1908): 201-2.
127 Ibid., 3, 12 (1908): 102.
128 Ibid., 172.
129 Ibid., 3, 11 (1908): 229-30.
130 Ibid., 3, 12 (1908): 179-86.
131 Barbara Mittler, *A Newspaper for China? Power, Identity, and Change in Shanghai's News Media, 1872-1912* (Cambridge, MA: Harvard University Asia Center, 2004).
132 Ibid., 363, 372-77, 398, 403, and 415.
133 Chang Tsun-wu, *China's Boycott against American Goods,* 51.
134 Joan Judge, *Print and Politics: "Shibao" and the Culture of Reform in Late Qing China* (Palo Alto, CA: Stanford University Press, 1996), 116-17.

Chapter 4: Confronting the "New"
1 Empresses Dowager Cian and Cixi were co-regents of the Tongzhi reign.
2 Li Xisuo, *Zhongguo liuxueshi lungao* (Beijing: Zhonghua shuju, 2007), 173 and 180.
3 The five human relationships are: ruler and subject, father and son, elder and younger brother, husband and wife, and friends. Zhang Zhidong, *Quanxuepian, Minggang, Neipian,* vol. 9 of *Jindai Zhongguo shiliao congkan,* ed. Shen Yunlong (Taipei: Wenhai chubanshe, 1966), 33.
4 *Fun,* 25 August 1897.
5 Ibid., 16 September 1898.
6 *Anecdotes,* 20 August 1898.
7 *Fun,* 26 September 1898.
8 Ibid., 3 October 1898.
9 Ibid.
10 Ibid., 14 and 15 October 1898.
11 Ibid., 4 and 5 October 1898.
12 Ma Guangren, *Shanghai xinwenshi* (Shanghai: Fudan daxue chubanshe, 1996), 158.
13 *Fun,* 15 July 1899.
14 Ma Guangren, *Shanghai xinwenshi,* 158.
15 *Allegories,* 2 February 1900.
16 *Anecdotes,* 6 February 1900.
17 Luo Zhitian, "Jindai Zhongguo shehui quanshi de zhuanyi: zhishi fenzi de bianyuanhua yu bianyuan zhishi fenzi de xingqi," in *Ershi shiji Zhongguo zhishi fenzi shilun,* ed. Xu Jilin (Beijing: Xinxing chubanshe, 2005), 133.
18 Wang Linmao, "Lun xinhai geming shiqi di shidaifu jieceng," in *Xinhai geming yu jindai Zhongguo – jinnian xinhai geming bashi zhounian guoji xueshu taolunhui wenji,* ed. Editorial Board of Zhonghua shuju (Beijing: Zhonghua shuju, 1994), 295-99.
19 Li Xisuo, *Zhongguo liuxueshi lungao,* 248-53. Zhang Pengyuan estimates more conservatively that over fifteen thousand Chinese went to Japan to study between 1904 and 1906. Zhang Pengyuan, "Qingmo minchu de zhishi fenzi," in *Ershi shiji Zhongguo zhishi fenzi shilun,* ed. Xu Jilin (Beijing: Xinxing chubanshe, 2005), 225.
20 *Splendid World,* 27 November 1901.
21 *Fun,* 23 August 1903.
22 Ibid., 8 January 1904.
23 Li Boyuan, *Wenming xiaoshi,* in vol. 1 of *Li Boyuan quanqi,* ed. Xue Zhengxing (Nanjing: Jiangsu guji chubanshe, 1997), 212-16.

24 Wu Jianren, "Wu Jianren ku," in vol. 8 of *Wu Jianren quanji*, ed. Haifeng (Harbin: Beifang wenyi chubanshe, 1998), 230.
25 *Splendid World*, 20 July 1905.
26 Dorothy Ko, *Cinderella's Sisters: A Revisionist History of Footbinding* (Berkeley: University of California Press, 2007), 17.
27 *Fun*, 2 September 1899.
28 In vol. 10 of *Illustrated Fiction [Xiuxiang xiaoshuo]* (Beijing: Beijing tushuguan chubanshe, 2006, reprint), 251-52.
29 Li Boyuan, *Wenming xiaoshi*, 278.
30 *Splendid World*, 24 June 1905. This article was also published in *Fun*, 24 June 1905.
31 Wu Jianren, *Xin shitouji*, in vol. 6 of *Wu Jianren quanqi*, ed. Haifeng (Harbin: Beifang wenyi chubanshe, 1998), 65.
32 Two such novels are *Yufuyuan* and *Saomizhou*, both published in *Illustrated Fiction*.
33 *Grove of Laughter*, 11 January 1907.
34 In vol. 2 of *Illustrated Fiction [Xiuxiang xiaoshuo]* (Beijing: Beijing tushuguan chubanshe, 2006, reprint), 3.
35 Wu Jianren, *Ershinian mudu zhi guaixianzhuang*, vol. 1 of *Wu Jianren quanji*, ed. Haifeng (Harbin: Beifang wenyi chubanshe, 1998), 195-96.
36 Li Boyuan, *Xingshiyuan*, vol. 10 of *Xiuxiang xiaoshuo*, ed. Li Boyuan (Beijing: Beijing tushuguan chubanshe, 2006), 264.
37 Kang Youwei, "Shang qingdi diwushu," in *Kangnanhai xiansheng yizhuo huikan*, ed. Jiang Guilin (Taipei: Hongye shuju, 1976), 92.
38 Liang Qichao, "Wenye sanjie zhibie," in *Ziyoushu* (Taipei: Taiwan zhonghua shuju, 1979), 8-9.
39 *Grove of Laughter*, 6 July 1902.
40 Quoted in Luo Zhitian, *Minzu zhuyi yu jindai Zhongguo sixiang* (Taipei: Dongda tushu gufen youxian gongsi, 1998), 257.
41 Luo Zhitian, "Jindai Zhongguo shehui quanshi de zhuanyi," 129.
42 This is a Chinese gesture showing sincerity and respect.
43 *Grove of Laughter*, 5 December 1902.
44 *Fun*, 25 December 1901.
45 Ibid., 5 January 1902.
46 *All-Story Monthly [Yueyue xiaoshuo]* 6, 21, supplement (1908): 38 (Shanghai: Shanghai shudian, 1980, reprint) (here and below, volume reference is to reprint edition, issue number reference is to original).
47 Li Boyuan, *Wenming xiaoshi*, 419.
48 Lin Mingde, *Wanqing xiaoshuo yenjiu* (Taipei: Lianjing chubanshe, 1986), 140.
49 Wu Jianren, *Shanghai youcanlu*, in vol. 3 of *Wu Jianren quanqi*, ed. Haifeng (Harbin: Beifang wenyi chubanshe, 1998), 478-79.
50 Wu Jianren, "'Xinan yixie – ziyou jiehun' pianhouping," in vol. 9 of *Wu Jianren quanji*, ed. Haifeng (Harbin: Beifang wenyi chubanshe, 1997), 227 and 233-35.
51 Wu Jianren, *Shanghai youcanlu*, 491.
52 Ibid., 489.
53 Ibid.
54 Ibid., 479.
55 Wu Jianren, *Wu Jianren ku*, 234-35.
56 *All-Story Monthly* 4, 14 (1908): 71.
57 Wu Jianren, *Wu Jianren ku*, 234.
58 Wu Jianren, *Shanghai youcanlu*, 479.

59 Chen Jianhua, *Geming de xiandaixing – Zhongguo geming huayu laolun* (Shanghai: Shanghai guji chubanshe, 2000), 202-13 and 204-6.
60 Quoted in Tang Xiaobing, *Global Space and the Nationalist Discourse of Modernity: The Historical Thinking of Liang Qichao* (Palo Alto, CA: Stanford University Press, 1996), 61. This book contains a detailed study of Liang Qichao's ideas on historiography.
61 Liang Qichao, "Shixue zhijieshuo," in *Liang Qichao shixue lunzhu sanzhong* (Hong Kong: Sanlian shudian, 1988), 10.
62 Liang Qichao, "Zhongguo zhi jiushi," in *Liang Qichao shixue lunzhu sanzhong* (Hong Kong: Sanlian shudian, 1988), 1-9.
63 Wang Fanshen, *Zhang Taiyan de sixiang (1868-1919) jiqi dui ruxue chuantong de chongji* (Taipei: Shibao wenhua chuban shiye youxian gongsi, 1985), 151.
64 Zhang Suiyang was the Tang official who fought heroically against the An Lushan rebels. Yue Wumu, also known as Yue Fei, was the Song general who fought against the Jin troops. Wu Jianren, *Qingbian*, in vol. 5 of *Wu Jianren qianji*, ed. Haifeng (Harbin: Beifang wenyi chubanshe, 1998), preface and 203-4.
65 *All-Story Monthly* 1, 1 (1906): 9-10.
66 Ibid., 11-4.
67 Wu Jianren, *Ershinian mudu zhi guaixianzhuang*, 828-29.
68 Ibid., 811.
69 *Fun*, 15 May 1899.
70 Ibid., 26 May 1899.
71 Ibid., 16 October 1897.
72 Li Boyuan, *Wenming xiaoshi*, 133-34 and 137.
73 *Grove of Laughter*, 11 January 1907.
74 Li Boyuan, *Wenming xiaoshi*, 395-96.
75 Wu Jianren, *Ershinian mudu zhi guaixianzhuang*, 612.
76 Ibid., *Xin shitouji*, 182.
77 *All-Story Monthly* 5, 17 (1908): 4-5.
78 Ibid., 4, 16 (1908): 117.
79 Wu Jianren, "'Xinan yixie – ziyou jiehun' pianhouping," 227 and 233-35.
80 *All-Story Monthly* 6, 21 (1908): 8.
81 *All-Story Monthly* 6, 22 (1908): 9-10. The three submissions are to father, husband, and son, and the four virtues are women's ethics, speech, appearance, and work skill.
82 Ibid., 6, 23 (1909): 79 and 84-85.
83 Ibid., 6, 24 (1909): 40-45.
84 Wu Jianren, *Ershinian mudu zhi guaixianzhuang*, 158-60.
85 Tang Xiaobing points out that Wu's meditations on qing follow a long philosophical tradition of "passionism" that during the late Ming period became a fully institutionalized Confucian code of social behaviour and propriety. Tang Xiaobing, *Chinese Modern: The Heroic and the Quotidian (Post-Contemporary Interventions)* (Durham, NC: Duke University Press, 2000), 26.
86 Wu Jianren, *The Sea of Regret*, tr. Patrick Hanan (Honolulu: University of Hawai'i Press, 1995), 103.
87 For further discussion of Liang Qichao's views on Madame Roland, see Tang Xiaobing, *Global Space and the Nationalist Discourse of Modernity*.
88 Michael Tsin, "Imagining 'Society' in Early Twentieth-Century China," in *Imagining the People: Chinese Intellectuals and the Concept of Citizenship, 1890-1920*, ed. Joshua A. Fogel and Peter G. Zarrow (Armonk, NY: M.E. Sharpe, 1997), 216.
89 Liu Shipei, "Lunjilie de haochu," in *Xinhai geming qianshinian jian shilun xuanji*, ed. Zhang Mudan (Hong Kong: Shenghuo dushu xinzhi sanlian shudian, 1962), 888.

90 Wang Fanshen, *Zhang Taiyan de sixiang*, 115-19 and 247-48.
91 Theodore Huters, *Bringing the World Home: Appropriating the West in Late Qing and Early Republican China* (Honolulu: University of Hawai'i Press, 2005), 171-72.
92 Joseph Richmond Levenson, *Liang Ch'i-ch'ao and the Mind of Modern China* (Cambridge, MA: Harvard University Press, 1959).
93 Perry Link, *Mandarin Ducks and Butterflies: Popular Fiction in Early Twentieth-Century Chinese Cities* (Berkeley: University of California Press, 1981), 178-81.

Chapter 5: Questioning the Appropriators
1 Luo Zhitian, "Jindai Zhongguo shehui quanshi de zhuanyi: zhishi fenzi de bianyuanhua yu bianyuan zhishi fenzi de xingqi," in *Ershi shiji Zhongguo zhishi fenzi shilun*, ed. Xu Jilin (Beijing: Xinxing chubanshe, 2005), 137-38.
2 Wang Xianming, "Shishen jieceng yu wanqing 'minbian' – shenmin chongtu de lishi quxiang yu shidai chengyin." *Jindaishi yanjiu* 1 (2008): 23.
3 Pierre Bourdieu, *Distinction: A Social Critique of the Judgment of Taste* (Cambridge, MA: Harvard University Press, 1987); and Edward Lipuma, Moishe Postone, and Craig J. Calhoun, eds., *Pierre Bourdieu: Critical Perspectives* (Chicago: University of Chicago Press, 1993).
4 *Anecdotes*, 21 March 1900.
5 Li Boyuan, *Wenming xiaoshi*, in vol. 1 of *Li Boyuan quanqi*, ed. Xue Zhengxing (Nanjing: Jiangsu guji chubanshe, 1997), 6.
6 *Grove of Laughter*, 5 August 1902.
7 Ibid., 6 October 1902.
8 In vol.1 of *Illustrated Fiction [Xiuxiang xiaoshuo]* (Beijing: Beijing tushuguan chubanshe, 2006, reprint), 275-76.
9 *Splendid World*, 23 June 1905.
10 Li Boyuan, *Wenming xiaoshi*, 113-14.
11 Ibid., 295-96.
12 Ibid., 335.
13 Ibid., 125.
14 *Fun*, 18 February 1899.
15 *Grove of Laughter*, 22 June 1907.
16 *Fun*, 5 December 1901.
17 Wu Jianren, *Ershinian mudu zhi guaixianzhuang*, vol. 1 of *Wu Jianren quanji*, ed. Haifeng (Harbin: Beifang wenyi chubanshe, 1998), 678-82.
18 Wu Jianren, *Shanghai youcanlu*, vol. 3 of *Wu Jianren quanqi*, ed. Haifeng (Harbin: Beifang wenyi chubanshe, 1998), 473-74.
19 *Allegories*, 27 August 1901.
20 *Grove of Laughter*, 6 July 1902.
21 Li Boyuan, *Wenming xiaoshi*, 319-21 and 322-25.
22 *Splendid World*, 6 June 1905.
23 Ibid., 1 October 1901.
24 Li Boyuan, *Wenming xiaoshi*, 424-25.
25 Wu Jianren, "Baixiangtu," in vol. 8 of *Wu Jianren quanji*, ed. Haifeng (Harbin: Beifang wenyi chubanshe, 1998), 449.
26 Li Boyuan, *Wenming xiaoshi*, 420.
27 Wu Jianren, *Shanghai youcanlu*, 444-45.
28 *All-Story Monthly [Yueyue xiaoshuo]* 3, 9 (1907): 140 (Shanghai: Shanghai shudian, 1980, reprint) (here and below, volume reference is to reprint edition, issue number reference is to original).
29 Cited in Xiong Xianjun, "Qingmo fumeiri liuxuesheng jiaoyu jixiao guiyin bijiao," *Hebei shifan daxue xuebao [Jiaoyu kexueban]* 9 (2007): 21.

204　Notes to pages 144-57

30　Bao Tianxiao, *Chuanyinglou huiyilu* (Taiyuan: Shanxi guji chubanshe, 1999), 197.
31　Ouyang Juyuan, *Fupu xiantan*, ed. Li Boyuan, 73, http://tinyurl.com/76qreus.
32　Li Boyuan, *Wenming xiaoshi*, 118-21, 129, and 237.
33　*All-Story Monthly* 4, 13 (1908): 227-29.
34　Ibid., 131-40.
35　Li Boyuan, *Wenming xiaoshi*, 140 and 143.
36　Ibid., 129-30.
37　*Grove of Laughter*, 31 December 1906.
38　Wang Xianming, "Shishen jieceng yu wanqing 'minbian,'" 30-31.
39　*Grove of Laughter*, 6 December 1906.
40　Li Boyuan, *Wenming xiaoshi*, 217.
41　*Fun*, 22 and 24 March 1899.
42　Ibid., 20 July 1899.
43　Ibid., 12 and 20 March 1899.
44　Ibid., 29 November 1901.
45　Wu Jianren, *Xin shitouji*, in vol. 6 of *Wu Jianren quanqi*, ed. Haifeng (Harbin: Beifang wenyi chubanshe, 1998), 324.
46　Li Boyuan, *Wenming xiaoshi*, 295 and 415.
47　*Grove of Laughter*, 10 July 1907.
48　Ibid., 24 July 1907.
49　Zhang Pengyuan, "Qingmo minchu de zhishi fenzi," in *Ershi shiji Zhongguo zhishi fenzi shilun*, ed. Xu Jilin (Beijing: Xinxing chubanshe, 2005), 223-31.
50　Luo Zhitian, "Jindai Zhongguo shehui quanshi de zhuanyi," 131 and 141.
51　Zhang Ziping, *Ziping zizhuan*, vol. 6 of *Zhongguo xiandai zizhuan congshu (ser.)*, ed. Zhang Yufa and Zhang Ruide (Taipei: Longwen chubanshe, 1989), 10.
52　Yang Guojiang, "Ershi shiji chunian zhishiren de zhishihua yu jindaihua," in *Ershi shiji Zhongguo zhishi fenzi shilun*, ed. Xu Jilin (Beijing: Xinxing chubanshe, 2005), 167.
53　Li Boyuan, *Wenming xiaoshi*, 129-30.
54　Ibid., 246-49.
55　Wu Jianren, *Wu Jianren ku*, in vol. 8 of *Wu Jianren quanji*, ed. Haifeng (Harbin: Beifang wenyi chubanshe, 1998), 231 and 232.
56　*Fun*, 23 May 1899.
57　Wu Jianren, *Shanghai youcanlu*, 455 and 474.
58　Pei Xiaowei, *Wu Jianren yenjiu ziliao huibian*, in vol. 10 of *Wu Jianren quanji*, ed. Haifeng (Harbin: Beifang Wenyi Chubanshe, 1998), 21.
59　Zhu Fusheng and Yao Hui, *Chenyingshi pingchuan* (Beijing: Tuanjie chubanshe, 1989), 38.
60　Bao Tianxiao, *Chuanyinglou huiyilu*, 454.
61　Li Boyuan, *Wenming xiaoshi*, 125-26.
62　*All-Story Monthly* 1, 1 (1906): 92-93.
63　*Grove of Laughter*, 4 June 1907.
64　Li Boyuan, *Wenming xiaoshi*, 160-61.
65　Wu Jianren, *Lixian wansui*, vol. 7 of *Wu Jianren quanji*, ed. Haifeng (Harbin: Beifang wenyi chubanshe, 1998), 38.
66　Wu Jianren, *Xin shitouji*, 59.
67　Li Boyuan, *Wenming xiaoshi*, 60.

Chapter 6: The Market, Populism, and Aesthetics

1　Ouyang Jian, *Wanqing xiaoshuoshi* (Hangzhou: Zhejiang guji chubanshe, 1997), 2.
2　Chen Pingyuan, *Zhongguo xiandai xiaoshuo de qidian: qingmo minchu xiaoshuo yanjiu. Wenxueshi yanjiu congshu* (Beijing: Beijing daxue chubanshe, 2005), 77.

3 Lin Mingde, "Mibu Zhongguo wenxueshi de yiye kongbai bianxu," in *Wanqing xiaoshuo yanjiu*, ed. Lin Mingde (Taipei: Lianjing chuban shiye gong si, 1988), 2.
4 Yuan Jin, *Yuanyang hutianpai* (Shanghai: Shanghai shudian chubanshe, 1994), 33.
5 Zunben Zhaoxiong, *Xinbian zengbu qingmo minchu xiaoshuo mulu* (Jinan: Qilu shushe, 2002), 1-2.
6 Pan Jianguo, "Qingmo Shanghai diqu shuju yu wanqing xiaoshuo," *Wenxue yichan* 2 (2004): 96-110.
7 Yan Tingliang, *Wanqing xiaoshuo lilun* (Beijing: Zhonghua shuju, 1996), 47.
8 Lin Mingde, "Mibu Zhongguo wenxueshi de yiye kongbai bianxu," 1-2; Leo Ou-fan Lee and Andrew J. Nathan, "Journalism and Fiction in the Late Ch'ing and Beyond," in *Popular Culture in Late Imperial China*, ed. David Johnson, Andrew J. Nathan, and Evelyn S. Rawski (Berkeley: University of California Press, 1985), 367; Guo Haofan, "Qingmo minchu xiaoshuo yu baokanye zhi guanxi tanlüe," *Wenshizhe* 3 (2004): 47.
9 Liang Qichao, "Yiyin zhengzhi xiaoshuoxu," in vol. 1 of *Yinbinshi wenji dianjiao*, ed. Wu Song et al. (Kunming: Yunnan jiaoyu chubanshe, 2001), 153; and Liang Qichao, "Lun xiaoshuo yu qunzhi zhi guanxi," in vol. 1 of *Yinbinshi wenji dianjiao*, ed. Wu Song et al. (Kunming: Yunnan jiaoyu chubanshe, 2001), 758-60.
10 Theodore Huters, *Bringing the World Home: Appropriating the West in Late Qing and Early Republican China* (Honolulu: University of Hawai'i Press, 2005), 103-20.
11 See *All-Story Monthly [Yueyue xiaoshuo]* 3, 9 (1907): 1-4 (Shanghai: Shanghai shudian, 1980, reprint) (here and below, volume reference is to reprint edition, issue number reference is to original); see also vol. 1 of *Illustrated Fiction [Xiuxiang xiaoshuo]* (Beijing: Beijing tushuguan chubanshe, 2006, reprint) (volume reference is to reprint edition), 109-16.
12 Lu Xiangyuan, *Gaochou zenyang jiaodong wentan: shichang jingji yu Zhongguo jinxiandai wenxue* (Beijing: Hongqi chubanshe, 1998), 156.
13 Xia Xiaohong, "Wu Jianren yu Liang Qichao guanxi gouchen," *Anhui shifan daxue xuebao (Renwen shehui kexueba)* 30, 6 (2002): 636-37.
14 Alexander Des Forges, *Mediasphere Shanghai: The Aesthetics of Cultural Production* (Honolulu: University of Hawai'i Press, 2007), 22-23.
15 *Fun*, 12 November 1897.
16 Wei Shaochang, ed., *Zhongguo jindai wenyi baokan gailan (II)*, in *Shiliao suoyinji*, vol. 30 of *Zhongguo jindai wenxue daxi* (Shanghai: Shanghai shudian, 1996), 193.
17 *Anecdotes*, 17 July 1898.
18 *Fun*, 29 July 1899.
19 Wang Xuejun, *Li Boyuan nianpu*, in vol. 5 of *Li Boyuan quanji*, ed. Xue Zhengxing (Nanjing: Jiangsu guji chubanshe, 1997), 168.
20 Wei Shaochang, "Qianben jingguo meitan xinxi," in *Li Boyuan yanjiu ziliao*, ed. Wei Shaochang (Shanghai: Shanghai guji chubanshe, 1980), 319.
21 Zhang Yilu, "Li Boyuan yishi," in *Li Boyuan yanjiu ziliao*, ed. Wei Shaochang (Shanghai: Shanghai guji chubanshe, 1980), 14-15. According to one author, the novel *Xianxia wuhuajian* was actually written before *Haishang fanhuameng (Dream of Shanghai Splendor)*; Xu Yin, "Zuojia baoren haishang shushisheng," in vol. 6 of *Ershi shiji Shanghai wenshi ziliao wenku*, ed. Liu Jianxin (Shanghai: Shanghai shudian chubanshe, 1999), 33.
22 *Grove of Laughter*, 2 April 1901.
23 Bao Tianxiao, *Chuanyinglou huiyilu* (Taiyuan: Shanxi guji chubanshe, 1999), 407.
24 Catherine Vance Yeh also discussed this in her book: *Shanghai Love: Courtesans, Intellectuals, and Entertainment Culture, 1850-1910* (Seattle: University of Washington Press, 2005), 214.
25 Perry Link, *Mandarin Ducks and Butterflies: Popular Fiction in Early Twentieth-Century Chinese Cities* (Berkeley: University of California Press, 1981), 117-18, 125.

26 Ibid., 151.
27 Both Yeh and Des Forges point to the leading role of the tabloid press: Yeh, *Shanghai Love*, 216; Des Forges, *Mediasphere Shanghai*, 108.
28 Li Jiuhua, "Lunwanqing wenyi qikan yu xiaoshuo fanrong," *Ningxia daxue xuebao (Renwen shehui kexueban)* 25, 5 (2003): 45. According to this author, *Illustrated Fiction* serialized sixteen novels, *All-Story Monthly* thirty-two, *New Fiction* nine, and *Grove of Fiction* four.
29 *All-Story Monthly* 1, 1 (1906): 3.
30 Letter to Liang Qichao from Huang Zunxian, 11 November 1902; quoted in Chen Pingyuan, *Zhongguo xiandai xiaoshuo de qidian*, 109.
31 In vol. 1 of *Illustrated Fiction [Xiuxiang xiaoshuo]*, 113-14.
32 Xia Xiaohong, "Wu Jianren yu Liang Qichao guanxi gouchen," 639-40.
33 *Fun*, 25 August 1897.
34 Li Boyuan, "Benguan bianyin Xiuxiang xiaoshuo yuanqi," in vol. 1 of *Ershi shiji Zhongguo xiaoshuo lilun ziliao (1897-1916)*, ed. Chen Pingyuan and Xia Xiaohong (Beijing: Beijing daxue chubanshe, 1989), 51-52.
35 *All-Story Monthly* 4, 13 (1908): 9-17.
36 In the late Qing, so-called vernacular Chinese contained classical Chinese. It was different from the vernacular Chinese that was promoted and practised in the May Fourth era.
37 Qin Shaode, *Shanghai jindai baokan shilun* (Shanghai: Fudan daxue chubanshe, 1994), 140.
38 Wo Foshanren, "Dianshu qitan fuji," in vol. 1 of *Ershi shiji Zhongguo xiaoshuo lilun ziliao (1897-1916)*, ed. Chen Pingyuan and Xia Xiaohong (Beijing: Beijing daxue chubanshe, 1989), 161-62.
39 Bieshi, "Xiaoshuo yuanli," in vol. 1 of *Ershi shiji Zhongguo xiaoshuo lilun ziliao (1897-1916)*, ed. Chen Pingyuan and Xia Xiaohong (Beijing: Beijing daxue chubanshe, 1989), 73-78.
40 Luo Zhitian, *Quanshi zhuanyi* (Wuhan: Hubei renmin chubanshe, 1999), 223 and 226.
41 Quoted in Luo Zhitian, "Jindai Zhongguo shehui quanshi de zhuanyi: zhishi fenzi de bianyuanhua yu bianyuan zhishi fenzi de xingqi," in *Ershi shiji Zhongguo zhishi fenzi shilun*, ed. Xu Jilin (Beijing: Xinxing chubanshe, 2005), 146.
42 Yuan Jin, "Shilun wanqing xiaoshuo duzhe de bianhua," *Mingqing xiaoshuo yanjiu* 59, 1 (2001): 18-28.
43 Jiaowo, "Yu zhi xiaoshuoguan," in vol. 1 of *Ershi shiji Zhongguo xiaoshuo lilun ziliao (1897-1916)*, ed. Chen Pingyuan and Xia Xiaohong (Beijing: Beijing daxue chubanshe, 1989), 335-36.
44 Yuan Jin, *Yuanyang hutiepai*, 40.
45 The schemes, based on harmonious combinations of flat and oblique tones in verses and sentences, have roots in single-syllable Chinese words and classical poetry.
46 See note 110 in Chapter 2 for details about the style of "bamboo twigs."
47 Chen Pingyuan, *Wanming yu wanqing: lishi chuancheng yu wenhua chuangxin* (Wuhan: Hubei jiaoyu chubanshe, 2002), 336.
48 Ouyang Jian, "Li Boyuan de wenxue zhilu," *Xuehai* 4 (1994): 88.
49 *Illustrated Fiction*, vol. 10, 260.
50 Barbara Mittler, *A Newspaper for China? Power, Identity and Change in Shanghai's News Media, 1872-1912* (Cambridge, MA: Harvard University Asia Center, 2004), 258 and 311.
51 Link, *Mandarin Ducks and Butterflies*, 5 and 189-92.
52 Some Chinese scholars define the genre broadly to include martial arts, detective, and exposé works of fiction that were hugely popular in the early twentieth century.
53 Link, *Mandarin Ducks and Butterflies*, 54.
54 Sun Yusheng, *Tuixinglu biji*, vol. 80 of *Jindai Zhongguo shiliao congkan*, ed. Shen Yunlong (Taipei: Wenhai chubanshe youxian gongsi, 1972), 139-40.

55 *All-Story Monthly* 1, 3 (1907): 1-10.
56 Ouyang Jian, *Wanqing xiaoshuoshi* (Hangzhou: Zejiang guji chubanshe, 1997), 4-5.
57 Hu Shi, "Jianshe de wenxue geminglun," vol. 1 of *Wenxue yundong shiliaoxuan*, ed. Modern Chinese Language Research Group, Beijing Normal University (Shanghai: Shanghai jiaoyu chubanshe, 1979), 78.
58 Lu Xun, *Zhongguo xiaoshuoshi lüè* (Beijing: Renmin wenxue chubanshe, 1956), 342.
59 Link, *Mandarin Ducks and Butterflies*, 196-97.
60 Roger Chartier, in his study of the French Revolution, uses the notion of appropriation to distinguish the construction of textual meanings by various "interpretive communities." Readers appropriated texts through acts of interpretation and by forming opinions and developing consciousness. He stresses the interconnection between the communities' positions in social relations of domination and their constructions of textual meanings. This perception is also instructive in analyzing how tabloid readers interpreted what they read. Roger Chartier, *The Cultural Origins of the French Revolution: Bicentennial Reflections on the French Revolution* (Durham, NC: Duke University Press, 1991).
61 Chen Wuwo, *Lao Shanghai sanshinian jianwenlu* (Shanghai: Shanghai shudian chubanshe, 1997), 374-75.
62 Wu Jianren, *Xinxiaolin guangji*, in vol. 7 of *Wu Jianren quanji*, ed. Haifeng (Harbin: Beifang wenyi chubanshe, 1998), 335.
63 Jianchan Zhuren, "Dushejuan ping yu," in vol. 1 of *Ershi shiji Zhongguo xiaoshuo lilun ziliao (1897-1916)*, ed. Chen Pingyuan and Xia Xiaohong (Beijing: Beijing daxue chubanshe, 1989), 112.
64 *Fun*, 2 October 1897.
65 Wang Xuejun, *Li Boyuan nianpu*, 155.
66 Sun Yusheng, "Li Boyuan," in *Li Boyuan yanjiu ziliao*, ed. Wei Shaochang, 18-19 (Shanghai: Shanghai guji chubanshe, 1980), 18.
67 Sun Yusheng, *Tuixinglu biji*, vol. 80 of *Jindai Zhongguo shiliao congkan*, ed. Shen Yunlong (Taipei: Wenhai chubanshe youxian gongsi, 1972), 132-33.
68 Hu Jichen, "Tongbei huiyilu," in *Wu Jianren yanjiu ziliao*, ed. Wei Shaochang (Shanghai: Shanghai guji chubanshe, 1980), 19. During his lifetime, Wu produced a large quantity of humour, including the collections *A New History of Laughter (Xinxiaoshi), New Comprehensive Stories of the Grove of Laughter (Xinxiaolin guangji), Humor (Qiaopihua), and Humorous Talks (Huajitan)*.
69 Alvin B. Kernan, *The Cankered Muse: Satire of the English Renaissance*, Yale Studies in English, vol. 142 (New Haven, CT: Shoe String Press, 1976), 1, 2, and 8.
70 Chen Wuwo, *Lao Shanghai sanshinian jianwenlu*, 33.
71 Mikhail Bakhtin, *Rabelais and His World*, tr. Helene Iswolsky (Bloomington: Indiana University Press, 2009).
72 Chen Pingyuan, *Zhongguo xiandai xiaoshuo de qidian*, 273.
73 This term is used in David Der-wei Wang, *Fin-de-siècle Splendor: Repressed Modernities of Late Qing Fiction, 1849-1911* (Palo Alto, CA: Stanford University Press, 1997), 43 and 200.
74 Des Forges, *Mediasphere Shanghai*, 85-86.
75 Wu Jianren, *Xin shitouji*, in vol. 6 of *Wu Jianren quanqi*, ed. Haifeng (Harbin: Beifang wenyi chubanshe, 1998), 7 and 58.
76 Guo Zhenyi, *Zhongguo xiaoshuoshi* (Shanghai: Shanghai shudian chubanshe, 1984), 552; see also Pei Xiaowei, *Wu Jianren yenjiu ziliao huibian*, in vol. 10 of *Wu Jianren quanqi*, ed. Haifeng (Harbin: Beifang wenyi chubanshe, 1998), 234-36. See also Gao Boyu, *Ershinian mudu zhi guaixianzhuang suoyin*, in vol. 10 of *Wu Jianren quanji*, ed. Haifeng (Harbin: Beifang wenyi chubanshe, 1998), 472-519.

77 Yeh, *Shanghai Love*, 19 and 250.
78 Yang Jiang, "Huiyi wode fuqin," in vol. 2 of *Yang Jiang zuopinji* (Beijing: Zhongguo shehui kexue chubanshe, 1993), 64-66.
79 Wo Foshanren, "Pou xinjin fanli," in vol. 1 of *Ershi shiji Zhongguo xiaoshuo lilun ziliao (1897-1916)*, ed. Chen Pingyuan and Xia Xiaohong (Beijing: Beijing daxue chubanshe, 1989), 280-81.
80 Wu Jianren, "Jinshinian zhi guaixianzhuang zixu," in vol. 3 of *Wu Jianren quanji*, ed. Haifeng (Harbin: Beifang wenyi chubanshe, 1998), 300.
81 Li Boyuan, *Boyuan shiwenji*, in vol. 5 of *Li Boyuan quanji*, ed. Xue Zhengxing (Nanjing: Jiangsu guji chubanshe, 1997), 28-29.
82 Yeh, *Shanghai Love*, 19-20.
83 Mittler, *A Newspaper for China?*, 100-4.
84 Jian, "Yunnan yecheng fubai," in vol. 1 of *Ershi shiji Zhongguo xiaoshuo lilun ziliao (1897-1916)*, ed. Chen Pingyuan and Xia Xiaohong (Beijing: Beijing daxue chubanshe, 1989), 283.
85 Wu Jianren, *Haishang mingji sida jingang qishu*, in vol. 6 of *Wu Jianren quanji*, ed. Haifeng (Harbin: Beifang wenyi chubanshe, 1998), 393.
86 Wu Jianren, *Shanghai youcanlu*, in vol. 3 of *Wu Jianren quanji*, ed. Haifeng (Harbin: Beifang wenyi chubanshe, 1998), 449.
87 *Fun*, 2 March 1902.
88 Wang, *Fin-de-siècle Splendor*, 215.
89 Sun Baoxuan, "Diary entry October 6, 1907 (lunar date)," in *Wangshanlu riji*, vol. 2 of *Zhonghua wenshi luncong zengkan* (Shanghai: Shanghai guji chubanshe, 1983), 1095.
90 Fan Boqun, "Teyuan shishi yaoqiu yihe shiren shihao: yipingyi Lu Xun, Hu Shi de youguan 'qianze xiaoshuo' lundian weizhongxin," *Suzhou keji daxue* xuebao (shehui kexue) 22, 1 (2005): 77.
91 Youhuan Yusheng, "Guanchang xianxingji xu," in vol. 1 of *Ershi shiji Zhongguo xioashuo lilun ziliao (1897-1916)*, ed. Chen Pingyuan and Xia Xiaohong (Beijing: Beijing daxue chubanshe, 1989, 1997), 72.
92 Pei Xiaowei, "Wu Jianren yenjiu ziliao huibian," 235.
93 Ye Xiaoqing, *The Dianshizhai Pictorial: Shanghai Urban Life, 1884-1898* (Ann Arbor: University of Michigan Center for Chinese Studies, 2003), 213-17.
94 Quoted in Wang, *Fin-de-siècle Splendor*, 354.
95 The four narrative aesthetics include simultaneity (multiple story lines of simultaneous installments), interruption (an essential feature of serialized narratives), mediation, and excess: Des Forges, *Mediasphere Shanghai*, 6-9.

Conclusion

1 Roger Chartier, *The Cultural Origins of the French Revolution: Bicentennial Reflections on the French Revolution* (Durham, NC: Duke University Press, 1991).
2 Douglas R. Reynolds, *China, 1898-1912: The Xinzheng Revolution and Japan* (Cambridge, MA: Harvard University Press, 1993).
3 Lin Yutang, *A History of the Press and Public Opinion in China* (New York: Greenwood Press, 1968), 17-18.
4 See, e.g., Jonathan Spence's book about the unusual way in which Emperor Yongzheng dealt with one case of subversive literature. Jonathan D. Spence, *Treason by the Book* (New York: Penguin, 2002).

Glossary of Chinese Terms and Names

Afanggong fu	阿房宫赋
Aiguobao	爱国报
Anhui ribao	安徽日报
Baling	巴陵
Bao Tianxiao	包天笑
Beiyang	北洋
Benguan lunshuo	本馆论说
buzhi	不治
buziyou wuningsi	不自由 毋宁死
Caifengbao	采风报
caizi yu jiaren	才子与佳人
celun	策论
Cen Chunxuan	岑春萱
Chen Boxi	陈伯熙
Chen Yingshi	陈英士
chenmin	臣民
chi	尺
chuanqi	传奇
ci	词
ci	辞
dabao	大报
Dagongbao	大公报
damalu	大马路
daminzu zhuyi	大民族主义
Danyuan shuyi	澹园述异
Daxue	大学
dazhong	大众
Deyujian	德育鉴
Dianshizhai huabao	点石斋画报
Dianshu qitan	电术奇谈

Dong Kang	董康
Duanchangbei	断肠碑
Eguo huangdi	俄国皇帝
Ershinian mudu zhi guaixianzhuang	二十年目睹之怪现状
fangzhen	方针
faren zhichu	发轫之初
fengchao	风潮
Fenglin	讽林
Fengshuangfei	凤双飞
Fengyuekong	风月空
fennei zhishi	分内之事
fenzhi	分治
Fozhaolou	佛照楼
fu	赋
Fu Chunyi	傅春宜
Fupu xiantan	负曝闲谈
Foshan shuyuan	佛山书院
Gang Ziliang	刚子良
Gao Taichi	高太痴
Gengzi guobian tanci	庚子国变弹词
geren tese	个人特色
gongde	公德
gonglun	公论
gongmin	公民
Gongzhong yanshuohui	公忠演说会
Gu Hongming	辜鸿铭
Gu Jiegang	顾颉刚
Guanchang xianxingji	官场现行记
Guanchang xiaohua	官场笑话
Guanchang yiban	官场一斑
Guantu xianxiang ji	官途现象记
Guantu xianxing ji	官途现行记
guo	国
guojia	国家
guomin	国民
guomin daode	国民道德
guoren	国人
Haishang fanhuameng	海上繁华梦
Haishang hualiezhuan	海上花列传
haishang laishisheng	海上濑石生

Haishang mingji sida jingang qishu	海上名妓四大金刚奇书
Haishang qishu	海上奇书
Haishang wenshe	海上文社
Haishang wenshe yuekan	海上文社月刊
Haitian hongxueji	海天鸿雪记
Han Bangqing	韩邦庆
Hangzhou Baihuabao	杭州白话报
Hanmanyou	汗漫游
hedeyou Zhongguo yifen	何得有中国一分
Henhai	恨海
Houguanchang xianxing ji	后官场现形记
Hu Baoyu	胡宝玉
Hu Fu	胡弗
Huajihun	滑稽魂
Huajitan	滑稽谈
Huang Ren	黄人
Huangchao zhanggu congtan	皇朝掌故从谈
Huanqiu Zhongguo xueshenghui	环球中国学生会
huaxuan	花选
huayi	华夷
Huodiyu	活地狱
Hutu shijie	糊涂世界
Jiang Fengqing	江峰青
jiedao sharen	借刀杀人
jieguo kaihua	结果开花
Jieyuhui	劫余灰
Jingguo meitan	经国美谈
Jitan	叽谈
jiuxue	旧学
juan	卷
kaishu	楷书
Kaiming zhuanzhilun	开明专制论
Kongzi gaizhikao	孔子改制考
kunqu	昆曲
Kushehui	苦社会
Laihan *or* Laigao	来函 来稿
Laocan youji	老残游记
li	礼
Li Boyuan	李伯元
Li Genyuan	李根源

Li Lianying	李莲英
Lian Mengqing	连梦青
Liang Dingfen	梁鼎芬
Liangjin yanyi	两晋演义
Lin Qinnan	林琴南
Liu E	刘鹗
Liu Juqing	刘聚卿
Liu Kunyi	刘坤一
Liu Shipei	刘师培
Lixian wansui	立宪万岁
Lu Chuanlin	鹿传霖
Ma Yukun	马玉昆
Meiguo dulishi biecai	美国独立史别裁
Menghualu	梦华录
Mengzi	孟子
mingshi	名士
mudi	目的
Nanting tingzhang	南亭亭长
Nanting xu	南亭序
nongbao	脓胞
Ouyang Juyuan	欧阳钜源
Pan Feisheng	潘飞声
Pang Shubo	庞树柏
pinghua	评话
pingtan	评弹
pipa	琵琶
Pouxinji	剖心记
Qian Qianyi	钱谦益
Qiaopihua	俏皮话
qidian	起点
qing	情
Qingbian	情变
qingguan	清官
qingguan	清馆
Qingyibao	清议报
Qingzhu lixian	庆祝立宪
qinqu	秦曲
Qiu Fengjia	邱逢甲
Qiu Jin	秋瑾
Qiu Shuyuan	邱菽园

Glossary of Chinese Terms and Names 213

qu	曲
Quanxuepian	劝学篇
Qubao	趣报
qun	群
qupai	曲牌
ren	仁
Renjing xueshe	人镜学社
Renjing xueshe guikuzhuan	人镜学社鬼哭传
riren	日人
Rulin waishi	儒林外史
sancong side	三从四德
sanxuan	三絃
Sanzijing	三字经
Saomizhou	扫迷帚
Shanghai Youcanlu	上海游骖录
shanzhen haiwei	山珍海味
shehui	社会
shehui daode	社会道德
Shen Xizhi	沈习之
Shenbao	申报
Sheshuo	社说
Shibao	时报
Shijie fanhuabao	世界繁华报
Shishe	诗社
Shishi fengwen	时事讽文
Shishi outan	时事偶谈
Shishi xitan	时事嬉谈
Shishi yanshuo	时事演说
Shiwubao	时务报
shoujiudang	守旧党
Shuhuashe	书画社
shuoshu	说书
sida jingang	四大金刚
side	私德
siwanwan tongbao	四万万同胞
siwanwan zhongguoren	四万万中国人
siwen bailei	斯文败类
Sun Baoxuan	孙宝暄
Sun Yusheng	孙玉声
Taixi lishi yanyi	泰西历史演义

tanci	弹词
Tancong	谈丛
Tiannan xinbao	天南新报
Tongmenghui	同盟会
Tongshi	痛史
Tongwen Guan	同文馆
tuanti	团体
wan	玩
Wang Kangnian	汪康年
Wang Wenshao	王文韶
Wang Xiaonong	汪笑侬
wangu dang	顽固党
wanshi	玩世
wanshi bugong	玩世不恭
Wanshoujie	万寿节
wanwu sangzhi	玩物丧志
Wei Bangxian	魏榜贤
weixindang	维新党
Wen Tingshi	文廷式
wenming	文明
Wenming xiaoshi	文明小史
wenming zhuanzhi	文明专制
Wenshe ribao	文社日报
woren	倭人
Wu Gang	鄥刚
Wu Jianren	吴趼人
Wu Jingzi	吴敬梓
Wu Tingfang	伍廷芳
Wuhu ribao	芜湖日报
Wulieshi xunlu	鄥烈士殉路
wulu	无路
Wutuobang youji	乌托邦游记
Wuxi	无锡
xi	溪
xi	西
Xi Xifan	席锡藩
Xia Zengyou	夏普佑
xiandai	现代
xiandaihua	现代化
xiandaixing	现代性

Glossary of Chinese Terms and Names 215

Xianxia wuhuajian	仙侠五花剑
xiaobao	小报
Xiaobao	笑报
xiaohanhui	消寒会
Xiaohua xinwen	笑话新闻
Xiaolin benzhi	笑林本旨
Xiaolinbao	笑林报
xiaominzu zhuyi	小民族主义
xiaoshimin	小市民
Xiaoxianbao	消闲报
Xin shitouji	新石头记
xindang	新党
xingminquan	兴民权
Xingshiyuan	醒世缘
Xinmin congbao	新民丛报
Xinminshuo	新民说
Xinshixue	新史学
Xinwenbao	新闻报
xinxi	新戏
Xinxiaolin guangji	新笑林广记
Xinxiaoshi	新笑史
Xinxiaoshuo	新小说
xinxue	新学
xinxuejia	新学家
xinxuetang	新学堂
xinzheng	新政
Xinzhongguo weilaiji	新中国未来记
xiren	西人
Xitan riji	嬉谈日记
Xiuxiang xiaoshuo	绣像小说
Xixiangji	西厢记
xixiao numa	嬉笑怒骂
xixue	西学
Xu Nianci	徐念慈
Xuangao	选稿
yang	阳
Yang Jiang	杨绛
Yang Shu	杨枢
yangqian	洋钱
yangren	洋人

Yanyi baihuabao	演义白话报
Yao Gonghe	姚公鹤
yi	夷
yi tianxiashi wei jiren	以天下事为己任
yifen	一分
yin	阴
Yinbingshi Zhuren	饮冰室主人
yiren	夷人
Yiwenshe	艺文社
yiwu	义务
youxi wenzhang	游戏文章
Youxibao	游戏报
Youxi Zhuren	游戏主人
Yu Dafu	俞达夫
Yuan Shikai	袁世凯
Yuan Xiangpu	袁翔莆
Yubei lixian	预备立宪
Yue Wumu	岳武穆
Yueyue xiaoshuo	月月小说
Yufuyuan	玉佛缘
Yunnan yecheng	云南野乘
yusheng	玉声
Yuyanbao	寓言报
zaju	杂剧
Zalu	杂录
Zeng Shaoqing	曾少卿
Zeng Guofan	曾国藩
zhang	丈
Zhang Biao	张彪
Zhang Suiyang	张睢阳
Zhang Zhidong	张之洞
Zheng Yimei	郑逸梅
Zhengwenshe	政闻社
Zhenjiang	镇江
zhina	支那
Zhinanbao	指南报
zhizhun zhouguan fanghuo, buxu baixing diandeng	只准州官放火, 不许百姓点灯
Zhongguo jinhua xiaoshi	中国进化小史
Zhongguo yifenzi	中国一分子

Zhongguo xianzaiji	中国现在记
zhongxindian	中心点
zhongxue	中学
zhongzu	种族
Zhou Bingyuan	周病鸳
Zhou Guisheng	周桂笙
Zhou Hao	周浩
Zhou Linzhi	周麟之
Zhou Shuren	周树人
zhuluo	猪猡
zhuquan	主权
zhuzhici	竹枝词
Zilin hubao	字林沪报
ziyou	自由
zixing	自性
zizhi	自治
Zizhi tongjian	资治通鉴
zongchen	宗臣
Zou Tao	邹弢
zoutou	走头
zoutou wulu	走投无路
zuguo	祖国
zuzhi	组织

Bibliography

Shanghai Tabloid Presses
Caifengbao [Anecdotes], 1898-1900
Shijie fanhuabao [Splendid World], 1901-7
Xiaolinbao [Grove of Laughter], 1901-10
Xiuxiang xiaoshuo [Illustrated Fiction], 1903-6 (Beijing: Beijing tushuguan chubanshe, 2006, reprint)
Xiuxiang xiaoshuo [Illustrated Fiction], 1903-6 (Shanghai: Shanghai shudian, 1980, reprint)
Youxibao [Fun], 1897-1908
Yueyue xiaoshuo [All-Story Monthly], 1906-9 (Shanghai: Shanghai shudian, 1980, reprint)
Yuyanbao [Allegories], 1901-3

All Other References
Albertazzi, Daniele, and Duncan McDonnell. *Twenty-First Century Populism: The Spectre of Western European Democracy*. New York: Palgrave Macmillan, 2008.
Allen, Robert C., Jean-Pascal Bassino, Debin Ma, Christine Moll-Murata, and Jan Luiten van Zanden. "Wages, Prices, and Living Standards in China, 1738-1925, in Comparison with Europe, Japan, and India." *Economic History Review* 64 (2011): 8-38.
Anderson, Benedict. *Imagined Communities: Reflections on the Origin and Spread of Nationalism*. London: Verso, 2006.
Bakhtin, Mikhail. *Rabelais and His World*. Trans. Helene Iswolsky. Bloomington: Indiana University Press, 2009.
Bao Tianxiao. *Chuanyinglou huiyilu*. Taiyuan: Shanxi guji chubanshe, 1999.
—. *Chuanyinglou huiyilu xubian*. Taiyuan: Shanxi guji chubanshe, 1999.
Bieshi. "Xiaoshuo yuanli." In vol. 1 of *Ershi shiji Zhongguo xiaoshuo lilun ziliao (1897-1916)*, ed. Chen Pingyuan and Xia Xiaohong, 73-78. Beijing: Beijing daxue chubanshe, 1989.
Bourdieu, Pierre. *Distinction: A Social Critique of the Judgment of Taste*. Cambridge, MA: Harvard University Press, 1987.
Boyte, Harry Chatten, and Frank Riessman. *The New Populism: the Politics of Empowerment*. Philadelphia: Temple University Press, 1986.
Chang Tsun-wu. *China's Boycott against American Goods (1905-06)*. Taipei: Academia Sinica, 1972.
Chartier, Roger. *The Cultural Origins of the French Revolution: (Bicentennial Reflections on the French Revolution)*. Durham, NC: Duke University Press, 1991.
Chen Boxi. *Shanghai yishi daguan*. Shanghai: Shanghai shudian chubanshe, 2000.
Chen Jianhua. *Geming de xiandaixing: Zhongguo geming huayu laolun*. Shanghai: Shanghai guji chubanshe, 2000.
Chen Pingyuan. *Ershi shiji Zhongguo xiaoshuoshi (1897-1916)*. Vol. 1. Beijing: Beijing daxue chubanshe, 1989, 1997.

–. *Wanming yu wanqing: lishi chuancheng yu wenhua chuangxin.* Wuhan: Hubei jiaoyu chubanshe, 2002.
–. *Zhongguo xiandai xiaoshuo de qidian: qingmo minchu xiaoshuo yanjiu. Wenxueshi yanjiu congshu.* Beijing: Beijing daxue chubanshe, 2005.
Chen Pingyuan, and Xia Xiaohong, eds. *Ershi shiji Zhongguo xiaoshuo lilun ziliao, 1897-1916.* Vol 1. Beijing: Beijing daxue chubanshe, 1989.
Chen Sanjing. "Xinhai geming qianhou di Shanghai." In *Xinhai geming yantaohui lunwenji.* Taipei: Zhongyang yanjiuyuan jindaishi yanjiusuo, 1983.
Chen Wuwo. *Lao Shanghai sanshinian jianwenlu.* Shanghai: Shanghai shudian chubanshe, 1997.
Chen Yushen. *Wanqing baoyeshi.* Jinan: Shangdong hubao chubanshe, 2003.
Chu Hong-Yuan, and Peter Zarrow. "Modern Chinese Nationalism: The Formative Stage." In *Exploring Nationalisms of China: Themes and Conflicts,* ed. C.X. George Wei and Xiaoyuan Liu, 3-26. Westport, CT: Greenwood Press, 2002.
Darnton, Robert. *The Forbidden Best-Sellers of Pre-Revolutionary France.* New York: Norton, 1996.
Des Forges, Alexander. *Mediasphere Shanghai: The Aesthetics of Cultural Production.* Honolulu: University of Hawai'i Press, 2007.
Dikötter, Frank. *The Discourse of Race in Modern China.* London: Hurst, 1992.
Dittmer, Lowell, and Samuel S. Kim. "In Search of a Theory of National Identity." In *China's Quest for National Identity,* ed. Lowell Dittmer and Samuel S. Kim, 1-31. Ithaca, NY: Cornell University Press, 1993.
Fan Boqun. "Teyuan shishi yaoqiu yihe shiren shihao: yipingyi Lu Xun, Hu Shi de youguan 'qianze xiaoshuo' lundian weizhongxin." *Suzhou keji daxue xuebao (shehui kexue)* 22, 1 (2005): 77-83.
Gao Boyu. *Ershinian mudu zhi guaixianzhuang suoyin.* In vol. 10 of *Wu Jianren quanji,* ed. Haifeng, 472-519. Harbin: Beifang wenyi chubanshe, 1998.
Gimpel, Denise. *Lost Voices of Modernity: A Chinese Popular Fiction Magazine in Context.* Honolulu: University of Hawai'i Press, 2001.
Gu Jiegang. *Gu Jiegang zishu.* Zhengzhou: Henan renmin chubanshe, 2005.
Guo Haofan. "Qingmo minchu xiaoshuo yu baokanye zhi guanxi tanlüe." *Wenshizhe* 3 (2004): 45-50.
Guo Zhenyi. *Zhongguo xiaoshuoshi.* Shanghai: Shanghai shudian chubanshe, 1984.
Haifeng, ed. *Wu Jianren quanji.* Vols. 3, 5, 6-10. Harbin: Beifang wenyi chubanshe, 1998.
Harrison, Henrietta. *China: Inventing the Nation.* Oxford: Hodder Arnold, 2001.
–. *The Man Awakened from Dreams: One Man's Life in a North China Village, 1897-1942.* Palo Alto, CA: Stanford University Press, 2005.
Henriot, Christian. *Prostitution and Sexuality in Shanghai: A Social History, 1849-1949.* Trans. Noel Castelino. New York: Cambridge University Press, 2001.
Hershatter, Gail. *Dangerous Pleasures: Prostitution and Modernity in Twentieth Century Shanghai.* Berkeley: University of California Press, 1997.
Hong Yu. *Jindai Shanghai xiaobao yu shimin wenhua yanjiu.* Shanghai: Shanghai shudian chubanshe, 2007.
Hu Jichen. "Tongbei huiyilu." In *Wu Jianren yanjiu ziliao,* ed. Wei Shaochang, 16-31. Shanghai: Shanghai guji chubanshe, 1980.
Hu Shi. "Jianshe de wenxue geminglun." In vol. 1 of *Wenxue yundong shiliaoxuan,* ed. Modern Chinese Language Research Group, Beijing Normal University. Shanghai: Shanghai jiaoyu chubanshe, 1979.
Huang Biao. *Haishang xinjuchao: Zhongguo huaju di xunli qidian.* Shanghai: Shanghai renmin chubanshe, 2003.

Huang Ko-wu. "Liang Qichao yu rujia chuantong: yiqingmo wangxue wei zhongxin zhi kaocha." *Lishi jiaoxue* 3 (2004): 19-23.

–. *Yige bei fangqi di xuanze: Liang Qichao tiaoshi sixiang zhi yanjiu*. Taipei: Zhongyang yanjiuyuan jindaishi yanjiusuo zhuankan, 1994.

Huters, Theodore. *Bringing the World Home: Appropriating the West in Late Qing and Early Republican China*. Honolulu: University of Hawai'i Press, 2005.

Iser, Wolfgang. *The Implied Reader: Patterns of Communication in Prose Fiction from Bunyan to Beckett*. Baltimore: Johns Hopkins University Press, 1978.

Jian. "Yunnan yecheng fubai." In vol. 1 of *Ershi shiji Zhongguo xiaoshuo lilun ziliao (1897-1916)*, ed. Chen Pingyuan and Xia Xiaohong. Beijing: Beijing daxue chubanshe, 1989.

Jianchan Zhuren. "Dushejuan ping yu." In vol. 1 of *Ershi shiji Zhongguo xiaoshuo lilun ziliao (1897-1916)*, ed. Chen Pingyuan and Xia Xiaohong, 73-78. Beijing: Beijing daxue chubanshe, 1989.

Jiao Runming, and Su Xiaoxuan. *Wanqing shenghuo lueying*. Shenyang: Shenyang chubanshe, 2002.

Jiaowo. "Yu zhi xiaoshuoguan." In vol. 1 of *Ershi shiji Zhongguo xiaoshuo lilun ziliao (1897-1916)*, ed. Chen Pingyuan and Xia Xiaohong, 332-38. Beijing: Beijing daxue chubanshe, 1989.

Judge, Joan. *Print and Politics: "Shibao" and the Culture of Reform in Late Qing China*. Palo Alto, CA: Stanford University Press, 1996.

Kang Youwei. "Shang qingdi diwushu." In *Kangnanhai xiansheng yizhuo huikan*, ed. Jiang Guilin, 91-101. Taipei: Hongye shuju, 1976.

Kernan, Alvin B. *The Cankered Muse: Satire of the English Renaissance*. Yale Studies in English, vol. 142. New Haven, CT: Shoe String Press, 1976.

Ko, Dorothy. *Cinderella's Sisters: A Revisionist History of Footbinding*. Berkeley: University of California Press, 2007.

Laclau, Ernesto. "Populism: What's in a Name?" In *Populism and the Mirror of Democracy*, ed. Francisco Panizza. London: Verso, 2005.

–. *On Populist Reason*. London: Verso, 2005.

Laitinen, Kauko. *Chinese Nationalism in the Late Qing Dynasty: Zhang Binglin as an Anti-Manchu Propagandist*. Surrey, UK: Curzon Press, 1990.

Lee, Leo Ou-fan, and Andrew J. Nathan. "The Beginnings of Mass Culture." In *Popular Culture in Late Imperial China*, ed. David Johnson, Andrew J. Nathan, and Evelyn S. Rawski, 370-73. Berkeley, CA: University of California Press, 1985.

–. "Journalism and Fiction in the Late Ch'ing and Beyond." In *Popular Culture in Late Imperial China*, ed. David Johnson, Andrew J. Nathan, and Evelyn S. Rawski. Berkeley: University of California Press, 1985.

Levenson, Joseph Richmond. *Liang Ch'i-ch'ao and the Mind of Modern China*. Cambridge, MA: Harvard University Press, 1959.

Li Boyuan. "Benguan bianyin Xiuxiang xiaoshuo yuanqi." In vol. 1 of *Ershi shiji Zhongguo xiaoshuo lilun ziliao, 1897-1916*, ed. Chen Pingyuan and Xia Xiaohong. Beijing: Beijing daxue chubanshe, 1989.

–. *Boyuan shiwenji*. In vol. 5 of *Li Boyuan quanji*, ed. Xue Zhengxing. Nanjing: Jiangsu guji chubanshe, 1997.

–. "Jinxian baochen." In vol. 5 of *Li Boyuan quanji*, ed. Xue Zhengxing. Nanjing: Jiangsu guji chubanshe, 1997.

–. *Wenming xiaoshi*. In vol. 1 of *Li Boyuan quanqi*, ed. Xue Zhengxing. Nanjing: Jiangsu guji chubanshe, 1997.

–. *Xingshiyuan*. In vol. 10 of *Xiuxiang xiaoshuo*, ed. Boyuan Li. Beijing: Beijing tushuguan chubanshe, 2006.

Li Jiuhua. "Lunwanqing wenyi qikan yu xiaoshuo fanrong." *Ningxia daxue xuebao (Renwen shehui kexueban)* 25, 5 (2003): 43-48.
Li Xisuo. *Zhongguo liuxueshi lungao*. Beijing: Zhonghua shuju, 2007.
Li Xisuo, and Qing Yuan. *Liang Qichao zhuan*. Beijing: Renmin chubanshe, 1993.
Li Yuzhong. "Wu Jianren shengping jiqi zhuzuo." In vol. 10 of *Wu Jianren quanqi*, ed. Haifeng. Harbin: Beifang wenyi chubanshe, 1998.
Liang Qichao. "Lun bianfa bizi pingmanhan zhijie shi." In vol. 1 of *Yinbin shi wen ji dianjiao*, ed. Wu Song, Lu Yunkun, Wang Wenguang, and Duan Bingchang. Kunming: Yunnan jiaoyu chubanshe, 2001.
–. "Lun xiaoshuo yu qunzhi zhi guanxi." In vol. 1 of *Yinbinshi wenji dianjiao*, ed. Wu Song, Lu Yunkun, Wang Wenguang, and Duan Bingchang. Kunming: Yunnan jiaoyu chubanshe, 2001.
–. "Shixue zhijieshuo." In *Liang Qichao shixue lunzhu sanzhong*. Hong Kong: Sanlian shudian, 1988.
–. "Wenye sanjie zhibie." In *Ziyoushu*. Taipei: Taiwan zhonghua shuju, 1979.
–. *Yinbin shi wen ji*. Taipei: Taiwan zhonghua shuju, 1983.
–. "Yiyin zhengzhi xiaoshuoxu." In vol. 1 of *Yinbinshi wenji dianjiao*, ed. Wu Song, Lu Yunkun, Wang Wenguang, and Duan Bingchang. Kunming: Yunnan jiaoyu chubanshe, 2001.
–. "Zhongguo zhi jiushi." In *Liang Qichao shixue lunzhu sanzhong*. Hong Kong: Sanlian shudian, 1988.
Lin Mingde. "Mibu Zhongguo wenxueshi de yiye kongbai bianxu." In *Wanqing xiaoshuo yanjiu*, ed. Lin Mingde, 1-3. Taipei: Lianjing chuban shiye gongsi, 1988.
–. *Wanqing xiaoshuo yenjiu*. Taipei: Lianjing chubanshe, 1986.
Lin Yutang. *A History of the Press and Public Opinion in China*. New York: Greenwood Press, 1968.
Link, Perry. *Mandarin Ducks and Butterflies: Popular Fiction in Early Twentieth-Century Chinese Cities*. Berkeley: University of California Press, 1981.
Lipuma, Edward, Moishe Postone, and Craig J. Calhoun, eds. *Pierre Bourdieu: Critical Perspectives*. Chicago: University of Chicago Press, 1993.
Liu Shipei. "Lunjilie de haochu." In *Xinhai geming qianshinian jian shilun xuanji*, ed. Zhang Mudan, 887-90. Hong Kong: Shenghuo dushu xinzhi sanlian shudian, 1962.
Lu Xiangyuan. *Gaochou zenyang jiaodong wentan: shichang jingji yu Zhongguo jinxiandai wenxue*. Beijing: Hongqi chubanshe, 1998.
Lu Xun. *Zhongguo xiaoshuoshi lüè*. Beijing: Renmin wenxue chubanshe, 1956.
Luo Zhitian. "Jindai Zhongguo shehui quanshi de zhuanyi: zhishi fenzi de bianyuanhua yu bianyuan zhishi fenzi de xingqi." In *Ershi shiji Zhongguo zhishi fenzi shilun*, ed. Xu Jilin, 127-61. Beijing: Xinxing chubanshe, 2005.
–. *Minzu zhuyi yu jindai Zhongguo sixiang*. Taipei: Dongda tushu gufen youxian gongsi, 1998.
–. *Quanshi zhuanyi*. Wuhan: Hubei renmin chubanshe, 1999.
Ma Guangren, ed. *Shanghai xinwenshi*. Shanghai: Fudan daxue chubanshe, 1996.
MacFarquhar, Roderick, and Michael Schoenhals. *Mao's Last Revolution*. Cambridge, MA: Belknap Press, 2006.
McGuigan, Jim. *Cultural Populism*. New York: Routledge, 1992.
Meng Yue. *Shanghai and the Edges of Empire*. Minneapolis: University of Minnesota Press, 2006.
Meng Zhaochen. *Zhongguo jindai xiaobao shi*. Beijing: Shehui kexue chubanshe, 2005.
Mény, Yves, and Yves Surel, eds. *Democracies and the Populist Challenge*. New York: Palgrave Macmillan, 2002.
Mittler, Barbara. *A Newspaper for China? Power, Identity, and Change in Shanghai's News Media, 1872-1912*. Cambridge, MA: Harvard University Asia Center, 2004.

Murata, Yūjirō. "Dynasty, State, and Society: The Case of Modern China." In *Imagining the People: Chinese Intellectuals and the Concept of Citizenship, 1890-1920*, ed. Joshua A. Fogel and Peter Gue Zarrow, 113-41. Armonk, NY: M.E. Sharpe, 1997.

Ouyang Jian. "Li Boyuan de wenxue zhilu." *Xuehai* 4 (1994): 86-89.

—. *Wanqing xiaoshuoshi*. Hangzhou: Zejiang guji chubanshe, 1997.

Ouyang Juyuan. *Fupu xiantan*, ed. Li Boyuan. http://tinyurl.com/76qreus.

—. "Guanchang xianxingji xu." In vol. 1 of *Ershi shiji Zhongguo xiaoshuo lilun ziliao, 1897-1916*, ed. Chen Pingyuan and Xia Xiaohong, 69-71. Beijing: Beijing daxue chubanshe, 1997.

Pan Jianguo. "Qingmo Shanghai diqu shuju yu wanqing xiaoshuo." *Wenxue yichan* 2 (2004): 96-110.

Panizza, Francisco. "Introduction: Populism and the Mirror of Democracy." In *Populism and the Mirror of Democracy*, ed. Francisco Panizza. London: Verso, 2005.

Pei Xiaowei. *Wu Jianren yenjiu ziliao huibian*. In vol. 10 of *Wu Jianren quanji*, ed. Haifeng. Harbin: Beifang wenyi chubanshe, 1998.

Pye, Lucien W. "How China's Nationalism Was Shanghaied." In *Chinese Nationalism*, ed. Jonathan Unger, 86-112. Armonk, NY: M.E. Sharpe, 1996.

Qin Shaode. *Shanghai jindai baokan shilun*. Shanghai: Fudan daxue chubanshe, 1993.

Reed, Christopher A. *Gutenberg in Shanghai: Chinese Print Capitalism, 1876-1937*. Vancouver: UBC Press, 2005.

Ren Fangqiu. *Zhongguo jindai wenxueshi*. Kaifeng: Henan daxue chubanshe, 2005.

Reynolds, Douglas R. *China, 1898-1912: The Xinzheng Revolution and Japan*. Cambridge, MA: Harvard University Press, 1993.

Rhoads, Edward J.M. *Manchus and Han: Ethnic Relations and Political Power in Late Qing and Early Republican China, 1861-1928*. Seattle: University of Washington Press, 2001.

Smith, S.A. *Like Cattle and Horses: Nationalism and Labor in Shanghai, 1895-1927*. Durham, NC: Duke University Press, 2002.

Spence, Jonathan D. *Treason by the Book*. New York: Penguin, 2002.

Su Tiege. "'Xinhainian' (Beijing) aiguobaosuozai wanqing xiaoshuo sanzhong shuluè." *Mingqing xiaoshuo yanjiu* 61, 3 (2001): 90-97.

Sun Baoxuan. "Diary entry October 6, 1907 (lunar date)." In *Wangshanlu riji*. Vol. 2 of *Zhonghua wenshi luncong zengkan*. Shanghai: Shanghai guji chubanshe, 1983.

—. *Wangshanlu riji*. Vol. 1 of *Zhonghua wenshi luancong zhongkan*. Shanghai: Shanghai guji chubanshe, 1983.

Sun Yusheng. "Baohai qianchenlu: xiaolin baoguan zhi huiyi." *Xinyebao*, 24 June 1934.

—. "Li Boyuan." In *Li Boyuan yanjiu ziliao*, ed. Wei Shaochang, 18-19. Shanghai: Shanghai guji chubanshe, 1980.

—. *Tuixinglu biji*. Vol. 80 of *Jindai Zhongguo shiliao congkan*, ed. Shen Yunlong. Taipei: Wenhai chubanshe youxian gongsi, 1972.

Taggart, Paul. *Populism*. Buckingham, UK: Open University Press, 2000.

Tanaka, Stefan. *Japan's Orient: Rendering Pasts into History*. Berkeley: University of California Press, 1995.

Tang Xiaobing. *Chinese Modern: The Heroic and the Quotidian: Post-Contemporary Interventions*. Durham, NC: Duke University Press, 2000.

—. *Global Space and the Nationalist Discourse of Modernity: The Historical Thinking of Liang Qichao*. Palo Alto, CA: Stanford University Press, 1996.

Tarumoto, Teruo. *Qingmo xiaoshuo yanjiu jigao*. Trans. Wei Chen. Jinan: Qilu shushe, 2006.

—. "Yūgi shujin sentei 'kōshi zuikyū kasen.'" *Shinmatsu shōsetsu kenkyū* 5 (1981): 15-25.

Townsend, James. "Chinese Nationalism." In *Chinese Nationalism*, ed. Jonathan Unger, 1-30. Armonk, NY: M.E. Sharpe, 1996.

Tsin, Michael. "Imagining 'Society' in Early Twentieth-Century China." In *Imagining the People: Chinese Intellectuals and the Concept of Citizenship, 1890-1920*, ed. Joshua A. Fogel and Peter G. Zarrow, 212-31. Armonk, NY: M.E. Sharpe, 1997.
Wang, David Der-wei. *Fin-de-siècle Splendor: Repressed Modernities of Late Qing Fiction, 1849-1911*. Palo Alto, CA: Stanford University Press, 1997.
Wang Fanshen. "Congxinmin daoxinren: jindai sixiangzhong di 'ziwou' yu 'Zhengzhi.'" In *Zhongguo jin dai sixiangshi de zhuanxing shidai*, ed. Wang Fanshen, 171-200. Taipei: Liangjing chuban shiye gufen youxian gongsi, 2007.
—. "Evolving Prescriptions for Social Life in the Late Qing and Early Republic: From *Qunxue* to Society." In *Imagining the People: Chinese Intellectuals and the Concept of Citizenship, 1890-1920*, ed. Joshua A. Fogel and Peter G. Zarrow, 258-78. Armonk, NY: M.E. Sharpe, 1997).
—. *Zhang Taiyan de sixiang (1868-1919) jiqi dui ruxue chuantong de chongji*. Taipei: Shibao wenhua chuban shiye youxian gongsi, 1985.
Wang Linmao. "Lun xinhai geming shiqi di shidaifu jieceng." In *Xinhai geming yu jindai Zhongguo: jinnian xinhai geming bashi zhounian guoji xueshu taolunhui wenji*, ed. Editorial Board of Zhonghua Shuju, 295-309. Beijing: Zhonghua shuju, 1994.
Wang Xianming. "Shishen jieceng yu wanqing 'minbian': shenmin chongtu de lishi quxiang yu shidai chengyin." *Jindaishi yanjiu* 1 (2008): 21-33.
Wang Xuejun. *Li Boyuan nianpu*. In vol. 5 of *Li Boyuan quanji*, ed. Xue Zhengxing. Nanjing: Jiangsu guji chubanshe, 1997.
Wang Yan. "'Xiuxiang xiaoshuo' gaikuang." In vol. 1 of *Illustrated Fiction [Xiuxiang xiaoshuo]*. Beijing: Beijing tushuguan chubanshe, 2006, reprint, 1-48.
Wei Shaochang, ed. *Li Boyuan yanjiu ziliao*. Shanghai: Shanghai guji chubanshe, 1980.
—. "Qianben jingguo meitan xinxi." In *Li Boyuan yanjiu ziliao*, ed. Wei Shaochang. Shanghai: Shanghai guji chubanshe, 1980.
—, ed. *Shiliao suoyin ji*. In vol. 30 of *Zhongguo jindai wenxue daxi*. Shanghai: Shanghai shudian, 1996.
—, ed. *Wu Jianren yanjiu ziliao*. Shanghai: Shanghai guji chubanshe, 1980.
—, ed. *Zhongguo jindai wenyi baokan gailan (II)*. In *Shiliao suoyinji*. Vol. 30 of *Zhongguo jindai wenxue daxi*. Shanghai: Shanghai shudian, 1996.
Weyland, Kurt. "Clarifying a Contested Concept: Populism in the Study of Latin American Politics." *Comparative Politics* 34, 1 (2001): 1-22.
Wo Foshanren. "'Dianshu qitan' fuji." In vol. 1 of *Ershi shiji Zhongguo xiaoshuo lilun ziliao, 1897-1916*, ed. Chen Pingyuan and Xia Xiaohong. Beijing: Beijing daxue chubanshe, 1989.
—. "Pou xinjin fanli." In vol. 1 of *Ershi shiji Zhongguo xiaoshuo lilun ziliao, 1897-1916*, ed. Chen Pingyuan and Xia Xiaohong. Beijing: Beijing daxue chubanshe, 1989.
Wu Jianren. "Baixiangtu." In vol. 8 of *Wu Jianren quanji*, ed. Haifeng. Harbin: Beifang wenyi chubanshe, 1998.
—. *Ershinian mudu zhi guaixianzhuang*. In vol. 1 of *Wu Jianren quanji*, ed. Haifeng. Harbin: Beifang wenyi chubanshe, 1998.
—. *Haishang mingji sida jingang qishu*. In vol. 6 of *Wu Jianren quanqi*, ed. Haifeng. Harbin: Beifang wenyi chubanshe, 1998.
—. *Huaji tan*. In vol. 7 of *Wu Jianren quanji*, ed. Haifeng. Harbin: Beifang Wenyi Chubanshe, 1998.
—. "Jinshinian zhi guaixianzhuang zixu." In vol. 3 of *Wu Jianren quanji*, ed. Haifeng. Harbin: Beifang wenyi chubanshe, 1998.
—. "Li Boyuan zhuan." In *Li Boyuan yanjiu ziliao*, ed. Wei Shaochang. Shanghai: Shanghai guji chubanshe, 1980.

–. "Lixian wansui." *All-Story Monthly* 2, 5 (1907): 167-80.
–. *Lixian wansui.* In vol. 7 of *Wu Jianren quanqi*, ed. Haifeng. Harbin: Beifang wenyi chubanshe, 1998.
–. *Qingbian.* In vol. 5 of *Wu Jianren qianji*, ed. Haifeng. Harbin: Beifang wenyi chubanshe, 1998.
–. "Renjing xueshe guikuzhuan." *All-Story Monthly* 3, 10 (1907): 232.
–. *The Sea of Regret.* Trans. Patrick Hanan. Honolulu: University of Hawai'i Press, 1995.
–. *Shanghai youcanlu.* In vol. 3 of *Wu Jianren quanqi*, ed. Haifeng. Harbin: Beifang wenyi chubanshe, 1998.
–. "Wu Jianren jun yanshuo," In vol. 8 of *Wu Jianren quanji*, ed. Haifeng, 237-38. Harbin: Beifang wenyi chubanshe, 1998.
–. "Wu Jianren ku." In *Wu Jianren yanjiu ziliao*, ed. Wei Shaochang, 2-9. Shanghai: Shanghai guji chubanshe, 1980.
–. "Wu Jianren ku." In vol. 8 of *Wu Jianren quanji*, ed. Haifeng, 227-37. Harbin: Beifang wenyi chubanshe, 1998.
–. "Wu Jianren zhi shanghuihan." *Shenbao*, 22 July 1905. Reprinted in Vol. 80 of *Shenbao yinyingben*. Shanghai: Shanghai shudian, 1985.
–. *Xin shitouji.* In vol. 6 of *Wu Jianren quanqi*, ed. Haifeng. Harbin: Beifang wenyi chubanshe, 1998.
–. "'Xinan yixie: ziyou jiehun' pianhouping." In vol. 9 of *Wu Jianren quanji*, ed. Haifeng. Harbin: Beifang wenyi chubanshe, 1997.
–. *Xinxiaolin guangji.* In vol. 7 of *Wu Jianren quanji*, ed. Haifeng. Harbin: Beifang wenyi chubanshe, 1998.
–. "Yiwang Hankou Ribao zhi zhubi Wu Woyao zhi Wuchang zhifu Liang Dingfen shu." In vol. 10 of *Wu Jianren quanji*, ed. Haifeng. Harbin: Beifeng wenyi chubanshe, 1998.
Xia Xiaohong. "Wu Jianren yu Liang Qichao guanxi gouchen." *Anhui shifan daxue xuebao (Renwen shehui kexueba)* 30, 6 (2002): 636-40.
Xiong Xianjun. "Qingmo fumeiri liuxuesheng jiaoyu jixiao guiyin bijiao." *Hebei shifan daxue xuebao (Jiaoyu kexueban)* 9 (2007): 19-23.
Xiong Yuezhi. "Lüelun wanqing Shanghai xinxing wenhuaren di chansheng yu huiju." *Lishi yanjiu* 4 (1997): 257-73.
–. "Zhengju biandong yu minxin xiangbei." *Shilin* (February 2000): 17-19.
Xu Xiaoqing. "Shuangchong zhengzhi wenhua rentong de kunjing: jiedu Liang Qichao minzu guojia sixiang." *Journal of Xiangfan University* 21, 1 (2000): 81-83.
Xu Yin. "Zuojia baoren haishang shushisheng." In vol. 6 of *Ershi shiji Shanghai wenshi ziliao wenku*, ed. Liu Jianxin, 33-36. Shanghai: Shanghai shudian chubanshe, 1999.
Xu Zhenyan. "Shixi xiuxiang xiaoshuo di duzhe dingwei." *Mingqing xiaoshuo yanjiu* 62, 4 (2001): 157-61.
Yan Tingliang. *Wanqing xiaoshuo lilun.* Beijing: Zhonghua shuju, 1996.
Yang Guojiang. "Ershi shiji chunian zhishiren de zhishihua yu jindaihua." In *Ershi shiji Zhongguo zhishi fenzi shilun*, ed. Xu Jilin, 162-75. Beijing: Xinxing chubanshe, 2005.
Yang Jiang. "Huiyi wode fuqin." In vol. 2 of *Yang Jiang zuopinji*, 57-108. Beijing: Zhongguo shehui kexue chubanshe, 1993.
Yao Gonghe. *Shanghai xianhua.* Shanghai: Shangwu yinshuguan, 1933.
Ye Xiaoqing. *The Dianshizhai Pictorial: Shanghai Urban Life, 1884-1898.* Ann Arbor: University of Michigan Center for Chinese Studies, 2003.
Ye Zhongqiang. "Youzou yu chengshi kongjian: wanqing minchu shanghai wenren de gonggong jiaowang." *Shilin* 4 (2006): 80-87, 131.
Yeh, Catherine Vance. *Shanghai Love: Courtesans, Intellectuals, and Entertainment Culture, 1850-1910.* Seattle: University of Washington Press, 2005.

Youhuan Yusheng. "Guanchang xianxingji xu." In vol. 1 of *Ershi shiji Zhongguo xioashuo lilun ziliao (1897-1916)*, ed. Chen Pingyuan and Xia Xiaohong, 72-73. Beijing: Beijing daxue chubanshe, 1989, 1997.

Yuan Jin. "Shilun wanqing xiaoshuo duzhe de bianhua." *Mingqing xiaoshuo yanjiu* 59, 1 (2001): 18-28.

—. *Yuanyang hutianpai*. Shanghai: Shanghai shudian chubanshe, 1994.

Zarrow, Peter. "Introduction: Citizenship in China and the West." In *Imagining the People: Chinese Intellectuals and the Concept of Citizenship, 1890-1920*, ed. Joshua A. Fogel and Peter G. Zarrow. Armonk, NY: M.E. Sharpe, 1997.

Zeng Xubai. *Zhongguo xinwenshi* [The journalistic history of China]. Taipei: Sanmin shuju, 1984.

Zhang Chun. "Youxibao: Wanqing xiaoshuo yanjiu ziliao de dafaxian." *Mingqing xiaoshuo* 4 (2000): 214-31.

Zhang Ming. "Minyin yu tianyi: xinhai geming de minzhong huiying sanlun." In *Xinhai geming yu ershi shiji de Zhongguo*, ed. Association of the Chinese Society of History. Beijing: Zhongyang wenxian chubanshe, 2002.

Zhang Pengyuan. *Liang Qichao yu qingji geming*. 2nd ed. Taipei: Zhongyang yanjiuyuan jindaishi yanjiusuo zhuankan, 1999.

—. "Qingmo minchu de zhishi fenzi." In *Ershi shiji Zhongguo zhishi fenzi shilun*, ed. Xu Jilin, 223-31. Beijing: Xinxing chubanshe, 2005.

Zhang Qiang. "Wu Jianren 'wenming zhuanzhi' sixiang tanwei." *Zhengzhou daxue xuebao* 4 (1996): 99-103.

Zhang Yilu. "Li Boyuan yishi." In *Li Boyuan yanjiu ziliao*, ed. Wei Shaochang. Shanghai: Shanghai guji chubanshe, 1980.

Zhang Yufa. "Cong gaizao dao dongyuan." In *Liang Qichao yu jindai Zhongguo shehui wenhua*, ed. Li Xisuo. Tianjin: Tianjin guji chubanshe, 2005.

Zhang Zhidong. *Quanxuepian, Minggang, Neipian*. Vol. 9 of *Jindai Zhongguo shiliao congkan*, ed. Shen Yunlong. Taipei: Wenhai chubanshe, 1966.

Zhang Ziping. *Ziping zizhuan*. Vol. 6 of *Zhongguo xiandai zizhuan congshu (ser.)*, ed. Zhang Yufa and Zhang Ruide. Taipei: Longwen chubanshe, 1989.

Zheng Yimei. *Shubao hua jiu*. Shanghai: Xuelin chubanshe, 1983.

—. *Yimei zazha*. Jinan: Qilu shushe, 1985.

Zhou Wu, and Wu Guilong. "Wanqin shehui." In vol. 5 of *Shanghai tonshi*, ed. Xiong Yuezhi. Shanghai: Shanghai renmin chubanshe, 1999.

Zhu Fusheng, and Yao Hui. *Chenyingshi pingchuan*. Beijing: Tuanjie chubanshe, 1989.

Zhu Junzhou and Huang Peiwei. *Zhongguo jindai wenyi baokan gailan (II)*. In *Shiliao suoyinji*. Vol. 30. of *Zhongguo jindai wenxue daxi*, in *Shiliao suoyinji*, ed. Wei Shaochang. Shanghai: Shanghai shudian, 1996.

Zunben Zhaoxiong. *Xinbian zengbu Qingmo minchu xiaoshuo mulu*. Jinan: Qilu shushe, 2002.

Zuo Songtao. "Shilun qingdai seqingye fazhan yu zhengfu yingdui." *Fujian luntan (Renwen shehui kexueban)* 4 (2003): 48-52.

Index

Note: "(f)" next to a number indicates a figure

1911 Revolution, 10, 23, 54-55, 83, 182, 183

activism. *See* movements
aesthetic populism. *See* populism, aesthetic
All That Is Empty (Fengyuekong), 96-97
All-Story Monthly (Yueyue xiaoshuo), 9; anti-Qing discourse, 56; on censorship, 82; on constitutional polity, 102; distribution, 18; diverse readership, 162; editorial policy, 167; on opium policy, 108; pro-reform novels, 118-19; and public education, 159; readership, 17; riddles, 41; serialized novels, 57, 157, 161-62, 164, 206n28; writers for, 15
Allegories (Yuyanbao), 7; flower elections, 30, 31; opera actor elections, 45; political columns, 55, 57; readers' contributions, 79; serialized novels, 35-36, 160-61
Anecdotes (Caifengbao), 34; attacks on reformers, 117; emergence, 3; flower election, 31; paired titles, 38; serialized novels, 160; writers for, 15
anti-American boycott, 106-7, 110
anti-imperialism, 86, 87-92; *vs.* ethnocentrism, 90-91; tabloid *vs.* mainstream press, 110
anti-Russian protest, 106, 107-8
appropriation: of foreign styles, 137-40; of New Learning, 136-37, 137-38, 141; of textual meanings, 207n60
Art and Literary Society *(Yiwenshe)*, 46, 50

bamboo-twigs ballad, 80, 164, 195n110
Bao Tianxiao, 15, 54, 78, 86, 143, 161

Bourdieu, Pierre, 136-37
Boxer Uprising, 7, 89, 179; criticism of, 90

capital: economic, 136, 144-48; social, 136, 141-44; symbolic, 136-37, 137-41
Cen Chunxuan, 62, 76
censorship, 81-82, 115, 117, 185
Chartier, Roger, 182-83, 207n60
Chen Pingyuan, 157, 172, 193n4
China: currency, 187n20; economic interests, 77; political groups, 73; social crisis, 124-25; terms for, 92, 197n42, 197n44; weights, 193n14, 193n32
Chinese Exclusion Act (US, 1882), 106, 107
circulation: of *Fun*, 3, 15, 29, 30, 49, 188n38; of *Guidance*, 5; of *Illustrated Fiction*, 17-18, 162; of mainstream newspapers, 1-2, 16, 18-19; of tabloids, 1-2, 15-19, 34-35, 162-67, 167-68
citizen *(guomin): vs.* national *(guoren)*, 95-96; new *(xinmin)*, 94, 97; role of, 99-105; women as, 131
citizenship, 94-95, 133; and nation-state, 99
collectivity *(qun)*, 94-95; and equality, 102-3; *vs.* individual, 99
conservatives *(shoujiudang)*, 73, 76, 88-89, 113, 118-19, 125-26, 130, 170, 183
constitutional polity, 99; *vs.* civilized/ enlightened autocracy, 103-4, 105; defined, 197n51; and local autonomy, 104; and people's rights, 100-3; problems of, 103-5
courtesans: books on, 30, 34; cemetery site for, 34; children, 31; and flower elections, 26-28, 29; and literati, 24; as motif,

38; news of, 34-35; numbers, 186n15; patrons, 28-29, 190n78; and tabloid circulation, 34-35

Des Forges, Alexander, 159, 173, 175-76, 206n27, 208n95
discourses: anti-imperialist, 86-92; anti-official, 54, 55-56, 56-57, 57-61, 62-73, 74-75, 76-77, 79-82; anti-Qing, 54-55, 56-57, 57-61, 62-73, 193n4; citizenship, 94-98; nationalist, 94-98, 99-105, 110-11; on New and Old Learning, 122-23
Dong Kang, 46, 47

education: access to, 149-50; and citizenship, 95-96, 98; Confucian, 13-14, 74-75; criticism of, 99-100; as elite institution, 149-50; public, 87, 158-59; and reading taste, 163-64; studying abroad, 77-78, 123, 129-30, 136-37, 141, 142-44, 150, 167, 200n19; superficial, 137-40, 140-41; visions of, 161-62; Western, 19, 74-75, 112-13; for women, 131
eight-legged essay, 73, 115, 158, 187n25
Emperor Guangxu: under arrest, 7; moral degeneration, 61; and print journalism, 1; reform measures, 71-72, 114-15, 117-18; support for, 91-92, 93
Empress Dowager Cixi: attacks on press, 117; and constitutional polity, 104-5; and Emperor Tongzhi, 112; extravagance, 79; gifts, 194n70; portrayals of, 62-64; and reform, 6-7, 19, 71-72, 115, 117-18
enlightenment: and China, 122-23; and history, 126-27; and marriage freedom, 130-31; pseudo, 137-39; of women, 129; and women's education, 131
entertainment literature, 5, 7, 9, 20. *See also* tabloid press

fiction: anti-imperialist, 86-87, 88; anti-officialdom, 54-56, 57; anti-reform, 124, 129-30; anti-reformer, 137-39, 141-43, 144-46, 150; anti-revolutionary, 148, 153; of censure, 179-80; classical *vs.* popular, 158; as educational tool, 157-59, 161-62; entertainment value, 162; historical, 100-1, 119, 128, 161; and news, 172-75, 176, 181-82; popularity of, 157-61; present-centred, 167; pro-reform, 118-19, 120, 121-22, 142; readership, 17-18;

and reality, 173, 174; satirical, 56-57, 58-59, 60-61, 64, 73-74, 77-78, 81; serialized, 15, 16, 17-18, 34, 35-36, 54-55, 57, 157, 159-62, 165, 166, 206n28; translated, 100-1, 119, 160, 163-64; types, 161, 163, 166, 193n6, 206n52
flower elections: as a fad, 30-33; first, 25-30; parallels with government examinations, 26, 27, 29; winners' lists, 27-28, 29
footbinding, 120, 121, 165
foreigners: attitudes towards, 86-92; Chinese as, 89; and Chinese values, 180-81; terms for, 90, 197n28
Four Buddhist Warrior Attendants *(sida jingang)* campaign, 33-34
Fu Chunyi, 70, 72
fun: culture of, 37-41, 41-46, 51-53; as essence of life, 24; fetishized, 37; legitimized, 45-46; playing *(wan)*, 24; playing with life *(wanshi)*, 24; as popular resistance, 51-53; in wordplay, 51-53
Fun (Youxibao), 3(f); anti-official discourse, 54-55; circulation, 3, 30, 188n38; distribution, 17; emergence, 2-4, 5-6; flower elections, 25-30; and Four Buddhist Warrior Attendants campaign, 34; leaf election, 30-31, 32; on nationalism, 86, 90; news reportage, 80-82, 166-67; offices, 42-43; paired titles, 38; popularity of, 16, 188n38; portrayal of gentry-capitalists, 148; readers, 15, 29, 30, 49; and reformers, 117, 142, 150; riddles, 41; satirical anecdotes, 57, 60; serialized novels, 159-60, 165; statement of purpose, 162; structure of content, 3-4, 6; writers, 15

Gang Ziliang, 73-74, 80-81
Gao Caiyun, 35-36
Gao Taichi, 13, 14, 47, 169; founds Poetry Society *(Shishi)*, 46
gender bias, 129-33
gentry-capitalist class, 146, 147(f), 148, 149-50
government examination system, 2, 12, 13, 19, 112, 115, 123, 149; and returning students, 143
Grove of Fiction (Xiaoshuolin), 161; works of fiction, numbers, 157
Grove of Laughter (Xiaolinbao), 7, 8(f); on constitutional polity, 102; distribution,

17; paired titles, 38; on people's rights, 100-1; popularity, 16; and reform, 76; riddles, 40, 41; satirical columns, 57; serialized novels, 55, 160, 166, 206n28; writers, 15

Hu Shi, 163, 167, 175
humour, 55, 57, 74, 78, 87, 100, 117, 161, 163, 169-73, 179, 181, 185, 207n68
Hundred Days' Reform, 1, 6-7, 73, 112, 114, 142; and print journalism, 1
Huters, Theodore, 134, 158

identity: national *vs.* ethnic/racial, 85-86, 89-90, 92
Illustrated Fiction (Xiuxiang xiaoshuo), 9(f); anti-Qing discourse, 56; circulation, 17-18; distribution, 18; diverse readership, 162; emergence, 9; on popularity of genres, 163; and public education, 159; satirical novels, 57; satirical sketches, 64, 65-68(f), 147(f); serialized novels, 118-19, 160, 161, 164, 165, 206n28; treatment of reformers, 152(f); works of fiction, numbers, 157; writers for, 15
imperialism: and Chinese nationalism, 85-86, 109-10; Japanese, 86, 87, 89; Russian, 86, 106, 108; types, 86-88, 145
International Settlement, 5; courtesans, 24; Fourth Street, 42-43, 191n98; opium smoking, 44; and tabloid press, 12

Jiang Fengqing, 70, 72
Jin Xiaobao, 26, 28, 33-34, 36, 47
Judge, Joan, 1, 17, 110

Kang Youwei: on enlightenment, 93, 122; initial public response to, 115-17; *Meditations on Confucius' Reform*, 113; on social role of fiction, 158; sympathy for, 137; tabloid community views of, 141-43

language: classical, 39, 158, 163-64, 206n36; dialects, 72, 73, 89, 162-63, 165, 187n26, 191n115; vernacular, 158, 162-64, 206n36
legitimacy: of elites, 181-82; of fun, 37, 51-52; of prostitution, 51-52; of Qing regime, 72, 83, 91-92; of the state, 22, 83

Li Boyuan, 10(f), 15, 18, 46, 54; on access to education, 149-50; anti-imperialist fiction, 86-87, 88; anti-Qing discourse, 60; anti-reform fiction, 124, 129-30; anti-reformer fiction, 137-39, 141-43, 144-46, 150; anti-revolutionary fiction, 148, 153; attacks on Kang Youwei, 117; and business community, 47, 48-49; and courtesans, 32-33, 34, 36, 190n48 (*see also Fun [Youxibao]*, flower elections); description of appropriators, 138-39; description of Fourth Street, 42; early years, 12, 13-14; fame, 48; founds Art and Literary Society, 46; founds *Fun*, 2-4, 5-6; founds *Guidance (Zhinanbao)*, 5; founds *Splendid World*, 7; on Gao case, 35; gimmicks, 30-31; and Imperial Academy, 46; on love, 35; pen names, 24, 37, 55; playful writings, 39, 169, 172; and public education, 159; *Records of Shanghai's Fragrances*, 30; reform theories, 114; on reforms, 73; satirical fiction, 56, 77, 78, 81; and *Shanghai Literary Society Monthly*, 38, 50; support for prostitution, 51-52; support for Qing regime, 92; support for reform, 118, 119, 120, 121-22; *tanci*-style novels, 164-65; view of reformers, 144
Li Boyuan, novels: *Awakening the Society*, 120, 165; *A Brief History of the Enlightenment*, 77, 88, 118, 120, 124, 139, 141-43, 150, 160, 173; *China Today*, 18; *The History of Flowers of the Erotic River*, 30; *Living Hell*, 56, 119, 160; *The National Incident of 1900*, 160, 165, 174; *Officialdom Unmasked*, 18, 54, 70, 78, 82, 160, 173, 175; *A Shanghai Swan's Tracks in the Snow*, 15
Li Hongzhang, 14, 70, 162
Li Lianying, 62-63, 81, 193n19
Liang Dingfen, 82, 195n86
Liang Qichao: on citizenship, 94-95, 104-5, 129, 133, 197n36, 197n86, 198n84; on constitutional polity, 101, 103; elite status, 85; on enlightenment, 122; ethnocentrism of, 91; initial public response to, 115-16, 117; nationalism/nationalist rhetoric, 90, 93, 99, 110, 197n26, 199n105; pen name, 142; promotion of fiction, 158-59, 162; promotion

of New Learning, 113-14, 134; sympathy for, 137; tabloid community views of, 141-43; theory of history, 126-27; and Western ideas, 181; vs. Wu Jianren, 104-5. See also New Fiction (Xinxiaoshuo); Qingyibao
Liang Qichao, writings: "On Enlightened Autocracy," 103; *Exhortation to Study*, 113; *Future of New China*, 162; *On the New Citizen*, 94-95; "New Historiography," 126-27; "Preface to Translating and Publishing Political Fiction," 158; *Reflections on Moral Education*, 95; "On the Relationship between Fiction and Popular Sovereignty," 158
Liang Xinghai. *See* Liang Dingfen
Lin Daiyu, 29, 33-34, 35
Link, Perry, 135, 161, 165-66, 167
literacy: of officials, 76, 97; of readers, 4, 17, 87, 158, 162-64
literary market: broad readership, 162-67; commercial, 156; present-centred, 167; and rise of fiction, 156-57, 157-62
literary societies, 46, 50. *See also specific literary societies*
literati: alienation of, 182-83, 207n60; audience of, 156; crisis of, 19-20; and fiction, 163-64; intellectual elite, 12, 19-20, 23, 93-95, 98, 112-14, 157, 178; last generation, 13; and New Policy, 136-37; ranks of, 12, 13, 20, 22; and the state, 182; of tabloid community, 12-15, 13-15, 15-19 (*see also* tabloid literati). *See also specific literati*
Liu Shipei, 133, 158
Lu Lanfen, 33-34, 35
Lu Xun, 38, 167

merry laughter and angry curses *(xixiao numa)*, 20-21, 169-71
Mittler, Barbara, 109-10, 165, 174
moral values: Confucian/traditional, 123-24, 125-26, 200n3, 202n81; traditional vs. foreign, 129-33, 180-81, 183-84
morality. *See* social morality
movements: anti-American boycott, 106-7; anti-British protests, 108-9; anti-Russian protest, 106, 107-8; nationalist, 103-5, 106-9; reform, 114-22 (*See also* reformers *[weixindang]*; reforms)

nation-state *(guo)*: concept of, 89-90; Confucianism and, 94-95, 113-14; as salvation, 93-95; sovereignty and, 99-105; Western values and, 94-95
nationalism *(minzu zhuyi)*: discourses, 94-98, 99-105, 110-11; vs. ethnocentrism, 92; imperialism and, 109-10; influence of the press, 110-11; little *(xiao)* vs. great *(da)*, 91; movements, 103-5, 106-9; sentiments, 85-86, 86-92, 93-94; versions of, 180
New Fiction (Xinxiaoshuo), 18, 158, 159, 161, 165, 166, 173, 206n28; works of fiction, numbers, 157
New Learning *(xinxue)*: Bookstores, 144; and commercial opportunities, 144, 148; and conspicuous display, 137-40; government-sanctioned, 137; and New Policy, 136-37; and officialdom, 143-44; vs. Old Learning, 122-23; positions on, 112-13; promoted, 117-19; and social values, 129, 150-54, 173; vs. traditional ethics, 123-24, 123-26. *See also* new-style schools; Western Learning *(xixue)*
New Policy *(Xinzheng)*, 7, 75, 80-81, 112-13
new-style schools, 12, 19, 74, 76-77, 80-81, 112, 113; enrollment, 149; and reformers' profits, 146, 147(f)
newspapers: anti-Qing discourse, 54-55; mainstream vs. tabloid, 5-6, 186n8, 187n24; and political consciousness, 5; as publishing houses, 50; readership, 1-2; role in the West, 115-16; in Song Dynasty, 184; views of, 1
novels. *See* fiction, serialized

officialdom, 193n4; exposed, 59, 61, 62, 64, 71-72, 78; and fiction of censure, 179-80; as motif, 54-56
Old Learning *(jiuxue)*, 13-14, 74-75, 113
Ouyang Juyuan, 6, 13, 15, 157; attacks on officials, 70; portrayal of reformers, 144; satirical novels, 56; writings, 31, 34, 38, 46

Paired Flying Phoenixes, 159-60
Pang Shubo, 15, 34
Pastime (Xiaoxianbao), 14, 34; criticism of *Shenbao*, 87; flower elections, 30; opera actor elections, 45; writers for, 15

patriotism, 92, 96, 126, 128, 162; of revolutionaries, 153-54
periodicals: anti-Qing discourse, 55-56; circulation, 1-2; entertainment, 5; entertainment vs. reform, 7, 9; of Liang Qichao, 94; literary, 9-10; and political consciousness, 2; readership, 17-18; Western historical fiction, 119
pinghua, 45, 191n115
politics: of the body/sexuality, 51-52; and entertainment, 171-73; journalistic importance of, 7, 9; participation in, 22; reforms and, 20; and tabloid growth, 6-7, 9; of tabloid literati, 52-53
populism: aesthetic, 20-21, 21-22, 176, 178; defined, 21-22; tabloid community and, 154, 166-68, 175-76, 183-84
prostitution, 24, 51-52, 60, 193n25, 193n31; and literacy, 187n31

Qing Dynasty. *See* Qing officials; Qing regime
Qing officials, 46, 194n69; anti-reform, 117; and China's decline, 10, 73-78, 179; and Chinese Exclusion Act, 106-7; education, 76-77, 118; exposed, 79-82, 195n116; fictional treatment of, 7, 57-61, 64, 65-68(f), 173, 193n4; moral degeneration, 54-55, 55-56, 56-57, 57-61, 62-73, 70; opium policy, 108; parallels with prostitutes, 51, 60, 193n25; priorities, 75-76; recruitment of, 143-44; and reforms, 73-78. *See also* officialdom
Qing regime, 22-23, 54-55; and constitutional polity, 99-100; demise, 82-84; legitimacy of, 72-73; reforms, 1-2, 123; support for, 91-92
Qingyibao, 94, 117, 119, 158
Qiu Shuyuan, 15, 34, 47, 169
queues, 118, 122, 130, 138-39, 153

race *(zhongzu)*: concept of, 89-90; racial discrimination (US), 107
reading public: changing attitudes, 45-46; as consumers, 156; diversity of, 4-5, 15-19, 162-66; drinking games, 39; influence on tabloid press, 166-68; interest in courtesans, 24-25; interpretations, 207n60; participation in flower elections, 25-30, 31-32; role in community,

179; as writers, 35, 38, 39, 43, 79, 115, 116-17
reformers *(weixindang)*: commercial opportunities of, 144; *vs.* conservatives, 73; economic capital of, 144-48; and family revolution, 129-31; fundraising scams, 144-45; hypocrisy of, 150-54; and New Learning, 137, 138-40; and new-style schools, 146, 147(f); organization, 80; social capital of, 141-44; tabloid community and, 181; and Western ethics, 123-24
reforms, 1, 6-7; anti-footbinding, 120-21; constitutional polity, 77-78; education, 123; in education, 19; of family relationships, 129-31; of justice system, 119; and nationalism, 90; and opportunities, 20; opposition to, 76, 123-24; pace of, 118-19; promoting, 114-22; public awareness of, 104-5; questioning, 122-25; *vs.* Republican revolution, 93; Western knowledge and, 113; in writing history, 126-29. *See also* New Policy *(Xinzheng)*
revolutionaries: condemnation of, 92; hypocrisy of, 150-54; *mingshi* type, 140-41; and New Learning, 137; social capital of, 148-49; tabloid community and, 181; treatment of Manchus, 63, 85-86, 91, 110, 141, 192n1; views of, 140-41
rights: and family relationships, 130; political, 195n106
Russia, 100-1
Russo-Japanese War, 87

satire, 179, 181; defined, 169-70; in early fiction, 176; in newspaper columns, 57-61, 62, 64, 73-74; in newspaper sketches, 65-68(f), 147(f); in novels, 56, 57, 62, 76, 77, 78, 81; and politics, 171-72
Shanghai: attractions, 24; city of fun, 24-25; cultural environment, 41; foreign concessions, 4; importance, 4; moral decay, 96; political environment, 10; publishing centre, 1-2
Shanghai Books and Press Guild, 107, 110
Shanghai Chamber of Commerce, 106, 108
Shanghai Literary Society *(Haishang wenshe)*, 38, 46, 50

Shen Xizhi, 13, 33, 36, 47, 50
Shenbao, 1, 2, 15, 16, 18-19, 87, 159, 161, 165
Shibao, 2, 18-19, 161
Sino-Japanese War, 86, 87
Social Darwinism, 89-90, 94
social morality: civilized, 104; Confucian *vs.* Western, 94-96; in crisis, 125; public *vs.* personal, 95-98; of revolutionaries, 150-54; theories of, 129-33; Western values and, 151. *See also* moral values
sovereignty *(zhuquan)*, 87, 199n105; popular, 107
Splendid World (Shijie fanhuabao), 7, 7(f); distribution, 17; exposé of Qing court, 71-72; flower elections, 31, 33; political columns, 55; popularity, 16, 78; prostitute columns, 193n31; readers' contributions, 49, 79; satirical anecdotes, 58, 59, 60-61; satirical columns, 57, 62; serialized novels, 54, 55, 160; theatre column, 44-45
Sun Baoxuan, 36, 46, 175
Sun Yusheng, 13, 14, 24, 32, 33-34, 44, 47, 78, 169, 190n67; attacks on Kang Youwei, 117; *Dreams in Splendid Shanghai*, 166; fame, 48; flower elections, 31; founds Poetry Society *(Shishe)*, 46; literary games, 39; novels, 30, 33, 160; and opera stars, 44, 45; pen names, 37-38, 192n127; support for prostitution, 51-52
superstition, 120, 121, 165

tabloid aesthetics, 168, 169-71, 171-72, 172-75, 181-82, 208n95; and anti-establishment populism, 175-76
tabloid community: activism, 79; attitudes toward reform/reformers, 113-14, 115, 117-22, 123, 137-41, 142-43; beginnings, 5-6; composition, 12-15, 15-19, 98, 178-79; concerns, 149-50, 167-68, 179, 183-84; interest in courtesans, 32-33, 36-37; interest in opera stars, 44; participation in politics, 83; pastimes, 31, 37-41, 41-46; Shanghai, 10; views of footbinding, 120-21; views of traditional values, 133-34; voyeuristic, 33-37. *See also specific members of tabloid community*

tabloid literati: activist voice, 79; anti-imperialist rhetoric, 86, 87-92; anti-Qing discourse, 56-57, 57-61, 62-73, 88-89, 99-100; and business community, 32-33; celebrity status, 48; in Changzhou, 13-14; on citizenship, 95-96; and courtesans, 24, 25, 51-52; in crisis, 19-20; as dissidents, 55-56; fame of, 47-48; *vs.* intellectual elite, 19-20, 85-86, 93-95, 94, 99, 126, 128-29, 129-33, 133-34, 133-35, 178; leadership role, 21-22; literary devices, 37-50, 40-41, 51-53, 89-90, 169-71; literary work and, 24-25; mercenary motives, 50; pen names, 37-38; positions on family values, 129-33; *vs.* reform journalists, 110-11; relationship with business community, 48-50; relationship with society, 46-50, 78-82; relationship with the state, 52; representational strategies of, 168, 169-71, 171-72, 172-75; social circles, 46-50; on social morality, 97-98; sources, 174; and style, 168; and women readers, 165. *See also specific tabloid literati*
tabloid press: anti-establishment stance, 166-68, 168-71, 171-72, 172-75; attacks on officialdom, 179-80; central theme, 24-25; and Chinese nationalism, 73-78, 85, 86-87, 90, 107, 109-11; circulation, 16-17, 17-18; competitions, 38-39, 41; contributors, 32, 36; costs *vs.* revenue, 6; disappearance, 10, 12; distribution, 17, 188n41; diverse readership, 162-63, 165-66, 167-68; fiction published in, 162-64; first/second waves, 7-12; in International Settlement, 42-43; legacy of, 185; magazines, 9-10; on new-style schools, 76-77; and news, 166-67; newspapers, 2-7, 2-9; photographs, 190n55; playful writings, 37-50, 51-53, 89-90, 169; and politics, 20-21, 101-2, 171-73; producers, 12-15; and public attitudes, 20, 22, 45-46, 52-53, 54-55, 78-82, 81, 83; and readers of fiction, 161; and reading market, 156, 165-66; and reality, 176; *vs.* "respectable" literature, 176; and rise of fiction, 156-57, 157-62; satirical anecdotes, 73-74; in Shanghai, 4; support for Qing regime, 91-92; theatre columns, 44-45; treatment of appropriators, 137-39; treatment of

reform/reformers, 115-16, 118-22, 125-26, 141-43. *See also specific tabloid publications*
Tan Sitong, 93, 133
tanci, 13, 17, 35, 56, 120, 181; defined, 164-65, 187n26
Tang Xiaobing, 126, 202n85
Tongzhi Restoration, 112, 200n1

voyeurism, 33-37

wanshi bugong, 52
Western Learning *(xixue)*, 13, 23, 73, 74-77, 76; in schools, 112-13. *See also* New Learning *(xinxue)*
women: as citizens, 131; place in reform theories, 120-21; as readers, 162, 164-65; and reform, 165; and social morality, 129, 131
wordplay, 37-41, 169, 172, 191n116
Wu Jianren, 9, 11(f), 197n28; on access to education, 150; activism, 82, 109, 110; anti-imperialist fiction, 88; anti-Qing discourse, 56, 60; anti-reform fiction, 124; anti-reformer fiction, 148; anti-revolutionary fiction, 92, 140-41, 153-54; on citizenship, 104-5; on civilized autocracy, 103-5; constitutional activism, 105-9; on constitutional polity *vs.* people's rights, 100-3; early years, 14; fame, 48; on family relationships, 131, 132-33, 202n85; on fiction as tool, 161-62; historical fiction, 128; on history writing, 127-28; on morality, 96-98; novels, 18, 34, 47; playful writings, 169, 172; portrayal of officials, 75; pro-reform fiction, 121; and public education, 159; satirical novels, 76, 78; satirical work, 57; social criticism, 97; support for Qing regime, 91-92; views of appropriators, 143
Wu Jianren, writings: *Apocalyptic Ember*, 128, 160; "Celebrating Constitutional Polity," 101; *Change of Heart*, 127-28, 131; *Complete Collected Works of Wu Jianren*, 57; "Cries of the Ghost from the Society of People's Mirror," 107; *Cutting the Heart Open*, 174; *Gallivanting in Yiunnan*, 174; *The History of Two Jin Dynasties*, 128, 160; *Humor*, 207n68; *Humorous Talks*, 207n68; "Long Live the Constitutional Polity," 102; *The Muddled World*, 160; *New Comprehensive Stories of the Grove of Laughter*, 207n68; *New History of Laughter*, 207n68; *The New Story of the Stone*, 103-4, 108, 134, 148; *Painful History*, 128, 162; "Preparing for the Constitutional Polity," 104-5; *Sea of Regret*, 128, 162; *Strange Events Eyewitnessed in the Last Twenty Years*, 18, 76, 78, 79, 97, 134, 159, 166, 173, 174, 175; *Touring Shanghai*, 88, 96, 100, 124-25, 151, 160, 174; *The Western Chamber*, 163; *The Wonder Book of Shanghai's Famous Courtesans*, 34, 160; *Wonders of Electricity*, 163; *Wu – the Railway Martyr*, 109
Wu Jingzi: *The Scholar*, 175-76

Xie Guixiang, 32, 33
Xinwenbao, 1, 14, 15, 16, 161

Yan Fu, 93, 94, 117-18, 158
Yanshi Goutu: *A Brief History of the Evolution of China*, 118; pro-reform novels, 118
Yeh, Catherine Vance, 4-5, 16, 52, 173, 174, 206n27
Yuan Jin, 4, 157
Yuan Shikai, 70, 71

zaju, 96, 198n66
Zarrow, Peter Z., 2, 95
Zhang Binglin, 127, 141
Zhang Garden teahouse, 32-33, 33-34, 43
Zhang Guo, 101, 199n94
Zhang Shuyu, 33-34
Zhang Sibao, 27, 28, 32, 36
Zhang Zhidong, 70, 71, 72, 81; on Chinese values, 133-34; on Old *vs.* New Learning, 113
Zhejiang railway affair, 108-9
Zhou Bingyuan, 13, 47, 169
Zhou Guisheng, 15, 143
zhuzhici, 80, 195n110
Zou Tao, 13, 46, 159-60

Contemporary Chinese Studies

Glen Peterson, *The Power of Words: Literacy and Revolution in South China, 1949-95*

Wing Chung Ng, *The Chinese in Vancouver, 1945-80: The Pursuit of Identity and Power*

Yijiang Ding, *Chinese Democracy after Tiananmen*

Diana Lary and Stephen MacKinnon, eds., *Scars of War: The Impact of Warfare on Modern China*

Eliza W.Y. Lee, ed., *Gender and Change in Hong Kong: Globalization, Postcolonialism, and Chinese Patriarchy*

Christopher A. Reed, *Gutenberg in Shanghai: Chinese Print Capitalism, 1876-1937*

James A. Flath, *The Cult of Happiness: Nianhua, Art, and History in Rural North China*

Erika E.S. Evasdottir, *Obedient Autonomy: Chinese Intellectuals and the Achievement of Orderly Life*

Hsiao-ting Lin, *Tibet and Nationalist China's Frontier: Intrigues and Ethnopolitics, 1928-49*

Xiaoping Cong, *Teachers' Schools and the Making of the Modern Chinese Nation-State, 1897-1937*

Diana Lary, ed., *The Chinese State at the Borders*

Norman Smith, *Resisting Manchukuo: Chinese Women Writers and the Japanese Occupation*

Hasan H. Karrar, *The New Silk Road Diplomacy: China's Central Asian Foreign Policy since the Cold War*

Richard King, ed., *Art in Turmoil: The Chinese Cultural Revolution, 1966-76*

Blaine R. Chiasson, *Administering the Colonizer: Manchuria's Russians under Chinese Rule, 1918-29*

Emily M. Hill, *Smokeless Sugar: The Death of a Provincial Bureaucrat and the Construction of China's National Economy*

Kimberley Ens Manning and Felix Wemheuer, eds., *Eating Bitterness: New Perspectives on China's Great Leap Forward and Famine*

Helen M. Schneider, *Keeping the Nation's House: Domestic Management and the Making of Modern China*

James A. Flath and Norman Smith, eds., *Beyond Suffering: Recounting War in Modern China*

Elizabeth R. VanderVen, *A School in Every Village: Educational Reform in a Northeast China County, 1904-31*

Norman Smith, Intoxicating Manchuria: *Alcohol, Opium, and Culture in China's Northeast*

Printed and bound in Canada by Friesens

Set in Futura and Warnock by Artegraphica Design Co. Ltd.

Copy editor: Frank Chow

Proofreader and indexer: Dianne Tiefensee